THEIR
DARKEST
HOUR

To Rupert Harding

THEIR
DARKEST
HOUR

THE HIDDEN HISTORY
OF THE HOME FRONT
1939–1945

STUART HYLTON

SUTTON PUBLISHING

This book was first published in 2001

This paperback edition first published in 2003 by
Sutton Publishing Limited · Phoenix Mill
Thrupp · Stroud · Gloucestershire · GL5 2BU

British Library Cataloguing in Publication Data
A catalogue record for this book is available from the British
Library.

ISBN 0 7509 3224 4

Typeset in 11/12pt Goudy.
Typesetting and origination by
Sutton Publishing Limited.
Printed and bound in Great Britain by
J.H. Haynes & Co. Ltd, Sparkford.

Contents

For nine months the land war had been a stalemate – while the home front had been a dreary catalogue of restrictions, regulations, frustrations and aggravations, all of which had achieved absolutely nothing. The German Blitzkrieg arrived just at the time when the 'Bore War', as it was dubbed, had reduced most of the civilian population to apathy. Home Intelligence reports . . . again and again reported apathy, boredom and irritation with the civil defence preparations. . . .

In March 1940, one person in ten was in favour of stopping the war immediately. . . .

Peter Lewis, discussing the state of the nation at the time of Dunkirk (*A People's War*, Thames Methuen, 1986)

Introduction

Rationing, blackouts, bombs, shortages of everything . . . such a diet would soon have destroyed the spirit of the people in most countries, but to the surprise and niggling annoyance of the Nazi regime, little Britain kept its pecker up and kept hitting back. Instead of whining and bemoaning its lot, we whistled as we worked and kept our spirits up with a string of memorable songs, both humorous and sentimental. If anything, the only secret weapon we ever possessed was our crackpot sense of humour which saw the funny side of almost everything. It flourished everywhere . . . at the Front, at work, in the bus queue and even in the air raid shelter. It became stronger under the most trying circumstances, and it was this as much as anything else which enabled us to 'keep on keeping on', and so led to the ultimate defeat of Hitler.

Roy Faiers, 'This was their finest hour',
This England, *Summer 1994*

Growing up as I did just after the Second World War, my picture of the home front during the war years was gained largely from the films of the time. Like the writer quoted above, I carried in my head a composite image of chirpy cockneys in the Anderson shelter, singing along to Vera Lynn on the radio as they made do and mended and the bombs burst all around them.

That image was dispelled for me in no uncertain terms several years ago, when I wrote a book about the war years as they were experienced in Reading, the town where I now live. My idealised picture was replaced by a reassuringly mixed view of the people and the times, in which grumbles, incompetence, bureaucracy and opportunism lived alongside the sacrifice and bravery that was undoubtedly part of the experience of those years.

This book stems from that revelation, and is my personal antidote to the excessive sentimentality which still exists in some quarters about the war years. It does not in any way aim to belittle the contribution those at home made to the war effort. But what it does try to do is to remind us that Britain won the war despite the best efforts of the bureaucrats, defeatists, profiteers and bigots among them.

In writing this, I was extremely fortunate in the wealth of published material available on the period, and I have included a section on my sources for the different parts of the book later on. In addition, I found a lot of material in local and national newspapers of the time. Two other contemporary sources were important to me, as they were for many other historians of the war before me.

Home Intelligence was, from early 1940, the Ministry of Information's machinery for keeping the government apprised of the thinking of the home population through the war years. They drew upon information gleaned by censors, looking at letters and monitoring telephone conversations; reports compiled by thirteen regional officers; bar room chatter and newspaper reports; grievances raised via MPs; reports from police duty rooms; BBC listener research; and talk picked up in newsagents and cinemas, and by agencies such as the WVS and the Citizens' Advice Bureau. Another important source for Home Intelligence was Mass Observation, set up in 1936 by Frank Jennings, Tom Harrisson and Charles Madge to apply anthropological techniques to the study of the home population. They started out by advertising in the New Statesman for volunteers to observe the views and behaviour of the public.

Thanks are due to the *Evening Standard* for permission to quote from the captions to the wartime cartoons of that splendidly satirical old bigot, Colonel Blimp. With one exception, the photographs in this book are reproduced with the permission of the Trustees of the Imperial War Museum, London. The one exception, the picture of bomb damage in Reading, is reproduced with the permission of Reading Central Library, which is part of Reading Borough Council. I have made every effort to track down any third party copyright, but if any have been inadvertently missed, please let me know via the publisher.

Last but by no means least, thanks are due to Rupert Harding, my editor at Suttons for this book and most of my previous work for them. In recognition of his help and encouragement over many years, this book is dedicated to him.

1

Over Here: Internees, Aliens, Fifth Columnists

The Nazis keep their concentration camps for their enemies; we use them for our friends.

G.M. *Trevelyan in a letter to* The Times

Aliens in the First World War

The treatment of foreign nationals living in Britain was one of the least glorious episodes of the First World War. About 67,000 Germans and Austrians were registered with the police by 9 September 1914, and at that time the government found good reason to intern only a tiny number of them. But by the spring of 1915 stories of atrocities in Europe, the Zeppelin raids and a hate campaign run by the newspapers led to mob violence towards 'foreigners'. Businesses owned by, or employing, Germans were attacked, foreigners were assaulted and the escalation of violence in the streets of Liverpool and West Ham after the sinking of the *Lusitania* resulted in 257 casualties.

Nobody was too great or too insignificant to evade the mob's anger. At one extreme, Prince Louis Battenberg, First Sea Lord and a distinguished public servant, was hounded out of office as a result of his German antecedents. At the other, innocent dachshunds found themselves being kicked in the street for the same reason. In May 1915 a petition bearing 250,000 signatures was presented to Parliament, calling for the immediate arrest of all aliens of military age. The government responded with large-scale internment – by the end of that year, some 32,274 were behind bars, and the last of them was not released until long after the war was over, in September 1919.

The scars that this left made many people determined to avoid similar excesses in the conflict that was brewing twenty years later.

Viscount Cobham, the Under-Secretary of State for War, told the House of Lords on 24 October 1939 that:

> It is not likely to happen, as there are far fewer enemy aliens, especially of military age, in this country than there were at the commencement of the last war, in spite of all the refugees. The figure I have been given, as being likely to be interned as enemy aliens, is somewhere between 1,000 and 1,500, as against a figure of over 29,000 during the last war.

Aliens in the Second World War

Britain's response to the German refugee problem in the run-up to the war was an honourable one. They accepted them in large numbers, at a time when many other countries refused them admission. By the outbreak of war, there were over sixty thousand refugees in Britain, in addition to other foreign nationals. Most were of German or Austrian origin and about half of them had come in during the nineteen months preceding the outbreak of war.

Tribunals were set up across the country in the early days of the war to identify those who were regarded as a potential threat to national security. They were classified into three groups. In Category A were those who were openly hostile to Britain, and they were to be interned within days of war starting. In Category B were the borderline cases, in particular those who had only recently arrived in the country. The remainder, Category C, had been in the country for at least six years and were generally political or racial refugees from Hitler.

The Tribunals started work in October 1939 and it soon became clear that there was considerable inconsistency in their decisions. One put all domestic servants into Category B, while another immediately interned anyone who was a socialist or a communist. Some interned anyone they thought would be vulnerable to blackmail, lest they be forced to act as German spies; others were locked up because they were in sensitive occupations. Some cases turned purely on chance factors: one man was thought to have been 'shopped' as a Fifth Columnist by a rival who wanted his job as a piano player. In another case a German who spoke no English was examined by a Tribunal which spoke no German, without the

FRIENDLY ALIEN

German Jewish Cambridge undergraduate Mark Lynton (formerly Max-Otto Loewenstein) recalls with amusement his Tribunal, in front of half a dozen First World War vintage officers and a judge. He was armed with a letter from General Sir Ernest Swinton, saying that he would be a reference for Lynton, despite never having met him: 'This geriatric gaggle set to in the finest Colonel Blimp tradition: What school had I been to (Cheltenham; very sound); did I play soccer or rugby there (rugby, of course; very good); did I play squash (I did; splendid); was I a member of the Officer Training Corps (forgot it was Cheltenham; silly question, of course, ha-ha); what was I studying in Cambridge (law; bit odd that, brainy chap, what? never mind). It went on in that vein until it came to references, and I handed over Swinton's note. Just as Guillebaud had forecast, it was reverently passed from hand to hand ("Sir Ernest? Why, I met him once near Cambrai in 1917"), and I was promptly certified as a "friendly alien".'

benefit of an interpreter. He was immediately interned on suspicion of being foreign.

The government had to issue additional guidance to try to standardise the results. Of the final total of 73,355 cases examined, 66,002 were put into Category C. Some 55,000 of these were recorded as refugees from Nazi persecution. The great majority of the remainder were category B and only 569 were classed as definite security risks.

Category B aliens were subject to a variety of controls. Their movements were restricted, they were subject to a curfew and could not own such things as maps, a wireless, a car or a bike. Thus, one Johannes Hofels found himself fined the considerable sum (for the day) of £10 plus 5 guineas (£5.25) costs for possessing maps of parts of Britain. Hofels, who was 65 and had lived in Britain since 1901, had been a member of the Auf Wiedersehen Rambling Club before the war. The club had been set up to promote Anglo-German friendship, but had understandably ceased activity in 1939.

Another case which attracted considerable interest was that of Wilhelm Solf, an Oxford student. The son of the former German Ambassador to Japan under the Weimar Republic, he was given a month's imprisonment, followed by internment, for photographing a crashed German plane. The case led to no fewer than four editorials, calling for a review of Category B aliens, in the *Daily Mail*.

The Myth of the Fifth Column

> It is extraordinary how we get circumstantial reports of Fifth Columnists and yet we have never been able to get anything worth having. One is persuaded that it hardly exists. And yet there is signalling going on all over the place and we cannot get any evidence.
>
> General Ironside, C-in-C Home Forces.

General Ironside illustrates the willingness of the authorities to believe in the existence of the Fifth Column in the absence of *any* evidence to support it. Lord Haw-Haw's* apparently intimate knowledge of events in Britain was often held to be proof of its existence, yet a Ministry of Information investigation in January 1941 could find 'no case . . . in which Haw Haw or any German wireless made predictions regarding a specific place or announced any detailed facts which . . . could not have been obtained through an explicable channel'.

The term Fifth Column came from the Spanish Civil War, when Nationalist General Emilio Moro claimed to have four armies converging on Madrid and a fifth column of secret nationalist sympathisers ready to support their cause within Madrid itself. Even in its first incarnation, the claim was untrue. It was designed to spread alarm and confusion among the opposing armies, and it had its desired effect, leading to a witch hunt and a self-inflicted purge among the opposition. The idea was a potent – but more or less totally groundless – one throughout the war years in Britain. No rumour was too wild to be denied circulation, though the story of a house full of blind alien refugees all being secretly armed with machine-guns must have stretched some people's credulity.

* Lord Haw-Haw was the name given to a number of broadcasters on the German propaganda stations, but it is primarily associated with William Joyce – see p. 90.

As Hitler made his way across Europe, the media eagerly reported the activities of Nazi sympathisers, real or imagined, in the countries that were overrun. This extract from the *Daily Express* account of the invasion of the Low Countries:

> As machine-guns came out of the sky like unnatural lightning, peppering the streets below, the Fifth Column crept out of their homes in their German uniforms, heavily armed. Holland had combed out the Fifth Column for weeks before but as the doors opened at 3 a.m. the men who had been proclaimed anti-Nazis and refugees from Germany held rifles.

In fact, German attempts to plant spies in Britain, both before and during the war, were quite spectacularly unsuccessful. Those few spies in place before the outbreak of hostilities were rounded up within the first few hours of war. A further two dozen or more were landed by boat or plane in September 1940. Almost without exception, they were captured within hours. Many were taken to a camp called 020 (the roman numerals for which are XX – or 'double cross'), which was run by MI5. The threat of the death penalty often persuaded the captured agents to 'turn' and work for the allies. One, a Dane called Wolf Schmidt, became the British agent 'Tate', and was able to persuade the Germans of the existence of a bogus minefield in the North Atlantic, to the great benefit of the convoys.

But the most successful of the turned spies was a Spaniard, Juan Pujol, codenamed 'Garbo'. He had applied to be a British spy but

---

STATELESS

In September 1939 all Germans living abroad received call-up papers for the armed forces. They were issued regardless of religion, race and other considerations. When, understandably, the refugee population in Britain did not respond to the call-up, the German authorities revoked their citizenship. The British government's response to this was to say that the German government's decree 'did not count' and that, in the British view, they were still Germans. This left the refugees technically stateless. When, later in the war, some of the refugees went on to serve in the allied armed forces, they were actually serving as what the British Government defined as 'enemy aliens'.

was turned down, so he pursued his career in espionage with the Abwehr, the German military intelligence organisation. His operating base for the Germans was the espionage capital of Europe – Lisbon – though the Abwehr thought he was actually in London. The British took him on and brought him back to England, where he ran a network of imaginary sub-agents (including one called Lady Smith-Jones) in a manner later associated more with soap opera producers.

Garbo's greatest triumph related to D-Day, when he managed to invent a whole army – the First United States Army Group, or FUSAG – and persuade the Germans that the main landing point was to be in the Pas de Calais. Not only this, but once the Operation Overlord landings in Normandy were under way, he even convinced them that Overlord was merely a diversion for the bigger landing that was to come. Thus, he delayed the Germans sending reinforcements to Normandy. Later, he was able to send back misleading information about the landing points of the V1 flying bombs, causing the Germans to make future flights fall short. For all these services to the German war effort, Garbo was awarded the Iron Cross in the final months of the war.

From the earliest days of the war there was lobbying for internment on a large scale. Lord Hailsham (the father of the politician Quintin Hogg) warned the House of Lords in November 1939 against interning only those against whom charges could be proved. Those left at liberty would, he said, guide the enemy, start fires and disrupt the work of the ARP authorities. But in general terms the *Spectator* on 19 January 1940 was still able to praise the absence of a witch hunt to any significant degree.

Early in 1940 scare stories began to appear in the press about the activities of the Fifth Column. The *Daily Sketch* blamed them for mysterious explosions in a gunpowder factory at Waltham Cross (20 January 1940), while the *Sunday Express* claimed that Germans in Britain were being blackmailed – by threats to their families at home – into spying (21 January 1940).

It was as the Germans broke through in the west that a hysterical campaign was begun in both the press and the corridors of government to imprison *all* enemy aliens. There were ulterior motives for both sources of pressure. The leading papers in whipping up anti-Fifth Column feeling were for the most part those owned by pre-war pro-Nazis and appeasers. During the 1930s Lord

Rothermere, who owned the *Sunday Dispatch* and the *Daily Mail*, had been a staunch supporter of Hitler as a 'bulwark against bolshevism', had run pro-fascist campaigns and was the patron of Princess Stephanie von Hohenloe, a confidante of Hitler who was eventually arrested in America by the FBI and interned. With the outbreak of war, such attitudes became deeply unfashionable, not to say embarrassing, and it may have been in an attempt to cover his tracks that Rothermere took such an aggressively anti-alien standpoint. Another press baron notable for his attacks on the aliens was another former appeaser, Viscount Kemsley, owner of the *Sunday Times* and other papers.

The rapid invasion of Norway and Denmark took British Intelligence by complete surprise, despite a wealth of evidence about Hitler's intentions, which they chose to ignore or misinterpret. Rather than admit their mistakes, intelligence sources preferred to blame a well-developed Fifth Column for the speed of Norway's collapse. Their case was given valuable impetus by the brief emergence of Vidkun Quisling, the former Norwegian War Minister turned Nazi collaborator, whose real influence was actually so minimal that he was kept in the dark about German plans before the invasion (General von Falkenhurst, in charge of the German invasion forces, had never even heard of him) and was largely ignored afterwards. American reports of a massive Trojan horse of Fifth Columnists, created by the Germans before the invasion, were based on the flimsiest of what turned out to be incorrect evidence, but such reports gained widespread and unquestioning acceptance in Britain. This extract from the *Yorkshire Post* in April 1940 gives an example of how the spectre of the Fifth Column was raised with a minimum of hard evidence and a maximum of innuendo:

Before attacking a country, Hitler always tries to undermine it from within. How does he enlist his sympathisers, ready to work for him when the hour strikes? Partly by a long continued policy of threats, which compels the chosen country to allow the organisation of a Nazi party, raised around a nucleus of German nationals in its midst. Partly by spreading fears of invasion, which tempt the unscrupulous and timorous to ensure their good standing with the invaders in advance. Local adventurers and ne'er-do-wells are attracted by the promise of fat jobs when the Nazis arrive.

The *Sunday Dispatch*, as the following extract shows, made particular attacks on communist sympathisers and members of pacifist organisations such as the Peace Pledge Union, whom they dubbed 'conchies' . . . who constitute 'an underground political force which endangers the very life of the nation':

> The seriousness of the menace in Glasgow, second city of the British Empire, can be judged from the message to the *Sunday Dispatch* from Lord Provost Dollan:
>
> Here there are more than two thousand subversive agents acting on instructions from Moscow. They disguise themselves as peace societies or genuine working class organisations. It is time they were shown up for what they are.

Nothing was too insubstantial or peripheral for them to use. The *Dispatch* ran stories about the pampered treatment alien internees received in prison and retailed backstairs gossip from domestic servants, whose (unnamed) German colleagues seemed to spend a good deal of time near important military establishments. Another day, the target would be Czech refugees who were spending government money on the production of (no doubt subversive) leaflets.

One of the most loathsome specimens in the field of anti-alien polemic was the writer Beverley Nichols, described by François Lafitte (author of the best-selling book of the time on internment) as 'ex-pacifist, ex-Buckmanite, ex-Mosley supporter, ex-pro Nazi'. This is one example of Nichols's work, from the *Sunday Chronicle* of 11 May 1941:

> Cast your eye for a moment on the Isle of Man; a delectable spot with plenty of good food; a spot where many of us would like to spend a short holiday. Well, there are some people who are spending a very long holiday there at the British taxpayers' expense, but they are not British. They are interned aliens, all avowed or suspected enemies of this country. The manner in which they are being coddled is driving many people on the island pretty well crazy. Our treatment of these people carries humanitarianism to the verge of insanity. . . .

Nichols goes on to speculate about the internees being allowed to breed generations of new Nazis in their mixed camps, a thought which must have been offensive and bewildering in equal proportions to the many middle-aged Jews living in their overcrowded, sexually segregated camps on the island. The *Daily Mail* also appealed on behalf of a 'public opinion' of their own invention: 'Disquiet about Britain's "Fifth Column" is growing . . . the people ask that doubtful enemy aliens should be immediately interned and all other aliens strictly examined. . . . The traitors of Norway have shown the perils of the enemy within.'

For good measure, the same article also alleged that the public were crying out for action against communists and 'peace cranks'. Extremes of public opinion were indiscriminately given space in the papers. One local paper carried a call for concentration camps to be established for enemy aliens in Britain, while the *Daily Mail* published a letter calling for them to wear distinctive armbands – a chilling echo of the Star of David that Hitler forced Jews to wear in public places in Germany.

Not all the newspapers were so rabid in their positions. *The Times* opposed large-scale internment in an editorial on 23 April 1940, and the *Daily Express* spoke out in ringing terms in favour of 'freedom' and 'liberty'. The latter's position may have been not entirely unconnected with the fact that its proprietor, Lord Beaverbrook, was having a relationship with a Jewish refugee at the time.

Mass Observation carried out a rather more systematic sampling of public opinion about the Fifth Column at about the same time. Far from the public baying for blood:

> We found that the majority of the people hardly recognised what the phrase meant. We also found that the level of ordinary people's feelings was much less intense than that expressed in some papers. Detailed interviewing in several areas in London and Western Scotland produced less than one person in a hundred who spontaneously suggested that refugees ought to be interned en masse.

Politicians none the less began to join the hue and cry. On 19 April some seventy Conservative MPs met at the Commons to discuss the problem of the Fifth Column. Some Labour MPs also became concerned, though their perspective on the problem was rather different. Whereas the Conservatives aimed their fire at aliens, communists and pacifists, the focus of Labour's concern was Oswald Mosley and the groups on the political far right. *Reynolds News*, which numbered Richard Crossman and J.B. Priestley among its editorial staff, was one of the few papers to follow the more socialist line. Crossman wrote that the Fifth Column would be found among: 'the rich and respected of the land. I can only explain the arrest of Social Democrats from Nazi concentration camps as a hysterical attempt to persuade public opinion that something is being done about a Fifth Column. It arouses my suspicion.'

However, *Reynolds News* and some of the papers on the left ran a campaign against British Fifth Columnists which was sometimes scarcely more responsible than that of the right-wing papers against the aliens. The *Manchester Guardian* became a particular champion of the refugees. By the end of 1940 they had published some 54 articles and leaders and 110 (overwhelmingly supportive) letters on the subject.

Some in the Civil Service shared the suspicion that the hysteria against enemy aliens was a blind to disguise real Fifth Column activity by British-born Nazi sympathisers. Moves were made to try to have aliens simply resettled as free people in other countries, rather than deported and interned. This was rejected, on the grounds that public opinion would not stand for such preferential treatment. If the German invasion were successful, the powers-that-be decided, the aliens should 'go down in the common ruin'.

At the same time as they tried to calm public sentiment, staff at the Home Office were being pressured by the security services. The latter maintained their belief in the danger of the Fifth Column, despite the lack of evidence. As a Joint Intelligence Committee report saw it, the absence of sabotage to date was some kind of bizarre proof of the existence of Fifth Columnists:

> We cannot rule out the possibility that Fifth Column activities in this country, at present dormant, might well play a very active and highly dangerous part at the appropriate moment selected by the enemy . . . the absence of sabotage up to date reinforces the view that such activities will only take place as part of a prearranged military plan.

Winston Churchill became Prime Minister on the same day that the Low Countries were invaded. This invasion again provided boundless (and mostly false) evidence of Fifth Column activity, much of it from people who should have known better. These included members of the Dutch government and their royal family (whose official report to their counterparts at Buckingham Palace made it clear that it was Dutch natives of a Nazi disposition, and not German nationals living within their borders, who had been the real problem – insofar as a Fifth Column could be held accountable at all for the invasion).

Particularly culpable was Sir Nevile Bland, the British Minister to Holland. He fled as the Germans invaded, and presented the Foreign Secretary, Lord Halifax, with a scaremongering story of murderous paratroops and Fifth Column activity – a story that enjoyed a wide currency in Britain. It was circulated immediately to the Cabinet, prompting Winston Churchill to call in Cabinet for:

> A very large round up of enemy aliens and suspect persons . . . it would be much better that these persons should be behind barbed wire. . . . Internment would probably be much safer for all German-speaking persons themselves since, when air attacks develop, public temper in this country would be such that such persons would be in great danger if at liberty.

Churchill's bullish approach to the internment of aliens was particularly ironic, given that the refugee population had generally been among his strongest supporters, bitterly opposed to the appeasement policies of Chamberlain.

Bland compounded his errors by repeating them on the radio and, via the Ministry of Information, to the press. Despite admitting to the Chaplain to the British Legation in The Hague that he could not identify a single case where a German refugee acted as a Fifth Columnist in Holland, Bland advised his listeners: 'Be careful at this moment how you put complete trust in any person of German or Austrian connection . . . if you know people of this kind, who are at large, keep an eye on them.' In fact, the example of Holland was fairly irrelevant to Britain in a variety of ways. They shared a land border with Germany and a hundred thousand totally unvetted Germans living in the country before war broke out. It would have been far easier to establish a Fifth Column there than in England.

All this hysteria delighted the Germans, who, learning of this new and unexpected source of 'support' within Britain, wasted no time in getting Lord Haw-Haw to broadcast bogus instructions to his non-existent army of Fifth Columnists. This in turn increased the paranoia among the British population, and so the spiral of hysteria went on. The Ministry of Information managed to add to the problem. After reporting to the government on 5 June that 'Fifth Column hysteria is reaching quite dangerous proportions', they promptly made it worse by publishing their own leaflet on the subject, guaranteed to set neighbour against neighbour. It said:

> There is a Fifth Column in Britain. Anyone who thinks there isn't, that 'it can't happen here', has simply fallen into the trap laid by the Fifth Column itself. For the first job of the Fifth Column is to make people believe that it does not exist. In other countries, the most respectable and neighbourly citizens turned out to be Fifth Columnists.

The Home Secretary, Sir John Anderson, tried vainly to resist this tide of opinion. As a former career civil servant, he was opposed to large-scale internment as much on the grounds of the administrative chaos it would cause as for its injustice. The research his officials carried out found little or no evidence to support the allegations of others about Fifth Column activity, at home or abroad.

But, right at the height of the struggle within the Cabinet, news broke of a spying scandal involving Anna Wolkoff, a naturalised British woman of Russian extraction, and Tyler Kent, an American Embassy official. They were tried in secret at the Old Bailey and received long sentences. There was later a suggestion that at the heart of the case there was some kind of political conspiracy involving MI5. If so, it had the desired effect of hardening the climate of opinion against enemy aliens. By May 1940 Mass Observation was reporting a change in the public's views about aliens, often coupled with increasing anti-Semitism.

The Home Secretary finally lost his struggle against large-scale internment. On 27 May all Category B aliens of German or Austrian origin were ordered to be rounded up and arrested, followed by Category C males in the weeks following 21 June. Although much of the pressure for this came from the security forces, the blanket approach illustrated the failure of the government intelligence services to sort out the security risks from the genuine refugees. Nor was there any evidence to link refugees to specific pieces of Fifth Column activity. Last, but not least, it exposed the lie (for example, in the *Sunday Express* of 9 June 1940) that the authorities had seized a full list of all the potential Gauleiters-in-waiting and Fifth Columnists in a raid on the British Union of Fascists' office.

To complete the process, pressure was successfully exerted for alien women to be included in the round-up. *The Times'* leader of 23 May quoted Kipling's remark about the female of the species being deadlier than the male, while Beverley Nichols made his own, more basic, appeal to the public's fears: 'German women, some of them pretty, are not above offering their charms to any young man, particularly if he works in a munitions factory or in a public works.' By late May Churchill's position on internees had hardened yet further. By now, he was 'strongly in favour of removing all internees out of the United Kingdom.'

But worse was still to come.

The Italian Connection

Even before the Italians joined the war, they were being indiscriminately vilified. This example is from the *Daily Mirror* in April 1940:

> There are more than twenty thousand Italians in Great Britain. London alone shelters more than eleven thousand of them. The London Italian is an indigestible unit of population. He settles here more or less temporarily, working until he has enough money to buy himself a little land in Calabria, or Campagnia or Tuscany. He often avoids employing British labour. It is much cheaper to bring a few relations into England from the old home town.
>
> And so the boats unloaded all sorts of brown-eyed Francescas and Marias, beetle-browed Ginos, Titos and Marios. . . . Now every Italian colony in Great Britain and America is a seething cauldron of smoking Italian politics. Black fascism. Hot as hell.
>
> Even the peaceful, law-abiding proprietor of the back-street coffee shop bounces into a fine patriotic frenzy at the sound of Mussolini's name. . . . We are nicely honeycombed with little cells of potential betrayal. A storm is brewing in the

Mediterranean. And we, in our droning silly tolerance, are helping it to gather force.

The treatment of the Italians was in some respects even more shameful than that of the other aliens. No real attempt was made even at the outset to screen them, to separate out the security risks from the others. The Acting Head of MI5, Brigadier Harker, wrote in May 1940:

> We have reason to suppose that the first act of war on the part of Italy might be an attempt to use the Italian fascist organisation for an attack on the key industries and key points in this country by the employment of gangster methods. We are therefore anxious that our arrangements should be made so as to forestall such attempts if possible.

They wanted the immediate arrest of 'all known suspects' and said that they had a list of 1,500 'desperate' and 'dangerous' characters. This list turned out to be fundamentally flawed. Not only did it include many prominent anti-fascists, it also failed to understand that membership of the Italian Fascists did not, in itself, make one 'desperate' and 'dangerous'. Even the Foreign Office understood this, as their memorandum from June 1940 shows:

> MI5's criteria for judging whether or not a person was a 'desperate character' more often than not resolved itself into mere membership of the Fascio. On being pointed out that membership of the Fascio was to all intents and purposes obligatory on any Italian resident abroad who desired to have any sort of claim to diplomatic or consular protection, they relented somewhat and limited their objection to Fascists of military age and special ardour. . . . As the discussion with MI5 proceeded there grew up a strong suspicion that in actual fact they had little or no information, let alone evidence, in regard to more than a fraction of the persons they had led the Home Secretary to describe to the Cabinet as 'desperate characters'.

But lack of evidence was not allowed to stand in the way. Immediately upon Mussolini's declaration of war, on 10 June 1940, Churchill issued the order 'Collar the lot!' Everyone on the MI5 list, plus all post-1919 residents, became eligible for internment. It was accompanied by a nationwide bout of xenophobic violence, reminiscent of the worst excesses of the First World War. The length and breadth of the country saw anti-Italian riots. Parts of Edinburgh were described as looking as if they had been bombed, and the police had to mount baton charges to disperse the crowds. Italian shops were wrecked and looted, in some cases with the terrified proprietors barricaded in upstairs. Children of Italian origin were victimised at school.

Italian businesses were quick to proclaim their loyalty. They would display signs saying 'this shop is entirely British' or 'the family owning this restaurant has sons serving in the British Army'. Bianchis in Frith Street, Soho, changed overnight from an Italian to a Swiss restaurant and a Leeds organ grinder put up a sign saying 'I'm British and the monkey is from India'.

This xenophobia rebounded on the British in one respect. One of their favourite daughters, Gracie Fields, was forced to quit Britain for the United States before her Italian-born husband, Monty Banks, and she officially became 'enemy aliens'.

The Internment Process

The process by which opinion was turned against alien refugees was disreputable enough, but the procedures by which they were detained were even more harsh and unjust. Even as Britain's ultimatum to Germany was running out, in September 1939, the exhibition halls at Olympia were being prepared for the reception of alien detainees. Arrests began even before war was formally declared, and the first batches rounded up on the instructions of MI5 contained an apparently random and potentially explosive mixture of ardent Nazis, Jews and political refugees. The latter included some people clearly arrested in error, such as Eugen Spier. As a member of the Focus for the Defence of Freedom and Peace before the war, Spier had advised Winston Churchill and helped inform his anti-appeasement stance. However, having influential friends did nothing to prevent his internment, and he found himself rubbing shoulders with the likes of Captain Schiffer, a senior Nazi police official and friend of Hitler. One man, who spoke no German and whose father had deserted his mother shortly after his birth, only learned of his German ancestry when they came to intern him.

Only a week before the outbreak of war, the government sub-committee responsible for the process belatedly realised that they would need separate camps for the pro-Nazis and the Jewish and other refugees. In consequence, these were not prepared in time. In some cases refugees were forced to endure the threats, abuse and violence of their Nazi fellow inmates for anything up to a year. The latter would jeer at the Jewish refugees' attempts to continue with their religious devotions, and would gather outside the accommodation of the Jews and refugees and lull them to sleep with the heart-warming sentiments of songs such as 'Wenn das Juden blut vom messer spritzt': 'When the blood of the Jews gushes forth from our knives, then everything goes twice as well.' Requests for segregation by the refugees themselves were repeatedly ignored by the authorities, as were anti-Jewish signs erected by the Nazis.

The process was conducted in a harsh and bureaucratic manner, given that many of these people had already suffered grievously in their home country. Families were split up, either as a consequence of being in different categories or because they were simply in different places at the time of arrest. They might even find themselves deported overseas without notice. The random nature of the process is illustrated by the case of a ten-year-old German Jewish boy, who was being sponsored by a British barrister to attend school at Winchester. But Winchester was in a prohibited area, and under the new restrictions an alien could not live there. Had the barrister chosen almost any other public school, the problem would not have arisen. However, before he could arrange for the boy's transfer, he had been interned and deported to Canada.

In another case a British woman had married a Category C German – a man whose loyalty to Britain was unquestioned. She was told that she could reclaim her British nationality within two months. Due to some bureaucratic muddle, this was not done and, when the new regulations came in, her husband was immediately arrested and she herself was declared an enemy alien. Others, who actually wanted to go overseas – who were in transit through Britain en route to some third country – were also caught up in the process and arrested.

As the numbers of interned aliens increased rapidly, the authorities were overwhelmed and forced to use the most unsuitable

SWISS MOVEMENT

Perhaps the most extreme and, in some respects, most ludicrous example of innocents caught up in the British policy towards aliens concerned two Swiss men. Named Eggler and Schmid, they were working in Belgium when the Germans invaded and they tried to cycle back to Switzerland. They were arrested as possible paratroops by the French, on the not particularly persuasive grounds that one of them was carrying a rucksack. They were handed over to the British, with whom they were made to travel, via the beaches of Dunkirk, to Dover, where they were promptly refused entry to Britain. Given that arrangements for returning people to the continent were, at that time, not entirely straightforward, they were then interned. It took a month for the Swiss authorities to find them and six to get them released to neutral Portugal.

accommodation for them. An unfinished housing estate at Huyton, near Liverpool, was requisitioned and surrounded by high barbed-wire fences. Twelve men were placed in each part-completed house with no furniture and just a sackful of straw each for a mattress. Others initially slept in tents beside the houses. Due to the shortage of coal for heating, they were allowed only one bath a month – which was perhaps just as well, since there was also a severe shortage of soap, towels and other basic materials. All cooking and eating had to be done in tents, whatever the weather.

Further investigation revealed that about a third of those interned on the estate were unfit to endure such treatment – the police had largely ignored Home Office instructions not to arrest the invalid or infirm. About 40 per cent of the inmates were found to be over 50 years of age, and many of them were considerably older. One house was completely filled with advanced tuberculosis cases. A single doctor, woefully short of medical supplies, served all the four thousand people living on the estate, assisted by whatever medical help the other inmates could provide. They were denied books, newspapers and wirelesses. Letters were delayed and censored.

Even worse conditions were faced by those housed in Warth Mills, a disused cotton mill in Bury. The floors where they slept were covered in cotton waste, oil and grease. The only light came through the glass roof, which was broken in many places, letting in the rain. Five hundred men shared eighteen cold water taps and filthy toilets, and they were half-starved – their evening meal consisting of a lump of bread, a small piece of cheese and a cup of tea. Few of the inmates had mattresses; most had to make do with a couple of (often verminous) blankets, and they shared this salubrious accommodation with rats. The Red Cross visited the site and complained about the conditions, as did Sir Walter Monckton from the Ministry of Information, who wrote: 'The two men who succeeded in committing suicide had already been in Hitler's concentration camps. Against these they held out, but this camp has broken their spirit.'

Others found themselves in tented camps or deported to the Isle of Man, where they became a poor substitute for the peacetime tourist trade. In Onchan camp they lived in grossly overcrowded conditions, two to a bed with others sleeping on the floors between the beds. No radios and, initially, no newspapers were allowed, and mail was delayed in a monstrous backlog of censorship that at one time reached a hundred thousand letters. A survey of those at Onchan gave some indication of the threat this group of evacuees posed to British security. Of the 1,491 inmates, 121 were artists or men of letters, 113 scientists or teachers, 68 lawyers, and 67 engineers; 1,230 of them were Jewish; 148 were married to British women, and no fewer than 1,080 of them had attempted to sign up in the British armed forces, to fight the Germans.

But even these spartan conditions were considered over-generous by the anti-alien lobby. It was claimed in the press that the prisoners on the Isle of Man were living in the lap of luxury, with private golf courses, beaches, cinema shows, the benefits of sea air and, of course, full hotel catering. Even the camp at Huyton was regarded as if it offered preferential treatment of some kind, with complaints voiced in Parliament about the aliens getting new homes while Britons continued to live in slums.

By a further irony, the Nazis who were interned enjoyed substantially better conditions, for a number of reasons. First, they had greater protection under the Geneva Convention, whereas the British could virtually make up their own rules for 'friendly' aliens. Secondly, the British government was afraid that, if they were harsh on Nazi internees, the German authorities might take retaliatory action against those British nationals interned in Germany.

MISSING CHILDREN

In the summer of 1939 my father sent us to Shottery near Stratford. My brother and I caught chickenpox. We were looked after by a German-Jewish doctor. He taught us how to make animals in plasticine – lions, elephants, horses and camels. He drew ink circles round the last pock marks on our arms and legs. We asked him where his children were. He cried. I asked my mother why he had cried. 'Don't ask so many questions!' she said. 'He cried!' said my brother. Then my mother cried. We were totally baffled.

Girl aged six, London, quoted in Westall.

More sinister was the suggestion that some of those responsible for their captivity felt greater sympathy for their Nazi inmates, as people who somehow 'stuck to their principles' in adversity (regardless of how distasteful those principles may be).

Swanwick, the first camp set up exclusively for interned Nazis, was a spacious manor house in Derbyshire, set in extensive grounds. All the older Nazis had their own rooms, with central heating and good plumbing. Moreover, the inmates effectively ran the place, with their own processes of censorship and discipline.

By the end of June 1940 the total number interned had reached 27,200. The Dominions were eventually persuaded to take substantial numbers of them, because it was felt that they constituted a major security risk if they remained in Britain. Over 11,000 internees were eventually shipped out. For many, the journeys to Canada or Australia proved hellish – and for a considerable number, they were to prove fatal.

Unlike the prisoners who were transported to the colonies in the nineteenth century, the internees were not even told where they were going. Some, as they were marched, at bayonet point, to the docks in Liverpool by soldiers, were pelted with rubbish by angry crowds. At the dockside, many had their valuables stolen or thrown into the sea. Those who managed to hold on to their possessions subsequently had them stolen by the crews on the ships or by their Canadian guards on their arrival.

They were packed on to the ships at twice or more their peacetime capacity. Even on board ship the discrimination continued, with the German army personnel getting the first claim on the cabins and the refugees often kept virtually imprisoned below decks throughout the voyage. Lynton describes a hellish crossing to Canada, during which an epidemic of dysentery broke out. Those who escaped the disease spent five solid days working naked in the sweltering heat below decks to clear up with their bare hands the mess left by the victims.

Throughout, their treatment seems to have been based upon the assumption that they were all virulent Nazis, which was far from the truth. A group of refugee monks found themselves jeered as they disembarked, in the belief that they were disguised Nazi paratroopers who had not yet had time to change out of their fancy dress since dropping on Holland! The Canadians, on receiving a bunch of supposedly desperate Nazi criminals, were surprised to find themselves controlling groups of callow schoolboys and left-wing sailors, about a third of whom demanded kosher food.

The cruellest fate awaited the men who left Liverpool on 1 July on board the *Arandora Star*. One day out from England, she was torpedoed and sank with the loss of 650 lives. The ship's normal peacetime capacity was 700 and there were lifeboats on board for 1,000 people (but not all of them proved capable of being launched). But for this voyage, the ship was packed with 1,564 people. No lifeboat drill had been explained to the passengers, many of whom were elderly and infirm.

Despite the death toll, the British press continued to attack the internees. According to the *Daily Express*:

> Soldiers and sailors . . . told of the panic among the aliens when they realised the ship was sinking. All condemned the cowardice of the Germans, who fought madly to get into the boats. 'The Germans were fighting with the Italians to escape, they were great hulking brutes', said one soldier. 'They punched and kicked their way past the Italians. We had to restrain them forcibly.' . . . 'But the Italians were just as bad. The whole mob of them thought of their own skins first. The scramble for the boats was sickening.'

Subsequent investigations showed this account to be entirely false. Just to complete the inglorious tale, Anthony Eden further tried to blacken their memory by claiming in the House of

Commons that all the passengers on the *Arandora Star* were either Italian Fascists or Category A Germans, and that none were refugees. He was reminded of the names of some of the prominent anti-Nazis who had gone down with the ship and duly promised to re-check his facts. He would not have been helped by the fact that the paperwork surrounding the departure of the ship had been in chaos, and nobody was sure precisely who was on it. Government inquiries were eventually launched, both into the deaths on the *Arandora Star* and into conditions at the Huyton internment camp.

The *Arandora Star* episode marked the beginning of the end of mass internment. The excesses of the press had begun to turn public opinion against internment. Many of the great and the good in the arts and literature, in particular, began to campaign against it, as much for the ham-fisted way in which it had been put into practice as for the basic principle. The anti-internment case began to get more of a hearing in the mainstream press. Michael Foot was able to write in the *Evening Standard* on 17 July 1940:

> If we intern German anti-Nazis who fought Hitler for years, why not also intern De Gaulle? This war is not about national frontiers; it is on a scale not seen since the Reformation. Instead of interning German political refugees we should use them as speakers to reach the hearts and minds of Germans and as underground fighters to spark off a revolution.

Public opinion shifted rapidly. Between mid-July and early August 1940 the proportion of the public in favour of wholesale internment fell from 55 per cent to about 30 per cent. In August Winston Churchill, once one of the most ardent 'internists' in the Cabinet, told the Commons, without a hint of irony or embarrassment, that he had always thought the 'Fifth Column danger somewhat exaggerated in this Island'. Sir John Anderson spoke more candidly to the Commons on 22 August:

> I am not going to deny for a moment that the most regrettable and deplorable things have happened. . . . They have been due partly to the inevitable haste with which the policy of internment, once decided upon, had to be carried out. They have been due in some cases to the mistakes of individuals and

to stupidity and muddle. These matters all relate to the past. So far as we can remedy mistakes, we shall remedy them.

During a parliamentary debate shortly before that, the government admitted that it knew of only one case (details unspecified) of a serious hostile act committed by an alien. Category C internees began to be released in significant numbers on 5 August. By the end of the month about a thousand had been set free, and by the end of the year almost nine thousand. Releases continued at about a thousand a month into 1941.

The Foreign Office belatedly set up a committee to advise on the welfare of internees and 'measures for maintaining the morale of aliens in this country so as to bind them more closely to our common cause'. Behind the scenes, the Foreign Office also launched a vicious attack on the ineptitude of MI5's part in the process, forcing an apology from the Chairman of the Joint Intelligence Committee.

The whole process had not only caused great hardship and injustice, and bureaucratic chaos, but had diverted significant resources away from any useful contribution to the war effort, and had denied the nation the efforts of a substantial and, for the vast majority, devotedly anti-Nazi group of people. For some, already burdened by the suffering they had undergone in their native country, anxieties about the safety of the families they had left behind and other factors, this treatment was the last straw.

The suicides in Warth Mills had succeeded in their grim mission. Another, 23-year-old Katherina Schwind, a domestic servant of Austrian descent, was found trying to gas herself. Her employer promptly moved her on to a couch and called not an ambulance, but the police. She was charged with attempted suicide and bound over to keep the peace (and, presumably, to stay alive) for twelve months.

Hitler, speaking at a Fuhrer Conference in July 1940, admitted: 'We cannot count that there would be much support at our disposal in England.' He found this out the hard way. Attempts to win over disaffected Welsh and Scottish Nationalists proved unsuccessful, and even the German contacts with the IRA in Dublin ended when the Irish government expelled the Germans' liaison officer.

In the absence of a spy network, much of the German intelligence about Britain and most of the European countries they conquered came from maps and guides that could be purchased in Berlin before the war. Studies of German intelligence sources after the war revealed the paucity and often inaccuracy of the information they possessed about Britain. Indeed, research carried out for UNESCO after the war indicated that, throughout western Europe, the idea of a Fifth Column on any significant scale had been a myth. Norwegian minefields 'defused' by Fifth Columnists had never been laid. Dutch bridges were not left undestroyed because of sabotage, but because the Dutch troops guarding them, expecting French reinforcements, had neglected to place any charges underneath them. False orders were never given.

One unexpected positive result of this whole unhappy process came from the fact that foreign nationals were not allowed to work on projects with direct application to the war effort. However, the more 'pure science' of atomic energy was not at that time covered by this war work rule, so a number of them went on to work on the Manhattan Project – which led in turn to the nuclear bomb and to the shortening of the war against Japan.

Anti-alien Feeling among the General Public

Anti-alien feeling may not have been widespread before the newspaper campaigns got to work, but it soon found fertile soil in which to grow. It was not always well directed. Many employers summarily dismissed their Hungarian staff on the outbreak of war, notwithstanding the fact that Hungary was a neutral country. They did not even meet their legal obligations to pay them wages in lieu of notice or their fare home, with the result that large numbers descended on the Hungarian Legation, looking for help. Seventeen 'enemy aliens' engaged in ARP work in Marylebone were sacked in May 1940 and the London County Council dismissed all Germans in its employ in early June.

Discrimination affected even the most long-standing and unimpeachable resident. This case was reported in the *Maidenhead Advertiser* in July 1940:

A petition, signed by some five hundred persons, has been forwarded to the Ministry of Home Security in regard to the continuance in office as Head A.R.P. Warden of Mr M.J. Speer, whose surname was formerly Mecklenburg. The view was expressed in the petition that it is wrong to permit persons of enemy origin or connection to occupy key positions in civil defence . . . to restore public confidence in the integrity and efficiency of our local civil defence services, we ask that . . . they appoint in Mr Speer's place a person without enemy taint.

And what was Mr Speer's dangerously subversive background? He had been born in Middlesex in 1883, his father having been a naturalised Englishman at the time of his marriage. The only time he had left his native shores was to fight the Germans during the First World War, where he distinguished himself by winning three medals and rising to the rank of staff sergeant. Mr Speer not unnaturally put the petition down to the activities of Fifth Columnists.

Following the outbreak of war, refugees continued to arrive in Britain at a rate of around 800 per month, until about 150,000 were living here. Only about a third of them were Jewish, but the blanket term 'refu-jew' was insultingly applied to them all, initially by the British Union of Fascists. Anti-Semitism grew during the war years. A survey in 1940 showed that 17 per cent of the population even agreed with Lord Haw-Haw's proposition that the Allies were fighting the war on behalf of Jews and capitalists. This Home Intelligence report from 6 May 1943 illustrates the problem:

During the last three weeks comment about Jews in this country appears to have increased slightly. Jews continue to be criticised for black marketing, escaping the call-up and 'displaying ostentatious wealth'. In London, the North Midland and North Western regions, there is said to be an increase in anti-semitism – 'the spreading of which is seemingly in some cases deliberately organised and fostered'; it is suggested that, in Hornsey, 'anti-semitism due to ignorance and prejudice is exploited by Fascist elements'. Reference is also made to 'undue prominence shown in the press to court cases against Jews'.

This anti-Semitism was despite public knowledge beginning to emerge of Hitler's ill-treatment of them in continental Europe.

ANTI-SEMITISM

I was travelling on the Tube to Edgware and people were getting up, making speeches. 'It's about time we caved in to Hitler. When all's said and done he's doing a good job, he's murdering all these bloody Jews.' They were probably Fascists.

Commercial traveller, quoted by Grafton.

At first, the Ministry of Information had been unwilling to publish the information about the concentration camps, because of the anti-Semitism in the country at large. Details of the appalling toll of lives were received from the middle of 1942, but it was not until 17 December that Anthony Eden announced them to the House of Commons. When he did, cynicism about the false German atrocity stories circulated during the First World War led a good number of the general public to disbelieve them.

Relationships between Jews and the rest of the population were complex. While those who were either positively pro-Jewish or actively anti-Semitic were both in a minority, opinion research suggests that a sizeable part of the population held views about Jews that were to varying degrees ambivalent. Mass Observation found evidence of anti-Semitism to some degree among more than 55 per cent of one of its survey populations.

What is clear is that anti-Semitism was much more institutionalised and respectable than it is today. People apparently found it easy to separate their anti-Semitism from their opposition to Nazism. A Mass Observation survey in January 1944 found 24 per cent of the population calling for stricter controls over the activities of British Fascists, while only 2 per cent of the same population saw the need for any curbs on anti-Semitism. Clubs and societies commonly had an open policy of excluding Jews, and A.J.P. Taylor has suggested that many people were 'annoyed at having to repudiate the anti-Semitism which they had secretly cherished', as a result of the Nazis' persecution of the Jews. A best-selling author like Douglas Reed could use openly and quite extremely anti-Semitic themes in his books – for example, *Insanity Fair*, published in 1938, had the Jews taking over London. Despite being forced by his publisher to tone down some of his worst excesses, Reed still attracted much criticism – as well as a huge readership – for fiction that was as racist as it was racy. He ended the war as foreign editor for Kemsley newspapers, despite being associated with some extreme anti-Semitic organisations.

He was far from alone. Another bestselling author, Warwick Deeping, featured crude caricatures of Jews in his 1941 book *The Dark House*, in which popular detective Sexton Blake pitted his wits against a 'Jewish financier' (the stereotype was so well established that it hardly needed further elaboration) who controlled both the Bank of England and the Bank of China. Improbably, Jewish characters even found their way into fiction as leading lights in the Gestapo. On the radio, a series of plays called *Born to be King*, broadcast in 1941–2 and written by Dorothy L. Sayers, portrayed the Jews of biblical times in such a hostile light that it led to complaints from the Jewish community, and to Jewish children being bullied at school for 'killing Jesus'. The BBC's response was to repeat the series over Easter 1943. This was a lapse from a generally creditable record on anti-Semitism by the BBC during the war years.

Anti-Semitism was not restricted to one part of the political spectrum. While it found its most virulent voice on the extreme right, mainstream Conservatives also displayed it to various degrees. Churchill himself had been a leading protagonist of the existence of a Jewish/Communist conspiracy in 1918, but now advised others in the party to 'be careful, whatever the temptation, not to be drawn into any campaign that might be represented as anti-Semitic'.

None the less a group of Conservative MPs lobbied against giving any refugees British nationality, since it would 'result in a permanent increase of our already over-large Jewish population . . . which was . . . a most unhealthy symptom in the body politic. The Jewish vote is so strong in some constituencies that the Member has no freedom of action.'

Not a single Jewish Conservative MP was elected in 1945. Even Lord Gort, who as High Commissioner for Palestine might have been expected to know better, was taken to task for making anti-Semitic remarks, but the complaints against him led to no disciplinary action from the government.

But anti-Semitism was also to be found on the radical left, where the Independent Labour Party attacked Jewish capitalism, among other things for causing the war. The ILP shared its anti-war position with the British Union of Fascists (BUF), and there had even been talk of a coalition between them in early 1939. The *Daily Worker* managed to condemn both anti-Semitism and Jewish financiers at the same time. Even after the liberation of the concentration camps there were those on the radical left who still believed that their main victims had been members of the German working classes.

The liberal centre opposed what it saw as Jewish exclusivity, and argued that the solution to prejudice was for them to become assimilated (that is, to give up their religion and their separate identity). Finally, well-meaning pacifist bodies such as the Peace Pledge Union were infiltrated by right-wing extremists, and their *Peace News* was given over to anti-Semitic attacks from the likes of the Duke of Bedford and the British National Party founder Edward Godfrey.

Among the lunatic fringes, wild views were held about Jewish plans for world domination. By 1943 some 70–80 per cent of German broadcasting time was given over to anti-Semitic material, including widespread publicity for the *Protocols of the Elders of Zion*. This told of a plot, dating from the time of King Solomon (and thus rather a long time in its gestation) for the Jews to overthrow Christianity and take over the world. Two editions of the *Protocols* were published and widely distributed during the war years. Running parallel to this was the school of thought that the present-day Jews were a mongrelised version of their biblical selves, and that the British were in fact the true descendants of God's chosen people.

The East End of London had one of the largest Jewish populations in Britain, and the fascists saw this area as their natural territory. If active anti-Semitism on a large scale was going to take root anywhere, it was likely to be here. In the event, the record of race relations there was patchy. In some cases, Jews and gentiles worked together to pursue common aims (as when the Stepney Tenants' Defence League successfully took on the slum landlords). In other areas, such as the Pembury Estate in Hackney, violence and attacks on Jewish property were used by the non-Jewish tenants in pursuit of a localised policy of ethnic cleansing. They were supported in this by the right-wing local newspaper, the *Hackney Gazette*. In more genteel areas of north-west London, similar sentiments took the form of a petition campaign, designed to remove aliens from the area.

Jews were prominent in the Civil Defence in the East End and, despite some initial tensions, appear generally to have worked well with their non-Jewish colleagues during the blitz. In the Tilbury shelter, Jews and gentiles united to persecute the local Indian population. Jewish shops were attacked in retaliation for the internment of leading fascists, and on one occasion, when a film at a Stepney cinema showed the Nazi persecution of the Jews, a racist element in the audience cheered, leading to a fight among the audience. But on the whole, the worst predictions of a breakdown in relations between the communities following bombing were not realised. Active anti-Semitism did not take root there on any large scale.

In the wider community, claims were commonly made that able-bodied Jews were displacing women and children in air raid shelters (something which George Orwell investigated and found to be groundless). The worst example of this occurred in March 1943 when 173 people were killed in front of Bethnal Green tube station. Some attempted to blame this disaster on panic among the local Jewish population. In fact, this was the non-Jewish part of the East End, the real heartland of the BUF, and the fact that only 3 per cent of those killed in the disaster were Jewish belies the rumour.

Jews were particularly accused of involvement in the black market. They were not helped in this by their strong association with consumer industries like food and clothing, where it was easy for a customer denied service by a genuine shortage to blame it on a Jewish conspiracy. Sections of the press seized upon these feelings. This is from the Janus column in the *Spectator*: 'There can be no doubt that a section, and a substantial section, of the Jewish community has a black record in this respect. It is not to anyone's advantage to keep complete silence in this matter.' Even normally sympathetic sources, like Cassandra in the *Daily Mirror*, echoed the concern: 'I have been examining the records of convictions for food misdemeanours, and it is impossible not to be struck by the number of Jewish offenders. Names like Blum, Cohen, Gold and the like occur with remarkable frequency.'

An analysis of black market prosecutions for the period April 1942 to May 1943 showed that, of more than 2,500 prosecutions, 10.9 per cent involved Jewish offenders. However, when this is compared to the proportion of businesses in Jewish ownership at the time, it appears that Jewish entrepreneurs were no worse (albeit no better) than their Aryan counterparts. The government did not publish these findings at the time, for fear of it being seen as Jewish propaganda. There is also some evidence that the newspapers were selective in the cases they publicised. For example, *The Grocer* in March 1942 reported forty-eight black market cases, only three of which involved Jews. However, it was these three cases that received some of the most extensive publicity in the wider press.

The Jewish community in Britain was, not surprisingly, sensitive to this current of opinion. In his 1943 Passover letter, the Chief Rabbi Dr J.H. Hertz warned: 'Though others are guilty of the same and even greater transgressions, they do not, in the eyes of the public, compromise their religious communities. But every Jew holds the good name of his entire people in his hand.'

The Jewish community, and its supporters such as the National Council for Civil Liberties, was active in trying to rebut anti-Semitic propaganda from whatever source (though the NCCL was simultaneously opposing Regulation 18B, which put the main peddlers of anti-Semitism behind bars, on the grounds of *habeas corpus*). How successful they all were is open to question, since their approach assumed that the holder of anti-Semitic views was susceptible to rational argument. They set up their own tribunal, to investigate the substance of the complaints being made against the community, but even this was turned against them by anti-Semites, who claimed that it was a device to by-pass established courts.

The Board of Jewish Deputies employed a public relations officer, whose main job was to go around London, correcting the behaviour of refugees – preventing them from speaking German too loudly, or warning Jewish restaurateurs against displaying German-language newspapers too openly in their premises.

The complaints against Jews were only silenced when the gates of Auschwitz and Belsen were opened to a horrified world.

Racial Prejudice

People cheerful and optimistic at weekend when Hitler failed to invade Britain on Friday as threatened. General feeling now that war will last a long time, as invasion cannot succeed and we shall then settle down to hammering away at Germany by RAF. . . . Most coloured people reported anxious to pull weight in war effort; unable to, except in St Pancras where twenty are Air Raid wardens. Some dismissals because of colour.

Home Intelligence report 22 July 1940.

Many British citizens had scarcely seen a black person before the arrival of the GIs in 1942. To them, this strange breed might as well have come from the moon. Their exotic nature is illustrated by the fact that some of them were successful in persuading the gullible locals that their skin had been artificially blackened for camouflage in night exercises, and that an injection would restore them to white on their return home.

Many of the problems stemmed from the fact that the American Army was far more racist than the host population. Most American states still practised their own form of apartheid. Among the white GIs, there were plenty who would not drink out of a glass previously used by a black person, and British branches of the Ku Klux Klan were not uncommon.

The subservience of many black GIs, born of years of discrimination and disadvantage in their own country, was taken by many Britons as politeness, as Home Intelligence reported in June 1944:

> Colonel Blimp explains: 'Gad sir, Lucy Houston is right! Those black troops are fine patriotic fellows – so long as they don't forget themselves and try to fight for their own country.'

Coloured troops . . . are praised. In some cases they are said to be better behaved and 'less sloppy' than the whites; also, in the Huddersfield area, better behaved than the British troops.

People deplore the association of coloured troops with white girls, but it is the latter who are censured. At the same time, it is suggested that the negroes might be provided with a contingent of coloured Auxiliaries, or more camp amenities so that they should spend less time out.

There is some concern at the relations between white and coloured troops and at reports of friction between them. Recent cases of coloured men being condemned to death for rape have aroused strong local protests on grounds of colour discrimination (S.W. Region). In Norwich there is resentment that certain restaurants will not serve negroes.

A Home Office Circular of 1943 warned that: 'Some British women appear to find a particular fascination in association with men of colour. The morale of British troops is likely to be upset by rumours that their wives and daughters are being debauched by coloured American troops.'

But the danger was not just in one direction. In May 1944 a black GI was sentenced to death for the alleged rape of a white woman. The *Daily Mirror* took up his cause, exposing inconsistencies in the woman's case. They produced evidence that the woman had been operating as a prostitute and had 'promised to make trouble for him' when he jibbed at a doubling of her usual rates. Faced by a petition from thirty thousand readers, General Eisenhower set aside the conviction for lack of evidence.

Some of the British also practised their own colour bar. After being bombed out in June 1941, Sir Hari Singh Gour, a British citizen, Vice-Chancellor of Nagpur University and a distinguished Indian legal authority, was refused accommodation at the Caernarvon Hotel because he was coloured – one of many such cases. Leary Constantine, the famous cricketer and a British government employee, suffered a similar fate at the Imperial Hotel while captain of the West Indies cricket team. Amelia King, a third-generation British black woman, was refused enlistment in the Women's Land Army on grounds of colour. The Colonial Office pressed the Home Secretary in the light of the Singh case for legislation making clear

> Colonel Blimp (as *maître d'hôtel*) explains:
> 'Gad sir! We can't have a coloured man here! It would take the minds of resident stinkers off their struggles for the ideals of the British family of free and equal peoples.'

the common law obligation on innkeepers and others to serve travellers of all colours.

About twelve thousand black GIs had arrived in Britain by October 1942. A War Cabinet memorandum from that time spells out the pressures this caused:

The Secretary for Foreign Affairs . . . undertook, with the approval of the War Cabinet, to press the USA authorities to reduce the number sent, but I believe he has met with little success. We are thus left to face the various problems to which their presence gives rise.

The policy of the United States military authorities in dealing with their coloured troops in this country is based on the modus vivendi which has been developed in the United States in the course of time as the result of conditions obtaining in that country. Their policy . . . rests on the principle of an almost complete separation between white and coloured troops. . . .

This policy may perhaps be fairly described as the combination of equal rights and segregation practised in the Southern States and is not generally known to the population of this country, who with little experience of a colour problem at home are naturally inclined to make no distinction between the treatment of white and coloured troops and are apt to regard such distinctions as undemocratic.

The War Office is thus faced with two incompatible theories, the disregard of either of which may have serious consequences. On the one hand the average white American soldier does not understand the normal British attitude to the colour problem and his respect for this country may suffer if he sees British troops and British Women's Services drawing no distinction between white and coloured. . . . Moreover, the coloured troops themselves probably expect to be treated in this country as in the Unites States, and a markedly different treatment might well cause political difficulties in America at the end of the war. It must be added that from the point of view of the morale of our troops, whether in this country or overseas, it is most undesirable that there should be any unnecessary association between American coloured troops and British women.

These considerations suggest that the War Office attitude toward the American coloured troops should be based on the view of the American Army authorities. . . .

To sum up, I would ask the endorsement of the War Cabinet of the policy I propose to follow in the Army. . . .

(a) To make full use of the American administrative arrangements for the segregation of coloured troops, but where those fail to make no official segregation against them.

(b) To give the Army through ABCA [Army Bureau of Current Affairs] a knowledge of the history and facts of the colour question in the USA and the USA Army.

(c) To allow Army officers without the issue of overt or written instructions to interpret those facts to the personnel of the army including the ATS and so educate them to adopt towards the USA coloured troops the attitude of the USA Army Authorities.

Officially the British government said it would not assist the US Army in enforcing segregation, but the Cabinet agreed not to object to that policy and to caution Britons against becoming too friendly with black GIs. Secretary of State for War Sir James Grigg wanted to go further. He proposed a guidance note for British servicemen which talked about the white American southerner's moral duty to the negro 'as it were to a child'. It spoke patronisingly of the negro's 'simple mental outlook' and his lack of 'the white man's ability to think and act to a plan'. The War Cabinet backtracked from the position of educating the troops in the ways of racism, and made it clear that no segregation in British public facilities would take place. Stafford Cripps drew up instructions for British service personnel which included the following:

The coming of American negro troops to this country may place members of the Services in difficult situations owing to the differences of outlook between the white American personnel and the British personnel as to the relationship between black and white people.

It has therefore been thought advisable to issue the following instructions as to the advice that should be given to the British Service personnel in this matter. . . .

It is necessary, therefore, for British men and women to recognise the problem and take account of the attitude of the white American citizen. This will prevent any straining of our amicable relations with the US Army through misunderstanding which knowledge and forethought can prevent. . . .

2. British soldiers and auxiliaries should try to understand the American attitude to the relationship of white and coloured people, and to appreciate why it is different from the attitude of most people in this country who normally come into contact with only an occasional Negro. . . .

7. There is no reason why British soldiers and auxiliaries should adopt the American attitude but they should respect it and avoid making it a subject for argument and dispute. They must endeavour to understand the American point of view and they must always be on their guard against giving offence.

8. There is certain practical advice which should be given as follows:

(a) be friendly and sympathetic towards coloured American troops – but remember that in their own country they are not accustomed to close and intimate relationships with white people.

(b) if you find yourself in the company of white and coloured American troops (as for example if American troops come into a canteen or bar where you are in the company of coloured Americans), make it your business to avoid unpleasantness. It is much the best, however, to avoid such situations.

(c) for a white woman to go about in the company of a Negro American is likely to lead to controversy and ill-feeling; it may also be misunderstood by the Negro troops themselves. This does not mean that friendly hospitality in the home or in social gatherings need be ruled out, though in such cases care should be taken not to invite white and coloured American troops at the same time.

(d) avoid arguments over the colour question; but if it comes up in discussions with American troops listen patiently to what the Americans have to say and, without necessarily agreeing with them, make up your own mind that you will not allow it to become an occasion for ill-feeling or open dispute.

Joan Pountney, a member of the Women's Land Army, describes another inter-racial fight in a pub:

The pub was packed with soldiers, British and American. I was sitting with some land girls at one table. A group of black servicemen were at another over the other side of the pub. One of the black chaps had been very kind to a friend of mine, giving her lifts and so forth. The Americans started to sing – 'Bless 'em all' – and my friend said, 'I'm going to buy him a pint to say thank you'. She got half way over with the pint when a British paratroop sergeant walked over to her and knocked the glass out of her hand, saying that the Americans singing a British song was an insult. That was it. They smashed the place to pieces. The landlord rushed over and told us to leave through his quarters. 'If you get caught up in this I'll be in trouble with your people,' he said. There were a good many men walking around with black eyes the next day.

Recorded in Tyrer.

(e) be on your guard against ill-disposed people who are out to use the colour question as a means of stirring up trouble between Americans and ourselves.

One of the first serious outbreaks of racially motivated trouble came in Launceston, Cornwall, in September 1943, where black and white GIs fought over white women who were not observing the US Army's colour bar. The following year, there were race riots in Manchester, after a black sailor was seen kissing a white girl at a railway station. More serious still, black GIs were driven out of a pub in Kingsclere, near Newbury, by white colleagues. They returned, armed, and in the fight which followed the landlord's wife was shot dead.

The black GIs left a more permanent memento of their time in Britain. It is estimated that there were some fifteen hundred mixed-race children in Britain at the end of the war. Most of their mothers could not join the army of post-war GI brides crossing the Atlantic, since mixed marriages were at that time still illegal in most American states.

2
The Evacuees

> The evacuation could have done on a major scale what a tiny handful of charitable societies had been struggling to do for years – to give the children of the slums a chance of a fuller, freer life in the open country. It left, instead, a scar on the national consciousness, the majority of hosts and guests alike looking back on the experience with a profound dislike. Two contrasting sides of Britain had been brought into enforced contact with each other and neither much liked what it saw.
>
> *E.R. Chamberlin*, Life in Wartime Britain

If race and nationality were divisive factors in wartime society, so too was the gulf between two sets of native Britons – the urban poor and rural England. As the last days of peace ebbed away in 1939, the government set in motion the largest mass movement of people ever seen in this country. Large parts of the population were to be removed from the nation's main towns and cities. From 7 a.m. on Friday nine key routes out of London became one-way streets, partly to assist those who were evacuating under their own steam. Normal bus and rail services were drastically curtailed or cancelled entirely, as three thousand special buses and four thousand trains were brought into operation by twelve thousand volunteer helpers. Passenger ferries were pressed into service to take some of the evacuees out of London by sea. Similar arrangements were being put into operation in provincial towns and cities, and news came from France that the people of Paris were also being moved out.

The Times reported that news of the evacuation had put a dampener on the stock market and that little trade had been done. They also gave an indication of the scale of the undertaking: 'By Monday evening, if all goes well, three million schoolchildren, mothers with infants, expectant mothers, invalids and blind persons will be in the safe reception areas with their temporary hosts.' It was, the paper emphasised, purely a precautionary measure which was bound in any case to take place before any international crisis had reached a final stage.

They told their readers: 'No one should conclude that this decision means that war is now regarded as inevitable' – but few were by then willing to believe that this was the case.

Planning for Evacuation

The journey from school to the station by crocodiles of schoolchildren on 1 September went relatively smoothly – most of them had had a rehearsal three days previously. But the plans for evacuation went back a long way further than that, to the days immediately following the First World War. The Germans made 103 air raids on Britain during that war, killing over 1,400 people and injuring almost 4,000. In the worst attack, by just seventeen bombers in 1917, 162 people were killed and over 400 injured. While these losses were relatively small in the context of the deaths that took place in the trenches, they had a huge impact on the general public, who found themselves in the front line for the first time.

The fear of bombing was compounded after the war by a series of wildly exaggerated estimates of its potential effects. The sub-text to these over-estimates was the political battle being fought by the fledgeling Royal Air Force to retain its independence as the third armed force. The estimates of the consequences of bombing grew steadily more wild as war approached. The first error in the debate was the belief in the invulnerability of the bomber. As Stanley Baldwin put it to the House of Commons in 1932:

I think it is as well for the man in the street to realise that there is no power on earth that can prevent him from being bombed. Whatever people may tell him, the bomber will always get through. The only defence is offence, which means you have to kill more women and children more quickly than the enemy if you want to save yourselves.

The second error related to the quantity of bombs an enemy was likely to drop. In 1924 it was assumed that the first twenty-four hours of any new war would see more than 300 tons of high explosive dropped on Britain – more than had been dropped in the whole of the First World War. By 1938 this estimate had risen to

100,000 tons of bombs in the first fourteen days of war. In the event Germany dropped a total 64,393 tons of bombs on Britain in the entire war. This was the equivalent of just 3 per cent of the bombs dropped by the Allies on Germany.

The likely impact of bombing was also wildly exaggerated. The official calculation as war approached was that every ton of bombs dropped would result in fifty casualties, a third of which would be fatal. This estimate was originally made by the Air Staff in 1924. But it was reinforced by the experience of Guernica, during the Spanish Civil War, where bombers attacked a defenceless village in daylight on a busy market day – hardly a reliable indicator of what would happen when Germany attacked England. By 1937 the Imperial Defence Committee was forecasting 1.8 million casualties, 600,000 of which would occur in the first two months, and a requirement for anything up to 2.8 million hospital beds. Insanity on a huge scale was also forecast, outnumbering physical casualties three to one. With forecasts like these, it was small wonder that the authorities concentrated on how they would bury the dead, rather than on meeting the needs of the survivors. It may also go some way to explaining Neville Chamberlain's unwillingness to confront Hitler.

Accordingly, during April 1939 the Ministry of Health very quietly issued a million burial forms to the local authorities, who in turn began stockpiling large supplies of coffins. These were made of papier mâché or stout cardboard, partly for ease of storage and partly because the authorities could not afford the £300,000-worth of coffin wood that they thought would be required in the first three months. In practice, bombing (including the V1s and V2s and long-range shelling) was to claim 60,595 lives during the entire war – the true figure was nearer to one than to fifty casualties per ton of bombs.

The final exaggeration related to the impact of bombing on civilian morale. Sir Hugh Trenchard, founding father of the Royal Air Force, told the Committee of Imperial Defence in 1923 that if people were subjected to enough bombing they would compel the government to sue for peace. J.F.C. Fuller, in the same year, put it rather more colourfully:

Picture if you can what the results will be; London for a few days will be one vast raving Bedlam, the hospitals will be stormed, traffic will cease, the homeless will shriek for help, the City will be in Pandemonium. What of the Government in Westminster? It will be swept away by an avalanche of terror. The enemy will dictate his terms which will be grasped like a straw by a drowning man.

This was the context in which the idea of evacuation evolved. From as early as December 1924 plans began to be prepared to move much of the civilian population out of the cities in the event of war. At this time there was no thought of Germany being in a position to attack Britain – France was assumed to be the most likely aggressor.

The idea of the government evacuating every child from London was decided not to be feasible, and the idea grew up instead that they would evacuate only the poorest. There were several reasons for this; first, they lived in the areas most likely to be bombed; secondly, they would be less well able to evacuate themselves. But also underpinning this decision were concerns about public order and the sanctity of property. As one of the sub-committees overseeing the Air Raid Precautions in the 1930s put it, those most likely to panic would in their view be 'the less stable in character of foreign elements within London as well as the very poor in east and southern London'. These groups were identified as 'foreign, Jewish and poor elements' and it was claimed that these would turn out to be 'the classes of person most likely to be driven mad with fright'. Similar concerns lay behind the decision to carry out evacuation before hostilities actually started. This was done in order to prevent people bolting and thereby causing a panic in the streets that would undermine the morale of the country, making it difficult to control. It was also feared that, if London were bombed, 'the poor might flock back into the wealthier areas where they would find prizes worth having'. But the committee took pains to point out that 'any discrimination against the foreign element or the poor was there for the sake of the whole'.

Winston Churchill, speaking in a Commons debate in November 1934, gave his view of the likely scale of the disruption bombing would cause:

We must expect that under pressure of continuous air attack upon London, at least 3 or 4,000,000 people will be driven out into the open country around the metropolis. This vast amount of human beings, far larger than any armies which have been fed and moved in war, without shelter and without food, without sanitation and without special provision for the maintenance of order, would confront the government of the day with an administrative problem of the first magnitude, and would certainly absorb the energies of our small army and our territorial force.

The plan for evacuation in the event of war was first made public in 1933. But the detailed organisation of it was left until much later. In January 1938 the Board of Education shifted responsibility on to local authorities for preparing evacuation schemes, but the confusion that this lack of central direction caused led them to withdraw that decision two months later. Councils were told not to draw up schemes until instructed to do so by the Home Secretary. The government finally set up the Anderson Committee to draw up evacuation plans in May 1938, but their recommendations were not approved by Parliament until the end of October 1938 – just ten months before the outbreak of war. By that time there had already been an unofficial mini-evacuation in September 1938, at the time of the Munich crisis. When the Anderson Committee handed over responsibility for implementing the scheme to the Department of Health, the Imperial Defence Committee was told: 'Evacuation plans are, at present, very backward.'

The evacuation plans were developed very much in secret. As a result, very little account was taken of the views of those whose cooperation would be vital to their success – the authorities in both the evacuating and the receiving areas, and the evacuee families themselves. Many of the mistakes that were made might at least have been identified, if not necessarily overcome, by obtaining those views. The authorities also took for granted the unquestioning cooperation of the teaching staff involved and failed to provide any expert monitoring of the billeting arrangements – this again being left to the teachers. Furthermore, the Anderson Committee failed to anticipate the hostility of working-class parents to the idea of sending their children to live with strangers. As a study for the Fabian Society in 1940 put it:

Surely only male calculations could have so confidently assumed that working-class wives would be content to leave their husbands indefinitely to look after themselves, and only middle-class parents, accustomed to shooing their children out of sight and reach at the earliest possible age, could have been so astonished to find that working-class parents were violently unwilling to part with theirs.

This unwillingness of inner-city people to part with their children produced one of the first cracks in the exercise. Only about a third of the expected number initially took up the offer of evacuation. This led to a radical telescoping of the departure times of trains that caused chaos in some of the reception areas. In some places, they waited for hours for trains that did not arrive, or arrived with many fewer, or different kinds of, evacuees than those expected. The arrangements in the reception areas were in any event relatively *ad hoc*, since local authorities were only given permission to spend anything on them three days before the exercise began.

The Anderson Committee had previously designated authorities as 'evacuation areas', 'neutral areas' or 'reception areas', according to the danger they were thought to face of being bombed. With the benefit of hindsight, the committee's designation of areas looks questionable in some cases. For example, Bristol, Plymouth and Nottingham were all defined as neutral areas, not to be evacuated – with what proved to be serious consequences for those populations.

Colonel Blimp explains: 'Gad sir! Colonel Pitt-Drivels is right! This billeting of children idea is damned nonsense. The poorer classes must be lacking in decent family instinct not to want their brats blown up with them.'

This was compounded in some cases by a confusion as to which authorities were to receive evacuees and which send them. It emerged that Essex authorities along the Thames Estuary were preparing to send their children away from what they thought might become a battle zone, at the same time as London authorities were preparing to evacuate some of their children to the relative 'safety' of these same areas. In some cases the final destination of the evacuees was a matter of pure chance. One group of schoolchildren from West Ham were scheduled to move to Somerset, but caused a near-riot on their non-corridor train when the driver failed to stop to allow them a toilet break. This forced the driver to make an unscheduled halt at Wantage, and it was here that the West Ham boys ended up spending their war years.

Billeting officers none the less made heroic efforts to place the new arrivals, though the process for doing so was variously likened to a Roman slave auction or a cattle market. Older, fitter boys and girls were more readily snapped up as potential farm or domestic labour. More appealing-looking children were chosen for their aesthetic value, while the less winsome, those with disfiguring diseases and those who stubbornly refused to be separated from one or more siblings proved to be far more difficult to place. Exhausted children would find themselves left in an ever-dwindling band of human 'remnants', pored over by unenthusiastic would-be hosts, and finally hawked from door to door with only the Billeting Officer's threat of compulsion securing some of them a lodging. Some were unplaceable even then; in Maidenhead, as no doubt in many other areas, a special home had to be set up for 'unbilletable boys', where they were given 'a course of correctional treatment under Mrs Porter, the Matron'. In the desperate effort to secure a roof – any roof – over their heads, no thought could be given to trying to match the backgrounds of host and evacuee.

All this differed markedly from the rosy picture presented of the evacuation in the press:

The reception in various districts of the evacuated schoolchildren was carried out with the same efficiency that characterised the departures. Competent nurses and reception officers saw that each child got milk and food before being taken to the billeting centres, from where the children were conducted to their temporary homes.

There was no confusion, the teachers who were in charge of the children paid close attention to the details of the arrangements that had been made beforehand. . . . So far no casualties have been reported. . . . For all but a few, it was an enthralling but happy adventure, and homesickness and shyness quickly fled at the sight of new faces, new surroundings

and new playmates. . . . Some of them were soon eating high
teas beyond their dreams and many went up later to bedrooms
larger and airier than they had thought possible.

This was far from the picture painted by many members of the
public. The Oxford academic R.C.K. Ensor kicked off what
turned into a near-hate campaign in the *Spectator*: his article
described the evacuees as follows: 'Many of the new arrivals were
the lowest grade of slum women – slatternly malodorous
tatterdemalions trailing children to match.' Others wrote to the
publication in similar vein, one contributor (using the
pseudonym 'A Victim') calling the *Spectator*: 'the only paper
which has broken the careful conspiracy of lies, organised on the
Nazi model, to blanket the hardships inflicted on the victims in
the "safe" areas', and going on to complain of the authorities
'thrusting filthy women and children into the homes of decent
cleanly [sic] people, who then had to give up their jobs to care
full-time for a couple of evacuees for the princely sum of 17s per
week.' Another anonymous contributor said: 'When I read the
Ministry of Health's unctuous and self-satisfied congratulations
on the success of the scheme, I can only wish some official of that
Ministry had been present here at our reception.'

    The enforced timing of the first evacuation – right at the end
of the school summer holiday – brought additional problems.
First, it was the height of the head-lice season, since several
weeks away from the ministrations of the school 'nit nurse' had
produced increased numbers of cases. This was compounded by
the children's close proximity to each other on the long train
journeys, creating infestations of epidemic proportions. It was
estimated that London evacuees had about a 35 per cent
incidence of head-lice, and one Medical Officer of Health in an
area receiving Liverpudlian evacuees ordered all the new arrivals'
heads to be shaved, when 50 per cent infestation rates began to
appear. Some hosts in rural areas were alleged to have used sheep
dip as an extreme cure for their guests' unwanted vermin. (There
were at this time unfounded fears among the general public that
head-lice could lead to the spread of typhus.)

    Health officers were appointed to examine the evacuees on
arrival, though the thoroughness of that examination may be
judged from the fact that, during the second (1940) evacuation,

they were supposed to check 480 children per hour. Rudimentary checks for lice and scabies were all that were possible, and any evidence this revealed of other potential problems was referred to a proper doctor for a closer look. There was good reason to expect that the general state of health of the evacuees would leave a great deal to be desired in other respects. Just before the war, in 1937, a survey of London schoolchildren had revealed that 67–70 per cent had bone disorders, 67–83 per cent had enlarged or septic tonsils and 88–93 per cent had malformed or decaying teeth. A quarter of them were deemed to be malnourished. At this time public school pupils were on average four inches taller than the rest of the school population, largely on account of their superior diet.

The timing of the evacuation also meant that many of the children had not yet been given their new clothes at the start of the school year – impoverished parents would have left their purchase to the last minute. It had also been a long, hot summer, so many of them would have travelled to their new homes with a very limited and particularly worn-out wardrobe. This problem was exacerbated by the evacuating authorities, which encouraged mothers not to pack too many clothes for their offspring, in an effort to cut down the amount of luggage to be carried.

Nor were the receiving local authorities encouraged to spend money on clothes for any new arrivals found to be lacking them, on the very reasonable grounds that everybody would then want some. They were authorised to spend just £1 per 200 children on the most extreme cases (and to do this without giving any publicity to their having done so), with the result that the burden often fell on the foster parent. For those who took up the burden of hosting an evacuee, the 10s per week allowance (8s 6d each if you took more than one child) was certainly not sufficient to reimburse the cost of clothing. Others just left their new guests to shiver.

Other shortcomings in the wardrobe department were the product of ignorance or grinding poverty. Little girls were found to possess no knickers; children were strangers to the concept of pyjamas, while one Scottish housewife found her new guests unwilling to climb between the clean white sheets she had put on the bed for them, on the grounds that sheets were 'for dead folk'. For those who were prepared to get into bed, bedwetting was a common problem – again often put down to some sort of degeneracy among the evacuees, but in fact more to do with stress (large numbers of the British Expeditionary Force, returning from Dunkirk, suffered a similar problem).

More worryingly, an estimated 10 per cent of the child evacuees were unfamiliar with the workings of a flush toilet and thought that a newspaper in the corner of the room performed the same function. Equally difficult were the cases where evacuees from more comfortable inner city homes were exposed to the extremes of rural poverty.

Colonel Blimp explains: 'Gad sir, Lord Mingy was right! To give the children of the unemployed enough to eat is to sap their sturdy British independence!'

Further tensions arose where the mothers of young children were evacuated. Two women sharing a kitchen often proved to be one too many, and rules (sometimes wholly Draconian and unreasonable rules) were set down for the terms of occupancy of the house. The following example of such house rules led to a prosecution:

No access to the kitchen or bathroom; loan of crockery refused; no laundry to be carried out on the premises; charge of 1s per week for electric light; all residents to be home by 10.30 p.m.; residents to be out of the house between 10.00 a.m. and 8.30 p.m. on Sundays; no smoking; absolute quiet at all times; residents also had to leave the house whenever the proprietor went to visit her invalid mother [though they were allowed to await her return in the porch or in the summer house in the garden].

This hostess (if such she can be called) was fined £15 and 3 guineas costs.

Even where less extreme restrictions were applied, the evacuee mother and her child would in many cases find themselves without any normal domestic responsibilities or their usual circle of social contacts. They might find themselves out of the house for many hours of the day, killing time. Few areas initially had any recreational facilities for them, and their enforced idleness no doubt added to the evacuees' reputation for fecklessness. This can be seen in the following report of a county organiser for the Women's Voluntary Service in one of the reception areas in September 1939:

I think this scheme is impracticable and unworkable, and it can never be successful. The low, slum type form the majority of the mothers, some of them out for what they can get, most of them dirty, many of them idle and unwilling to work or pull their weight. No arrangements whatever have been made for them by the local authorities from the social point of view. They have nowhere to go, and walk the streets tiring out themselves and their tiny children. . . .

The general feeling is that people can cope with the children and in time can get them clean and disciplined, but the mothers who are not a good influence are a great drawback. . . .

There is nowhere for them to go. That they are a bad slum type and expect 'the pub and the pictures' on the doorstep is not the point. Some arrangements should be made immediately for a mothers' club or recreation room for them. . . .

I feel that the dirt and low standard of living of the evacuees from big industrial cities of Leeds and Hull has been an eye-opener and an unpleasant shock to the inhabitants of an agricultural county like Lincolnshire, who had no idea that such terrible conditions existed.

The Women's Institute made its protests known through a report called *Town Children through Country Eyes*, compiled from the experiences in some 1,700 of their branches of the appalling condition and habits of the evacuee children. Copies were sent to Health and Education Officers of all the towns and cities from which evacuees were sent.

One complaint the report may not have mentioned was that some of the evacuated women – with their alleged fondness for a good time in all its respects – also became rather too attractive to some of the more easily led menfolk in the reception areas. In the eyes of some in the host areas, evacuees also became synonymous with crime. Thus, one mother felt able to plead in mitigation for

---

A LIVERPOOL EVACUEE'S FIRST POSTCARD HOME

Dear Mum,

I hope you are well. I don't like the man's face much. Perhaps it will look better in daylight. I like the dog's face best.

her son, brought up before the court for the theft of a mouth organ: 'He is a good boy at home. I think he has been associating with evacuees.'

In Chester the local representative for the National Society for the Prevention of Cruelty to Children tried to have an 8 p.m. curfew imposed on the city's new guests. He was told that the magistrates had no such powers, and that he should direct his idea to the Home Secretary.

There were those who saw evacuation as an opportunity for social engineering on a large scale. This correspondent to *The Times*, for example, wanted to see the most disadvantaged children taken away from their parents entirely and placed into care:

> In the course of my work I have, in the last few years, attended many trials at the Central Criminal Court, and I am always nearly horrified by the low mental and physical standards of the accused persons. Stunted, misshapen creatures, only capable of understanding the very simplest language and quite incapable of thought, moved by impulses at the best sentimental, at the worst brutal. During a trial when the accused and witnesses are of this sub-human sort, it is as though a flat stone in the garden had been raised and pale, wriggling things, that had never seen the light had been exposed.
>
> These children, of whom the country residents so reasonably complain, are bound to grow up into just such sub-human savages, unless we seize this opportunity of saving them. . . . War has lifted the flat stone – these disgraces to our educational system have been forced out into the light. . . .

All manner of other problems were laid at the doors of the evacuees. It was said that their presence in local schools prejudiced the chances of local children getting scholarships for direct grant schools; that evacuation had disintegrated the life of the country and disrupted the trade of the urban areas, in both respects weakening the nation's war efforts; transport and communications had been disrupted, and (for reasons which are not immediately obvious) the government's market schemes for meat and fish had failed because of them; verminous evacuees had contaminated the wallpaper, furniture and bedding in their billets, leading to demands for compensation; helpless husbands, unable to look after themselves after their wives had been evacuated, were calling for more communal feeding; jury trials could not function in urban areas subject to substantial evacuation (the 1939 Administration of Criminal Justice Act actually made provision for trials to be held before juries of seven people – rather than twelve – at the Central Criminal Court); and local authorities were suffering loss of revenue.

Even insurance proved to be an unexpected complication. Early in 1940 the insurance companies announced that they would invoke a 'war clause' if householders made claims on their home or contents insurance resulting from the presence of evacuees. Despite exhortations from the British government, only one company – Lloyds – withdrew that clause. This proved to be a significant problem in at least one case. A church organisation, the Society for Waifs and Strays, bought two properties in Morthoe for the housing of evacuees. They were poorly supervised, and by the end of the war vandalism damage to them from the inmates was estimated at £1,500. A reluctant government found itself being badgered to honour claims such as these.

Objections to receiving evacuees took all forms. Didcot Parish Council pleaded exemption on the grounds that there were government stores and a railway junction (both potential bombing targets) nearby. A local authority in Wiltshire argued its case for not taking them in terms of the local shortage of domestic servants. For some, the dispute was more ideological. This letter to the *North Wales Chronicle* in January 1939 was from the Welsh Nationalist Party:

The indiscriminate transfer of English people into Wales will place the Welsh language, and even the very existence of the Welsh nation, in jeopardy. The national welfare of the Welsh people should be a matter of first consideration by the authorities who are planning evacuation into the countryside. We, as Nationalists, demand that there should be no transfer of population into Wales which would endanger Welsh nationality. If England cannot make its emergency plans without imperilling the life of our little nation, let England renounce war and grant us self-government.

Small wonder that Hitler saw the nationalist parties as possible territory for Fifth Column activity. However, the Welsh Nationalists were not opposed to all evacuation. They protested against the decision of the Anderson Committee to designate south Wales as a 'neutral' area, and thus not to be evacuated, and called upon children from the valleys to be moved to safety (in rural Wales, naturally). They also wanted the children of Welsh expatriates in England to be evacuated to the land of their fathers, for a proper upbringing.

The Welsh antipathy to foreigners was reciprocated by some of their visitors. One Catholic priest from Liverpool called for children billeted in chapel-going Wales to be repatriated, since he felt that the physical danger they faced in Liverpool was far outweighed by the spiritual danger of exposure to such a heretical environment. Other Liverpool children found themselves thrown into Welsh village schools where both the religion and the language in which the lessons were taught were foreign. Some rose to the challenge, becoming fluent Welsh speakers and competing successfully in Eisteddfods.

Not everyone reacted with horror and resentment towards the

A LONDON EVACUEE SEES HIS FIRST COW

Much fun was made of the evacuees' ignorance of country matters. This item, quoted in Westall, appeared on the BBC News on 29 October 1939:

'The cow is a mamal [sic]. It has six sides, right, left, an upper and below. At the back is a tail, on which hangs a brush. With this, it sends the flies away so they do not fall in the milk. The head is for the purpose of growing horns and so that the mouth can be somewhere. The horns are to butt with and the mouth is to moo with. Under the cow hangs the milk. It is arranged for milking. When people milk, the milk comes and there is never an end to the supply. How the cow does it, I have not realised but it makes more and more. The cow has a fine sense of smell; one can smell it far away. This is the reason for the fresh air in the country.

'The man cow is called an ox. It is not a mamal. The cow does not eat much but what it eats, it eats twice so that it gets enough. When it is hungry it moos and when it says nothing it is because its inside is full up with grass.'

evacuees, as this letter shows: 'I never knew that such conditions existed, and I feel ashamed of having been so ignorant of my neighbours. For the rest of my life I mean to try and make amends by helping such people to live cleaner and healthier lives.' The author could perhaps afford to take a more positive view, as he was not likely to be asked to take any evacuees himself. It was from Neville Chamberlain to his sister.

Supervision of the evacuated children became an increasing problem. Initially, around 103,000 inner city teachers and volunteer helpers were evacuated to look after the 827,000 primary school evacuees, a pupil:teacher ratio of 8:1. However, many of these volunteers proved to be unsuited to the job and 32,000 had been dismissed by the middle of 1941. Together with natural wastage among the teaching staff, this meant that the pupil:teacher ratio dropped to more like 100:1. Repeated government circulars urged host authorities to visit the home of each evacuee on at least a monthly basis, but this was often disregarded. Even where it was done, much could happen to the children between visits, and intimidation of the evacuees could prevent the authorities from finding out what was really going on.

There are many vivid accounts published of evacuees' experiences – good and bad. It would be impossible to say whether the good experiences outweigh the bad, but where they were bad, they could be very bad indeed. One former evacuee recalled, as a ten-year-old child, trying to cut her own throat with a knife (which fortunately turned out to be too blunt for the purpose). In another family of nine, the eldest five were sexually assaulted, an experience which meant that one of them was still receiving counselling forty years later. A man in Swanage was found guilty of indecently assaulting the three evacuees in his care, offering in his defence the improbable explanation that he was simply using them in bed as human hot water bottles.

The failure of heavy bombing to materialise in the early months of the war led many evacuees to abandon their new living arrangements. The *Maidenhead Advertiser* reported in February 1940:

It is now known that, generally speaking, 59 per cent of the mothers and children moved to safety on the eve of the war have returned home. Locally, of course, the figure is more like

EVACUEES' TALES

I was soundly beaten at least once a week with sticks, poker, wooden spoon – whatever was at hand – mostly when the husband was at work. It was hard to endure this physical and mental abuse and I often thought of suicide by drowning myself in the fen drain a couple of hundred yards from the house. . . . I suffered from severe headaches and vomiting and trembled continuously with anxiety. I had outbreaks of sores on my scalp, face and body as well as hurting all over from the beatings. I was always hungry and had a bad case of intestinal worms of which only I was aware.

John, aged about five, quoted by Wicks.

Every item was stolen. All our toys, all our clothing that would fit members of other families, and they dictated our letters. . . . My sister Anne had beautiful long hair and it was falling out. And my hair started falling out. And scabs were coming on our heads and bodies.

London boy, quoted by Grafton.

It was there that I had my first experience with a man that was not quite nice. He would tuck me in of a night and fondle me. I was terrified. Mind you, he never forced me. He would just say that I was an evacuee and if I said anything he would send me back to where I'd be bombed. . . . Then one day I really got frightened. I thought he was going to put his thing inside me and I got really scared.

Maureen, aged twelve, quoted by Wicks.

80 per cent, both in the Borough and the rural district, an appalling percentage. Something like half a million children evacuated to safe areas are still there, but about 43 per cent of the 734,883 school children evacuated have returned. . . . It is time to ask whether evacuation has been such a failure as to determine expert and general opinion that no such movement of children must be attempted again.

Evacuation was originally planned as a temporary and quasi-military operation to save children and mothers from a few weeks of intensive bombing. Whitehall did not foresee a complete and prolonged dislocation of normal education, and emergency education policy has been and is being built together in bits and pieces, generally following rather than leading public opinion and the education authorities. . . .

According to official figures, almost 900,000 evacuees had returned home by 8 January 1940. But the drift back to the cities brought new problems. The government had worked on the assumption that there would be total evacuation by the target groups. (Compulsory evacuation had been considered, but public opinion and the difficulty of enforcing it led the government to shy away from the idea.) Most of the inner-city schools had been closed, so those children who had stayed behind or had returned from evacuation were free to roam the streets all day and, if they were so inclined, get up to mischief. The Home Secretary was eventually forced to allow head teachers to reopen inner-city schools, always assuming they were not counted among the two-thirds of all inner-city schools taken over by ARP wardens or other parts of the war effort. Some, such as the Chief Education Officer for Sheffield, resorted to more radical solutions:

I knew we had 55,000 children and no schools open . . . we appealed for 5,000 school rooms in private houses, for which we paid 2s 6d a week, and we moved the desks and furniture from the schools into those houses. The children were divided into groups of twelve and each group was taught for an hour and a half a day . . . they spent another hour and a half in the local library.

Instead, the government tried to force evacuation by the back door, by means of making life as unpleasant as possible for those who remained in the cities. In London it became illegal to take your children into the tube shelters during the 'epidemic period' from 15 January to 31 March. No clue was given as to what the expected epidemic was and none was subsequently reported. This was coupled with increased enforcement of legislation relating to child abuse, school attendance and measures against those living in unsanitary conditions. Life in the tube shelters was also more closely regulated. You needed a ticket from the authorities to occupy a place in them and you could be ejected from them, if the authorities saw fit.

The Poor Housing the Poor

> We find over and over again that it is the really poor people who are willing to take evacuees and that the sort of bridge-playing set who live in such places as Chorley Wood are terribly difficult about it all.
>
> WVS Regional Administrator

While the evacuation programme gave some of its participants a terrifying view across the gulf that divided the classes, for the most part the official scheme involved the poor housing the poor. Some owners of large country homes threw open their doors generously to the newcomers, but Home Intelligence reports in June 1941 showed that billeting officers were generally afraid to press the owners of large country houses to take evacuees, for fear of reprisals. They would have to live in that community after the war. The use of local agents as billeting officers was generally felt to be 'a bad idea' for this reason, and local or central government officers were suggested instead. One billeting officer even tried to discourage one big house owner from taking evacuees, for fear that he would be 'letting down' the owners of other big houses locally, who were holding out against it. More generally, the fact that only a quarter of the original offers of billeting were taken up, owing to the lower than expected numbers of evacuees, meant that the burden was falling unevenly on a small proportion of households. A campaign was run to move the evacuees about, to share the burden more equally.

The End of Evacuation

The scheme was a long time ending – at least officially. Delayed by the V1 and V2 flying bombs, it was April 1945 before the government issued Circular 68/45, which set out the arrangements for bringing the evacuees home. However, many of them had not waited for the government's permission – in the six months to March 1945, it was estimated that 600,000 out of the 1.04 million remaining evacuees had repatriated themselves. For many of the rest, things were far less straightforward. Many were returning to areas which had suffered widespread devastation from the bombers, and pre-war housing problems were exacerbated by the chronic post-war shortage of housing in the urban areas. By August 1945 there were still 76,000 evacuees with no homes to return to.

Some children – an estimated 5,200 – were still left unaccounted for when the scheme was ended in March 1946. Many were believed to have been orphaned by the blitz. Others, who for example had changed billets without informing the authorities, were effectively 'mislaid'.

But even those who could return often found it hard to readjust. For the evacuees, some were traumatised by their experiences of poverty or child abuse; conversely, for those who had passed the war years in a more comfortable billet, the return to urban deprivation could be an equal shock. Children who had grown used to the countryside found it hard to re-adapt to a harsher urban environment; some parents found it difficult to adjust to the loss of a child-free independence. For others, the bond between child and parent had been broken entirely; they met at the railway station as strangers, and some even failed to recognise each other at all. For those returning from evacuation overseas, the drabness of austerity Britain was sometimes the hardest thing to bear.

The Problems with Evacuation

At least some of the problems resulting from evacuation can be laid at the door of appeasement. Chamberlain and his Cabinet were desperate not to be seen to be putting Britain on to a war footing, lest it undermined their efforts to negotiate peace terms. This was one of the main reasons why the preparations were made in secret; as a result, key players were not consulted and did not tie their parts of the programme together. It also put the evacuation scheme in direct conflict with other government programmes, for example where the demands of evacuation were made on communities whose housing supply was already being stretched by the demands of billeted service personnel.

The other reason for secrecy was concern that the very sight of the preparations would cause widespread panic among the people. During the Munich crisis, there had been panic buying and a flight from the cities, with 150,000 people heading for the hills of Wales. Earlier planning for air raids had even toyed with the idea of throwing a giant police and army cordon around London, to prevent a mass evacuation. However, in the end, secrecy about war preparations could hardly be consistent with digging a million feet of slit trenches in the capital's parks and issuing the entire population with gas-masks.

A degree of panic also entered into the execution of the scheme, in particular because it was done before there was any firm indication of the German intention to commence bombing. This stems back to the wildly exaggerated estimates of the effects of bombing, discussed earlier. At least some of the resentment of the hosts might have been eased, had they been able to see a good reason for the cities being evacuated.

The planning of the evacuation also concentrated on the arrangements in the evacuation areas, rather than on those at the reception end. This was perhaps inevitable, given the much more diffuse nature of the reception areas and the limited resources of many of the rural district councils who were charged with making the arrangements. At this time, the ability of any authority, in particular the smaller rural ones, to deliver social services was very limited by modern standards. This was still the era of the Victorian Poor Laws – in 1939 a hundred thousand people were still cared for in workhouses. Such arrangements as the receiving authorities did make were not helped by the fact that the numbers and types of evacuees delivered to them often differed wildly from what they had been led to expect.

Nor had the (presumably) middle-class people who organised the arrangements had the slightest inkling of the shock waves this enforced breaking down of the class barriers would create. Their initial assumption, that working-class mothers would be as willing as their middle-class counterparts to part with their young children, proved wrong, leading to the piecemeal nature of the evacuation and the problems associated with that. And if any of them entertained fond notions that it would lead to a breaking down of class barriers, this was soon dispelled by the wave of recrimination among the hosts against what they saw as feckless and work-shy parents, who let their children leave home in such a state of health, hygiene and dress.

Evacuation and the Rich

Those who could afford it made their own evacuation plans. In addition to the official evacuation scheme, an estimated two million people made such arrangements. Some were able to stay with family or friends in less dangerous parts of the country, while those who had the money bought or rented somewhere safe. Out-of-the-way hotels advertised their services to 'the sensitive and artistic' who wished to be well out of the conflict. These became derisively known as 'funk holes', and the *Daily Express* journalist Nathaniel Gubbins created the fictional population of the 'Safe Hotel'. *The Times* said: 'The hotels are filled with well-to-do refugees, who too often have fled from nothing. They sit and read and knit and eat and drink, and get no nearer the war than the news they read in the newspapers.'

> Colonel Blimp explains: 'Gad sir, Lucy Houston is right! We need 5,000 more planes, otherwise how can the upper classes fly to Scotland when the bombing of London begins?'

Private evacuees also took up a good deal of the accommodation that might otherwise have been available for the government scheme. Potential hosts often decided that they represented a 'nicer class of person' than the urban poor that might be visited upon them under the official scheme. A 1939 survey showed that 18 per cent of all the billeting accommodation in England and Wales had been pre-booked seven months before the war broke out. In desirable areas like West Sussex, Berkshire and Herefordshire, the figure was over 25 per cent. Constantine Fitzgibbon recalls:

> . . . a constant stream of private cars and London taxis driving up to mother's front door in the Thames Valley in the September of 1939, filled with men and women of all ages, in various stages of hunger, exhaustion and fear, offering absurd sums for accommodation in her already overcrowded house and even for food. This horde of satin-clad, pinstriped refugees poured through for two or three days, eating everything that was for sale, downing all the spirits in the pubs, and then vanished.

PET EVACUEES

In some cases, pets were treated better than human evacuees. Many people were killing their pets as war broke out and evacuation started. Prompted by this, the Animal Defence League started a scheme for evacuating dogs. The Duchess of Hamilton threw open the grounds of her Dorset estate to them and 176 dogs were eventually resident there. The staff even wrote to the owners at intervals, informing them of the progress of their pets. But for those pets who could not get away from it all, there was always: 'Bob Martins Fit and Hysteria Powders in ARP cartons to calm cats and dogs in air raids.'

Overseas Evacuation

Safer still were non-combatant countries. It was reported that, in the forty-eight hours leading up to the start of the official evacuation, some five thousand people had embarked at Southampton for the United States, and places on board any remaining ships were at a premium.

Offers to give a home to a British evacuee child came from all over the Americas and the Commonwealth. American corporations offered to take the children of their UK employees; American doctors offered to take the children of their professional counterparts in Britain; Rhodes scholars were encouraged to offer places to the children of Oxbridge and other dons; Douglas Fairbanks Junior proposed setting up a colony of British actors' children in Hollywood. The elite Cambridge Tutoring School in New York offered to take a hundred British boys at the bargain price of £100 each, but specified that: 'Boys from a cultural background only can be accepted. Sons of army and navy officers and professionals would be welcome.' They even offered to send the private yacht of one of their patrons to collect the boys, but this elitist offer was not taken up. While the Commonwealth countries were generally happy to receive a cross-section of British youth, the Americans were more likely to want children from 'a better background'.

There was criticism, from Labour MPs and others, of the elitist nature of private evacuation arrangements, the cost of which placed them far beyond the means of the ordinary citizen. Initially, offers from overseas governments to take British children through some official scheme were dismissed by the government as 'good hearted but impracticable'. The idea was ruled out for fear that it would result in panic and defeatism, and lead to resentment among those left behind. There were also practical problems, such as the shortage of space on ships to transport them, the lack of military vessels to provide an escort, and the resultant danger of the exercise.

None the less a parliamentary committee was set up to examine the question in more detail, under Geoffrey Shakespeare MP. It reported to the War Cabinet on 17 June 1940, and it was while they were actually making their presentation that news was brought in to the Cabinet Room of France's surrender. Churchill was said – perhaps not surprisingly – to have been so preoccupied with the news of the surrender that he failed to notice that a decision had been made about the evacuation matter.

The result was that an organisation – the Children's Overseas Reception Board (CORB) – was set up, to coordinate the evacuation of children, principally to America. The scheme was drawn up with a strongly egalitarian emphasis, with at least 90 per cent of the intake coming from state schools, and particular priority being given to children from poorer backgrounds and the most vulnerable areas. News of this scheme was made public on 19 June, and by mid-morning a queue 3,000 strong had formed outside the CORB offices. They were forced hurriedly to issue a statement to try to calm the rush – emphasising the dangers involved and the limited numbers of spaces available.

It had little effect. By 4 July they had received a total of 211,548 applications, almost 200,000 of them from state-aided schools and almost 50 per cent of the applications meeting the eligibility criteria. On that day, the government closed the waiting list and temporarily suspended the scheme, because of the lack of Royal Navy escorts for the convoys concerned. Private evacuations meanwhile continued unabated, and there were further complaints in Parliament that the CORB scheme had just been a ruse to allow the government to get the children of the well-to-do out of the country without undue criticism.

There were further delays later that month, and it was 21 July before the first of CORB's evacuees could sail. They were taken to Liverpool, where they were housed in children's homes and schools, pending their departure. (Private evacuees leaving from Liverpool at the same time were, by contrast, put up at the Adelphi Hotel.) It did not take long for the dangers involved in the enterprise to become clear. On 1 August the ship *Volendam*, with 321 evacuees among its 606 passengers, was torpedoed. Fortunately, the damage was not terminal and the ship was towed back to port by tugs. However, it transpired that *Volendam* had been sailing in a vulnerable position at the head of one of the lines of the convoy, and she was also carrying a cargo of wheat that made her a legitimate target for the U-boats.

But Worse was to Come

On Friday 13 September 1940 the Glasgow-built ship *City of Benares* pulled out of Liverpool, bound for Canada. It was an inauspicious date for such a hazardous journey. Three hundred passengers were on board, including a large group of child evacuees. Six hundred miles out, at ten o'clock on a moonlit night, the ship was struck by a torpedo on the port side, immediately below the children's quarters. One child was killed outright and many more were injured. Attempts were made to lower the boats, but eleven of the twelve took in water as they hit the rough sea. One, containing the captain, sank completely. Most of the children remained calm, but the largely Indian crew panicked. They were among the first into the boats and, once there, most took no further part in the rescue. The nearest civilian ship to them, the SS *Marina*, was also torpedoed, and the nearest Royal Navy ship, the destroyer *Hurricane*, was sixteen hours away – despite the fact that the *City of Benares* was supposed to be escorted.

Almost immediately, bad weather set in. Rain and hail added to the waves that were sweeping over the boats faster than the survivors could bail. They found themselves up to their knees or even their chests in water. It became dangerous to move in the boats, since a foot in the wrong place could mean capsize and people being swept overboard.

In one of the boats Michael Rennie, a 23-year-old theology student, found himself in charge of fourteen children and two adults. In the days that followed, he repeatedly dived overboard to rescue one or other of his party who had been swept out of the boat. It was after fourteen days in the lifeboat that they saw the Royal

Navy coming. Rennie leapt to his feet, waving and shouting 'Hurrah! Here comes the destroyer, thank God!' They were his last words. Fatally weakened by his ordeal, he lost his balance and fell overboard. Efforts by the others in the lifeboat to save him were futile. The government turned a deaf ear to calls for him to be awarded a posthumous George Cross, and his parents were even made to repay the loan he had taken out to get him through university.

A happier fate awaited the Catholic priest Father O'Sullivan, who was in bed with chronic seasickness when the torpedo struck. He rounded up his party of children and they were rescued after eight days in the lifeboat. Back in England, he found that he had been declared dead, and had the grim satisfaction of reading his own glowing obituaries.

There were 84 children among the 260 people who died on the *City of Benares*, and world opinion was outraged. The Germans first tried to deny the event entirely, then accused the British of using the children as a shield to try to secure safe passage for legitimate military targets. This disaster effectively marked the end of the government-sponsored overseas evacuation scheme.

The government had not at any stage been happy about the scheme. As Winston Churchill put it:

I must frankly admit that the full bearings of this question were not appreciated by the British Government at the time it was first raised. It was not foreseen that the mild countenance given to this plan would lead to a movement of such dimensions and that a crop of alarmist and depressing rumours would follow at its tail, detrimental to the interest of national defence.

At home, the scheme was regarded as pushing the panic button. Abroad, the Germans made propaganda out of it, and used the Americans' increasing involvement to cast doubts on their neutrality. However, private evacuations continued after this time, until late 1941. It is thought that some 17,000 private evacuees were sent abroad after June 1940. The elitist nature of this trade was by now very clear; social gadfly Henry 'Chips' Channon recalled in his diary for June 1940 visiting Euston station, dispatching his offspring on the train to Liverpool Docks: 'There was a queue of

Rolls-Royces and liveried servants and mountains of trunks. It seemed that everyone we knew was there.'

The list of evacuees did indeed read like a version of *Who's Who*. As well as Channon's son (Paul Channon, later himself a Conservative cabinet minister), there were the wife and children of Lord Mountbatten, the son of the Minister of Information, Duff Cooper, and members of the Guinness, Rothschild and Hambro families. Also among those evacuated were future politicians Jeremy Thorpe and Shirley Williams. At least three sitting MPs fled the country. This export industry became a sufficient embarrassment for the British government to lead the Home Secretary, Sir John Anderson, to suggest scrapping the exit permit scheme, to avoid accusations of elitism. However, the Cabinet rejected this as 'unduly drastic'.

The warmth of the welcomes for British children began to cool more than somewhat as the war went on. The Americans had their first taste of rationing after Pearl Harbor, further dampening their enthusiasm for their guests. By 1944, Lord Halifax, who had by then become British Ambassador to the United States, reported that 'nearly every evacuee family is . . . producing a festering spot of anti-British feeling'.

Their hosts had not expected them to stay for more than a year, but once the threat of invasion receded, the British government seemed strangely reluctant to take its citizens back. One of the reasons given for this was the danger involved in shipping them back, though this was greatly reduced compared with the risks faced on the outward journey.

Wealthy people evacuating their children to the Dominions when invasion threatened in 1940 increased class animosity at the time. Home Intelligence reported on this in July 1940, when the CORB scheme had originally been postponed:

There is great disappointment at the postponement of the plan for evacuating children to the Dominions. There was initial resistance among the public to sending children abroad: vigorous publicity overcame that resistance, and the results of a statistical survey showed that the parents of approximately 1,000,000 children were prepared for them to go. The effect of a reversal of policy has promoted sharp recrimination against the rich, whose children were enabled to sail.

Now, as parents waited anxiously for the return of their children, there was a further public outcry against the 'White Ensign' scheme, whereby the children of the rich and influential could get a preferential passage home on a Royal Navy ship. The government tried to play down the adverse publicity, claiming rather implausibly that they had no control over decisions made by individual captains. Thomas Cook also operated a scheme for shipping children back, for those for whom money was no object. Even the most nightmarish passages across the Atlantic, where the passengers faced everything from wet bedding and inedible food, through to sexual harassment and the theft of their luggage by the crew, commanded a hefty premium. Some American hosts were so keen to be rid of their young guests that they paid the fare for their parents!

But many could not afford to pay, and had no sponsor. By the end of 1943 there were almost twelve thousand women and children waiting to get back from the USA and Canada. Some waited over two years for a passage. The British government insisted on negotiating a safe conduct permit from the Germans before launching an official repatriation programme – something they had tried and failed to negotiate in the much more dangerous conditions of 1940. This further fuelled the speculation that, in the original evacuation, the British government had gambled with the children's lives against the possibility of drawing America into the war.

3
Class War

Socialism is, in its essence, an attack not only on British enterprise but on the right of an ordinary man or woman to breathe freely without having a harsh, clumsy, tyrannical hand clapped across their mouth and nostrils.

Winston Churchill, election broadcast, 4 June 1945.

The war of politics

The gulf between the classes manifested itself in many ways other than the evacuation scheme. Britain entered the war a deeply divided society. The depression of the 1930s had seen hunger marches and other demonstrations on the streets of London. Attempts by the government to address unemployment and poverty through measures such as the Land Settlement Association – military-style camps to train the unemployed for a career in an agricultural industry that was itself in deep recession – had ended in a shambles, with accusations of them being 'slave camps'. Rent strikes in the East End of London ended in battles between the tenants and the police. The most basic social services were either severely means-tested or available only through charity or the Victorian institutions of the Poor Law.

The idea that party political differences were shelved for the duration of the war is some way from the truth. Entrenched political divisions were maintained throughout the conflict, at times threatening the wartime coalition and, at one point, actually bringing down the Conservative government that had led the nation into war. Part of the problem lay in the personalities of the wartime prime ministers. Taking Neville Chamberlain first, there can rarely have been a prime minister less capable of uniting the parliamentary parties against a common enemy. Chamberlain had utter contempt for socialism and took little trouble to hide it. As Attlee put it: 'He always treated us like dirt.' Even his own side acknowledged his shortcomings in this respect. His Chief Whip, David Margesson: 'He engendered personal dislike among his opponents to an extent almost unbelievable. . . . I believe the reason was that his cold intellect was too much for them, he beat them up in argument and debunked their catchphrases.'

Some on the Labour side before the war were almost more inclined to blame Chamberlain than Hitler for the forthcoming hostilities. Ernest Bevin, then leader of the Transport and General Workers' Union, put it thus to the 1939 Labour Party Conference:

> Behind Chamberlain are the bankers; they are the principal supporters of appeasement for Germany. They do not want justice for the German masses – that is quite a different thing. I am anxious to prevent this movement fighting for the preservation of the Paris Bourse, the London Stock Exchange, the Amsterdam Exchange and Wall Street.

Similar views were picked up by Home Intelligence from working-class respondents, reflecting on the possibility of Hitler invading: 'He won't hurt us; it's the bosses he's after; we'll probably be better off when he comes; he robs the rich to pay the poor; German victory would only harm the wealthy.'

The government even considered plans for a campaign to highlight the sufferings of the rich in wartime, but wisely abandoned the idea. The Ministry of Information's Home Morale Emergency Committee none the less saw class feeling as a major factor undermining war morale and proposed that:

> . . . something might be done to diminish the present predominance of the cultured voice upon the wireless. Every effort should be made to bring working-class people to the microphone and more frequent use should be made of left-wing speakers to counteract the propaganda of our enemies regarding imperialism and capitalism.

The labour movement had bitter memories of war and its aftermath. After the sacrifices made by millions of the working classes on the fields of France and elsewhere in 1914–18, they saw war profiteers make huge fortunes while their people were forced into unemployment and poverty by the post-war depression. Chamberlain proposed some modest preparations for war – controls over wages, strikes and labour supply – during the early part of 1939.

Even he realised that he needed cooperation from the labour movement for these preparations, and that this would not be forthcoming without some controls over profiteering. Chamberlain therefore promised 'to take the profit out of war', by introducing an excess wartime profits tax. This came in, at a rate of 60 per cent, at the outbreak of war. But when he set up a Ministry of Supply in July 1939 to implement some of these proposals, its advisory panel was drawn solely from the management side of industry – no trade union representatives were invited to take part.

The class war thus continued scarcely unabated into the early 'phoney war' period of the conflict. Certain concessions were made by the Conservative government to reduce the normal acrimony of party dispute – shadow ministers were taken to some extent into the confidence of their opposite numbers in government – but Chamberlain's whole pursuit of the war was based upon the premise that it would all blow over without too much serious fighting. His view was that Hitler would not dare to expose his people to the potential suffering of a second major conflict in twenty years. He therefore attempted to conduct the war with a minimum of disruption to 'business as usual'. This meant giving as few concessions as possible to the opposition, so that there was less to unpick later. It certainly excluded setting up the kind of coalition government established by Lloyd George in 1916 (in which one of the most conspicuous failures had been the Co-ordinator for National Service – one Neville Chamberlain).

Gradually, pressure grew for greater control of the economy and for more vigorous efforts to put it on a war footing. Under Chamberlain, the whole management of the economy seemed positively amateurish. Even the government's Chief Economic Adviser, Lord Stamp, was only a part-time appointment. The half of the week he did not devote to steering the nation's economy was given over to running the London and North Eastern Railway.

Even the early proposals to put Britain on a war footing ran into difficulty, so deep was the class divide. The economist Keynes proposed introducing compulsory saving, to take some of the spending power of the working class out of the economy in order to fund the war effort. Even though this was to be offset by minimum standards of living for the lower-paid, Ernest Bevin opposed it. He anticipated the workers being asked to fund the prosecution of the war and then being faced with bearing the burden of unemployment afterwards. At the same time the Conservatives instinctively recoiled from greater state planning of the war economy. So, in the early part of 1940, little progress was made in preparing for a war that seemed an awfully long time coming.

Meanwhile the tensions in Parliament were starting to re-emerge. The main parties had entered into a pact to ensure that by-elections would not be contested, leaving the sitting party to replace vacancies. By the spring of 1940 Labour's dislike of the Chamberlain government was such that the party conference had no fewer than fifty-one resolutions on the agenda to abandon the by-election truce.

> Colonel Blimp explains:
> 'To preserve British liberty, we must lock up the entire British Labour Party.'

When Chamberlain was displaced as prime minister, it was not the votes of his own party that finally unseated him. For two days after the confidence vote, Chamberlain still entertained hopes of leading a coalition of some description. It was Attlee's telephone call, saying that Labour would not serve in a Chamberlain-led government, that forced his resignation. By this time, the pressure for coalition was irresistible and Labour, although heavily outnumbered in Parliament, were able at last to extract their revenge on a hated prime minister.

That is not to say that Labour's relations with Churchill were anywhere near idyllic. His track record was, from a Labour perspective, perfectly appalling. During his previous time as Home Secretary, in 1910, he was credited in Labour mythology (wrongly, as it happens) with having instructed troops to fire on striking miners at Tonypandy. He had also been bitterly opposed to the General Strike of 1926, editing the strike-breaking newspaper, the *British Gazette*. On foreign policy, Churchill had advocated the use of force to put down the Russian Revolution, had ridiculed Gandhi and praised both Mussolini and Franco. The ideological gulf between him and Labour was to remain vast throughout the war.

Churchill was not even particularly secure among his own party, prior to rejoining the Cabinet. His own constituency party had agreed to continue supporting him in 1938–9 by only a single vote, and his active support within the parliamentary party was limited to a tiny group. However, as war approached and his stand against appeasement was vindicated, he began to rehabilitate himself in public opinion. By May 1939, 56 per cent of the population wanted him back in the Cabinet (though a significant 26 per cent did not). Even then, he was not an obvious choice for prime minister. In April 1940, 57 per cent of the public were still in favour of Chamberlain remaining as prime minister, and on his departure the following month, the majority of the party establishment (and the royal family) favoured Lord Halifax as his successor. It was only the fact that Halifax did not want the job that created the opening for Churchill.

Chamberlain may have thought that the war could be conducted as an extension of normal business but, even among those who accepted the need for a more radical approach, party interests were not abandoned for the duration. Each side always had at the back of its mind the resumption of normal party politics at the end of hostilities. As Churchill put it to a meeting of senior Conservatives in March 1942, when the war was over, he wanted the Conservatives to be seen as 'the main part of the rock on which the salvation of Britain was founded and the freedom of mankind regained'.

Clearer thinkers among the Conservatives foresaw the sea change that the war would bring to the political scene. Robert Boothby wrote to Lloyd George in the following terms, expressing views that were also, to varying degrees, being articulated by others, such as Eden and Butler:

Nothing is more certain than that this war will mark the transition from monopoly capitalism to socialism. . . . You cannot hope to go through a world convulsion of this magnitude without fundamental changes in the social as well as the economic structure. It is inconceivable to me that our present hereditary system, or our 'caste' system of education, can survive the struggle without drastic modification. In the case of Churchill, any diminution of the power of the governing class will involve a clash between his natural instincts and his imagination.

Labour moved quickly to articulate its aims, both for the war and for the peace that would follow. They published their document, *Labour's Aims in War and Peace*, during the period of the phoney war. The *Birmingham Mail*, speaking from Chamberlain's heartland, was predictably scathing about its programme of nationalisation, increased public works and improved social services:

> Where . . . will the money come from? The answer, alas, is far from reassuring at the moment. For the raising of revenue for the prosecution of its vigorous social policy, the Labour Party proposes to revise dramatically the system of death duties, to steepen the graduation of income tax and to tax excess profit and 'all other forms of wealth'. With the best will in the world for the England that is to be, our own optimism wavers a little at this point.

Churchill and the Conservatives had, to a far greater degree, to be persuaded that the aim of the war was something more than just beating Hitler. They kept much more silent about the world after the war and, when peace arrived, tried to cry 'foul'. An exhibition entitled 'How the people were told a story' claimed in 1947 that socialist propaganda was promoted during the war years despite an alleged truce between the parties.

In these political terms, the conduct of the war can be seen as a long preparation for the election of 1945. One of the reasons for Labour's outstanding electoral success in that year was that they were associated in the public's mind with the successes of the war and with the reforms that were to follow it, while the Conservatives were seen as the 'old guard', still associated with the discredited policy of appeasement, and with many of the problems of the war years.

Class War in the Work Place

This was seen as the first real 'total war', in the sense that virtually every other aspect of life was subjugated to the war effort. It was a war that would be won as much in the factories as on the battlefields. But Britain in the 1930s had been riven with deep class divisions that were thrown into sharp relief by the recession. Far from the war effort sweeping away these divisions, they continued to bubble to the surface, despite the strict controls the government was theoretically able to exert over industrial unrest in wartime. The days lost to strikes increased throughout 1942, 1943 and 1944.

While the numbers fell somewhat in 1945, they were still at twice the 1939 level.

In part, this illustrates the strong position organised labour found itself in during the war, with government and employers both preferring to concede wage demands rather than lose war production. Bevin in particular saw a relatively light touch with industrial disputes as being part of the price he was willing to pay for the Draconian controls he exerted over other areas of industrial life.

Colonel Blimp explains: 'Gad sir, Henry Ford was right! Trades unionism is just a plot by the workers to stop employers treating them well of their own free will.'

Class resentment is illustrated by a Home Intelligence report of August/September 1941:

There is 'considerable resentment among women who are already working that the middle and upper classes are still being allowed to "get away" with voluntary war jobs, as drivers, helpers in canteens, etc.' which can be made to look like whole-time work – 'but if such women want time off, there is never any difficulty with their getting it'. (This is contrasted with the great difficulty experienced by women factory workers in doing their household shopping. This problem is causing 'more and more discontent' and is thought to be 'seriously holding up the supply of woman-power'. Trades union representatives again complain that 'very few factories are giving facilities for shopping to their women workers'). The opinion appears to be general that compulsion is most needed 'among the women in the income groups in which the wage earner is receiving from £400 upwards'.

But, for some, the class-ridden British way of doing things was by divine appointment. Lieutenant-Colonel R.C. Bingham provoked a lively correspondence in *The Times* in January 1941 with the following:

Never was the old school tie and the best that it stands for more justified than it is today. Our new armies are being officered by classes of society who are new to the job.

The middle, lower-middle and working classes are now receiving the King's Commission. These classes, unlike the old aristocratic and feudal (almost) classes who led the old army, have never had 'their people' to consider. They have never had anyone to think of but themselves. This aspect of life is completely new to them, and they have largely fallen down on it in their capacity as army officers.

. . . Man management is not a subject which can be 'taught'; it is an attitude of mind, and with the old school tie men this was instinctive and part of the philosophy of life.

If public schoolboys had the divine right to become officers, the ladies of the same class even had their own branch of the Armed Forces. The Voluntary Aid Detachments (VADs) consisted of some four thousand middle- and upper-class women who volunteered to do basic nursing and other duties for the Armed Forces. This gave them exemption from less desirable war work, such as munitions manufacturing. Proposals in 1942 to merge them with the predominantly working-class Auxiliary Territorial Service (ATS) led to a storm of protest – what one observer referred to as a 'monsoon in Mayfair' – in which a host of influential people were mobilised against the merger. Mary Stocks, a Labour Party supporter, lobbied Clement Attlee on the subject:

The present VAD agitation is a social ramp boiled up by a few influential people on behalf of the wives and daughters of their friends. The VADs themselves ought to be ashamed to make such a fuss about the precise terms on which they will serve their country in wartime. I do hope someone will say this good and hard if the government allows a parliamentary discussion.

The armed forces were generally bastions of class prejudice. In the army, public school alumni were fourteen times more likely than their state-educated counterparts to be officers. In the Air Force, pilots of the officer caste were awarded the Distinguished Flying Cross for valour and got first-class rail travel. Equally brave Sergeant Pilots had to settle for the Distinguished Flying Medal and the third-class carriage. The Navy reserved half the places in its officer cadet scheme for public schoolboys. As First Lord of the Admiralty, Churchill had intervened in their selection process, personally

interviewing three youths who
had come in the top twenty of
three hundred applicants, but had
been rejected as 'unfit for naval
service'. He found that two were
the sons of non-commissioned
sailors, while the third had
rendered himself ineligible by
possessing a slight cockney
accent. Churchill got them
admitted but, as soon as he was

Colonel Blimp explains:
'Gad sir, *The Times* is right!
Fine sort of democracy this
is, where young gentlemen
of the Officer Training
Corps haven't the right to
be officers without serving
in the ranks. Class
distinction, that's what it is.'

safely moved upstairs as prime minister, the Admiralty reverted to
its pre-1913 policy of restricting 'lower deck' promotions.

Mass Observation visited the industries of the north in 1942 and
found that pre-war attitudes of class struggle survived, undiluted by
the war:

> The most striking feature of the industrial scene here is the
> survival of strictly peacetime procedure in the conflict between
> employers and men, which is still today the predominant
> conflict here. One looked or listened in vain for any sign of a
> unity binding all parties in the fight against Germany. From the
> men, one got the fight against the management. From the
> management, one experienced hours of vituperation against
> the men. Both sides claimed to be only concerned with
> improving the situation to increase the strength of the struggle
> against fascism, but nevertheless, the real war which is being
> fought here today is still pre-war, private and economic.

Home Intelligence had found similar problems the previous year on
a visit to Merseyside:

> The workers' idea (possibly distorted) of the employers'
> attitude to the war effort appears important. It seems their
> patriotism is overshadowed by their unwillingness to make
> profits for the employers whom they regard as their natural
> enemies. Propaganda impressing workers of their importance,
> rather than encouraging their war effort, appears merely to
> incite them to use their increased bargaining power, whilst the
> recent publicity given to slacking in factories is regarded as an

organised attempt by capitalists to throw the blame on workers to cover their own shortcomings. Keen workers with too little to do are said to be suffering from a sense of frustration which is leading to the feeling 'What's the use?'

> Colonel Blimp explains: 'Gad sir, Lord Nuts is right! The working class should be ashamed to ask for shorter hours, when the upper class is slaving themselves to the bone at dinners and balls.'

Efforts to drive up productivity sometimes met with resistance, and the two sides of industry each had its own explanation for the problem. The President of the Board of Trade, writing to the prime minister in June 1941, had no doubt that the solution was for Churchill to tell the workers to pull their socks up:

For some time I have heard from various industrialists with whom I am in touch stories that the workers in various vital industries are no longer putting forward their best efforts, and that there is an increasing slackness becoming apparent. In the last week or two such statements have become more numerous and are now coming to me from men in whose judgements I rely, and I therefore feel obliged to pass on this information.

The remedy suggested is always the same, namely that you should make a personal broadcast to the labour employed in vital industries, urging them to put forward an effort comparable to what they did last year.

But a *Daily Mirror* reporter, smuggled into the Vickers shipyard in Barrow in July 1940, found a very different picture, and came back with an indictment of management so damning that it could not be printed in its entirety at the time. It was recalled in Cecil King's war diary, *With Malice Towards None*:

Seventy five per cent of the workforce he saw were doing nothing at all. Many had done no work for weeks and some not even for months, and all the men were completely fed up. There was ample material, willing and skilled men and quantities of machinery, but practically no output. One gun, which had been completed, was out in the rain and had been out for at least two months. Fourteen men he found asleep in a pocket in a big gun mounting.

Similar mismanagement was reported by a Liverpool girl, and quoted by Grafton:

I went to work for Rootes, in their aircraft factory. I think they were making De Havilland Mosquitos. To be quite truthful I don't remember doing anything there. The hardest job I had was hiding away from the bosses. I was paid for nothing. I can picture to this day sitting under one of those aeroplanes.

The Minister of Labour, Ernest Bevin, thought one of the problems was that the workforce was hungry:

It seems to be a case of one person telling another until they have made each other believe it. That there is a lethargy mainly due to physical conditions is true. We have run the food supply too low for the people on these heavy metal industries; their energy has been sapped and no appeals can make up for it.

The pressures of the war certainly took their toll of the labour force. The Ministry of Health Annual Report for 1942/3 spoke of complaints from around the country of a general increase in minor illness – reports of crowded surgeries and out-patients, more absenteeism and more complaints of feeling fatigued or 'run-down'. Sickness benefit claims were running above pre-war averages, even despite the absence of those workers now serving in the armed forces. A sample survey showed that 37 per cent of respondents thought their health worse than before the war and only 10 per cent thought it was better. Diet was blamed, and 10 per cent of the population was at that time classified as being malnourished or worse, but the pressures of long working hours and the other demands of war work were also beginning to tell on the labour force.

The 'low state of health' of many people is commented on. . . . The wartime diet is regarded as the main cause; and to this are ascribed skin troubles, 'flu with bronchial or pneumonic symptoms, and the inability of people to throw off chills.

Complaints of physical and nervous fatigue have been reported frequently during the past month. Absenteeism and industrial unrest are attributed partly to the strain of long working hours combined with extra Civil Defence and household duties. Many feel the need of a 'real holiday' – women workers who are 'carrying on a double job' are particularly mentioned.

But Bevin seemed to come to the conclusion that under-achievement was partly a result of the labour force not feeling stressed enough. What they needed was rather more of a threat of invasion!

All the reports show that there is no defeatism and very little evidence of war weariness. Hard work, alterations in mode of life and various inconveniences are accepted as a necessary part of the war effort. . . .

But in the absence of military operations close to the country there is no fiery enthusiasm or sense of urgency among war workers collectively. . . . The possibility of defeat has not entered the heads of most workers, with the result that they are carrying on quietly, rather than urgently, more interested and concerned with their personal interests, their pay packets, their trade union activities, politics after the war, their food and minor comforts. They are anxious for victory but do not see the war as a major issue in their individual lives. There is not sufficient consciousness of their personal responsibility for achieving victory and of the need therefore to sacrifice their personal interests.

The long hours seen in industry were not reflected in government circles. As Neville Chamberlain's Private Secretary, John Colville was appalled to find that the staff at 10 Downing Street started work at 'the disgustingly early hour of 9.30 a.m.' Hugh Dalton had to issue instructions that his staff at the Ministry of Economic Warfare should be at their desks by 10.00 a.m., and until November 1940 the Foreign Office did not start until 11.00 a.m. Key government and senior military staff took

MELT-DOWN

Last week, the railings around Alexandra Park, Manchester, were taken down to the munitions melting pot. Last night, the watchman walked his three mile beat round the park with a bunch of keys, locking the six heavy iron gates. He will lock the gates every night until he receives orders to stop.

Daily Express, 20 June 1940.

Others did not even keep their gates. Earl Baldwin, the former Prime Minister Stanley Baldwin, had the ornamental gates to his home requisitioned for the war effort by his pre-war foe, Lord Beaverbrook. They had been presented to him by a grateful electorate. This was a particularly vicious piece of revenge for long-remembered slights. Baldwin tried to appeal to Parliament to keep them, and a fellow Conservative MP gleefully told the House that he needed them 'to protect him from the just indignation of the mob'.

extended leave, regardless of imminent threats of invasion or major military initiatives.

Food and Privilege

While the very poorest in society were generally better nourished during the war years, for most people the wartime diet was probably more dispiriting than actually unhealthy. Home Intelligence reports from the middle years of the war none the less point to public concerns about the wartime diet and its effects upon productivity.

People are inclined to blame 'vitamin deficiency in the wartime diet' for the prevalence of skin troubles, indigestion, colds and general debility, and to feel some resentment of official statements that 'The health of the nation is better than before the war.'

The shortage and lack of variety of food was a preoccupation throughout the war, and one's ability to overcome those shortages was one of the clearest divisions between the classes. As the war started, the introduction of rationing was seen by some as a measure that would balance out some of the grosser inequalities. Others, including Winston Churchill and a number of MPs from both major parties, felt that the image of 'starving Britain' that rationing would convey gave a propaganda coup to the Germans. The *Daily Express* ran a vigorous campaign against rationing:

> The public should revolt against the food rationing system, that dreadful and terrible iniquity which some of the Ministers want to adopt. There is no necessity for the trouble and expense of rationing because there may be a shortage of this or that inessential commodity. Why should old women be forced to wait here and there before the shops for their supplies? This form of folly is difficult and almost impossible to understand.

However, the experience of this East End grocer in the autumn of 1939 illustrates just how gross the inequalities of a free market could be:

> It is bringing all the rich people in from the West End to take the poor people's food. I came back from lunch this morning and found a beautiful car outside. A lady and her husband were carrying 28 pounds [of sugar] each – and the chauffeur was carrying 28 pounds on each arm. I made them put it all back again and gave them 3 pounds each. I don't think that sort of thing is right – they take the poor people's food. They don't give the poor people a chance.

Before state rationing was introduced, not all shopkeepers were prepared, like this man, to operate their own, informal system. There were plenty who were happy to put their prices up and sell to whoever could afford it, in whatever quantities they wanted to buy. Others gave preferential service to favoured customers, saving goods 'under the counter'. By the same token, shopkeepers ran the risk of being unfairly vilified by their customers, some of whom were ready to condemn any price rise, however justified, as 'profiteering': 'One week there was two boats of oranges sunk and that affected the market, of course; the price went up and you can imagine the complaints.'

However, only food supplied in large enough quantities to be available to the masses was rationed. For those with the money to pay for it, there was always a more or less ready supply of luxury foodstuffs. As this breathless correspondent for *Shopping News* reported: 'The mouthwatering displays of foodstuffs at Fortnum and Mason's this week made me wonder whether rationing need worry anybody. If you're short of anything in the food line I'll be surprised if you can't get it here.'

One disincentive to ordinary people might have been the prices luxury foods attracted in wartime. Grapes could be as much as £1 a bunch, a melon 10–15s and a bottle of wine costing 5s before the war was going for £1 5s. Even so, the diaries of 'Chips' Channon recall a dinner party in 1944 at which nineteen car-loads of people dined on oysters, salmon, dressed crab, minced chicken and enough alcohol to get happily drunk. While such events may have been the exception, they tended to multiply in the telling and fuelled the resentment of ordinary rationed members of the public in proportion.

At the other extreme, civil servants worked out an absolute minimum diet, for introduction in the event of dire emergency. It was supposed to be the minimum necessary to sustain life, and consisted of a mixture of bread, potatoes, oatmeal, vegetables – all in very small quantities – and ⅗ pint of milk. Churchill was shown this 'basal diet', as it was called, and was horrified. He commented: 'Almost all the food faddists I ever knew, nut-eaters and the like, have died young after a long period of senile decay.' The scheme was rapidly abandoned.

One option for avoiding rationing, not affordable for the ordinary member of the public on a frequent basis, was eating out. Coupons were not needed for restaurant meals. During the early years of the war newspaper photographs of ostentatious consumption in restaurants were not banned by the censor, but as food supplies got

---

FOOD, GLORIOUS FOOD...

Pig bins were provided on street corners. An army of inspectors kept an eye on them, to ensure that nothing suitable for human consumption was being placed in them. Should such delicacies as bacon fat or bread crusts find their way there, local residents would be questioned, and it was even not unknown for bins to be staked out, in the hope of catching the guilty party in the act.

tighter, the censor yielded to public sensibilities and discouraged them. The Ministry of Food considered the possibility of requiring individuals to surrender their ration tickets in restaurants but dismissed it as an administrative impossibility. However, the problems it was causing greatly exercised the mind of the Minister of Food. Lord Woolton wrote in his diary in March 1942:

> I went to see the Chancellor of the Exchequer about luxury feeding in restaurants. There is a great press outcry against meals in expensive hotels, the conclusion being that people who pay 10s or thereabouts for a meal must be getting a good deal of food for that money, and there's agitation abroad about the inequality of a system that allows wealthy people to feed very adequately off [outside] the ration. We shall have to do something about this, but I don't think the solution is a tax on meals.

Administratively impossible or not, the 1945 Annual Congress of the Women's Co-operative Guild called for rationing to be extended to restaurant meals:

FUNNY FOOD

We never starved, but we ate some bloody funny things. Best was American dried egg. You poured a thin trickle into the frying pan, then as it cooked it blew up like a balloon, till it was two inches thick, like a big yellow hump-backed whale. And we had whale meat, that tasted strongly of fish, unless you soaked it for twenty-four hours in vinegar, after which it tasted of vinegar. But there was so much of it – great big bloody steaks as big as your plate – that we didn't care what it tasted like.

Boy, Tyneside, quoted in Westall.

I had never seen or eaten a banana. Where I lived there was a prisoner-of-war camp behind us. One day I was walking to the shops when a prisoner called us to the fence and offered us three bananas (for my sister and my brother). Not knowing how to eat it, we peeled the banana, ate the skin and threw the inner away.

Girl aged six, quoted in Westall.

In view of the cuts in rations which will press with particular hardship upon the working class, the Congress of the Women's Co-operative Guild calls for the adoption of a points scheme for restaurant meals. We have yet to hear of the wholesale dismissal of chefs employed by the upper classes, whose duty it will now be to cook one shilling's-worth of meat, and two pennyworth of corned beef with one ounce of cooking fat per person. We realise that people with money and influence go short of nothing, as there is still unrationed food such as poultry and game, and meals can be obtained in hotels and restaurants. We also protest at the hypocritical propaganda of the BBC and the press in trying to make us believe that everyone is on the same rations.

The memoirs of the wealthy at that time reveal that they were able to live very well indeed. As the invasion threat reached its height in September 1940, Harold Nicolson recorded in his diary: 'Dine with Guy Burgess at the Reform and have the best cooked grouse that I have ever eaten.' 'Chips' Channon recalls the Dorchester Hotel during the blitz:

Half London seemed to be there. . . . I gave Bob Boothby a champagne cocktail in the private bar . . . our bill must have been immense, for we had four magnums of champagne. London lives well; I've never seen more lavishness, more money spent, or more food consumed than tonight, and the dance floor was packed.

One partial solution was a chain of government-run eating establishments, where the general public could get a nourishing meal for a modest price. However, Churchill reacted strongly (and probably rightly) against Lord Woolton's suggestion of calling them 'Communal Feeding Centres', a term which Churchill condemned as 'an odious expression, suggestive of Communism and the Workhouse'. Instead they became 'British Restaurants'.

Even named thus, they did not avoid suspicion on the part of the public, some of whom saw them as an attempt to introduce collective feeding by stealth. At holiday seasons, too, when they were closed, there were questions asked about what was happening to the food normally supplied to them, and why it was not coming through to the public in the form of increased rations?

Another of the mechanisms used by the government was the maximum charge of 5s for a meal consisting of a single main course. 'Superior' restaurants were later exempted from this maximum, leading to a spate of overcharging among 'middling' restaurants. All sorts of devices were used to evade this limit. The Dorchester, for example, charged a 7/6 cover charge and an extra 2/6 for dancing. Wild overcharging for any wine consumed was commonplace, and one establishment was fined for charging a cloakroom fee (the 'cloakroom' being a row of hooks in the restaurant itself). Five shilling maximum charge or not, 'Chips' Channon again notes paying £10 for lunch for three people at Claridges. Again, Home Intelligence reflected public outrage at the apparent inequalities, in March 1942:

There is growing evidence of a feeling among certain sections of the public that 'everything is not fair and equal and that therefore our sacrifices are not worth while'. In particular, there is some belief that the rich are less hit by rationing than 'ordinary people' for the following reasons:

(a) they can eat at expensive restaurants.

(b) they can afford to buy high priced goods in short demand, such as salmon and game.

(c) they can spend more on clothes and therefore use their coupons more advantageously.

(d) they receive preferential treatment in shops, as 'people giving large orders are favoured and poorer people wanting "little bits" are refused'.

(e) they receive preferential treatment as regards petrol rationing. To quote a postal censorship report: 'we can see the Big Bugs riding in their posh cars and poor beggars can't get petrol for business'.

The feeling of inequality of 'sacrifice' between the Services and civilians, frequently mentioned in these reports, continues. Ill-feeling between the two is said to be growing as tales of slacking in factories, high wages and black markets increase the belief among Service men that civilians are not pulling their weight.

LUXURY GOODS

Anything deemed to be a luxury item was subject to substantial reductions in the quantity manufactured. A team of civil servants based in an office in Leicester Square struggled with the philosophical teaser 'what is a luxury?' Thus it was that hair nets, cosmetics and any underwear fancier than the Utility variety came into short supply. At the same time, a host of new products, some of them arguably of little more use to the war effort, found their way on to the market. Wartime shoppers, starved of normal consumer goods, had to console themselves with such things as leather ID card and ration book covers; personalised gas mask holders; Buckley's Balm, for the treatment of the effects of the mustard gas that was never used on us; and anti-vermin jockstraps and gas-proof suits.

This sense of inequality even translated itself to the police tendency to be much stricter on breaches of drinking and gambling laws in working mens' clubs than they were over similar establishments for the rich. This was even reflected in Defence Regulation 44C, which allowed them to prosecute establishments whose attractions could affect the ability to operate of those engaged in essential war work. Presumably, similar concerns did not apply in relation to the drones gravitating to the kind of gentlemen's clubs portrayed by P.G. Wodehouse. Another Regulation – 55C – gave the police virtual *carte blanche* to close down any establishment to which they took a dislike. The mere name of a club – such as the Boogey Woogey, the Paradise or the Hi-de-Hi – could be enough to get it the kiss of death from the licensing authorities.

Despite the ostensible equality of everyone having the same number of rationing coupons, the system still worked in favour of the better-off. With clothes rationing, for example, they were able to afford better-made and therefore longer-lasting clothes for their coupons, which was important when so few new clothes could be obtained. Thus, the richest people were able to expand their wardrobes during the war years, while those of the poorest were reduced. For the very poorest, who could not even afford the cheapest new clothes, their clothing ration books simply became another desperate source of black market cash, to keep them from immediate destitution. Some rationing was even avoided in the interests of the relatively privileged. Back-bench Conservatives successfully opposed domestic fuel rationing, on the grounds that it was the people with the biggest houses who would suffer most from it.

Business as Usual – the 1945 Election

In 1945 the public got their first chance in ten years to express their views through the ballot box. It was an election conducted in considerable chaos. Vast numbers of the electorate were scattered around the world in the armed forces, and the electoral registers at home had been thrown into disarray by the wartime mobility of the population.

The conventional wisdom, even among Labour supporters, was that a grateful nation would give the victory to the man who was seen to have won them the war. Opinion polls forecasting a Labour landslide and even by-elections producing huge Labour swings during the latter months of the war were disregarded, especially by the Conservatives themselves.

Churchill mounted one of the most ill-judged campaigns in modern electoral history. His first election broadcast claimed that the introduction of socialism into Britain would require some form of Gestapo. In that same radio broadcast, which one commentator claimed cost the Conservatives a million votes, he predicted that a Labour government would erode people's savings, and also referred patronisingly to 'you, listening to me in your cottages'. . . .

Mass Observation summed up the public's view of this broadcast: 'It would be difficult to exaggerate the disappointment and genuine distress aroused by this speech. . . .' Attlee, commenting on the speech the following day, reflected the widely held view as to who was behind the Conservative election campaign: 'The voice we heard last night was that of Mr Churchill, but the mind was that of Lord Beaverbrook.'

Whichever hands were pulling the strings, the great war leader had completely lost his way once peacetime politics were resumed. As Labour left-winger Ian Mikardo put it during the election campaign: 'I yield to no man in my admiration of Mr Winston Churchill. I think he is the greatest war minister this country has had since William Pitt, but I am not disposed to have another war to give him an opportunity of exercising his talents again.'

These views were reflected in opinion polls. As early as February 1944 Mass Observation had found that 62 per cent of the population was against Churchill as a post-war prime minister. They found that the public saw him as: 'No man of peace, domestic policy or human detail.'

In contrast to Churchill's vituperative campaign, Labour concentrated on the future, did not attack Churchill personally and did not even put up a candidate against him in his own constituency. But if the Labour leadership was not being provoked into conducting a class war through the election campaign, the demand for radical change was strong among the Labour rank and file. Their candidate for Pudsey and Otley was a young Army Major, one Denis Healey. He told the 1945 Labour Party Conference:

> The upper classes in every country are selfish, depraved, dissolute and decadent. These upper classes in every country look to the British Army and the British people to protect them against the just wrath of the people who have been fighting underground against them for the past four years. There is very great danger, unless we are very careful, that we shall find ourselves running with the Red Flag in front of the armoured car of Tory imperialism and counter-revolution.

The election results showed the extent to which the population had been polarised during the war years. Labour took 47.8 per cent of the vote and 393 seats, the Conservatives 39.8 per cent and 213 seats. The middle ground, represented by the Liberals, was all but destroyed. Despite going to the polls with great confidence, with the coup of having William Beveridge as one of their candidates (already an MP, having taken Berwick in a by-election in October 1944), they took just 9 per cent of the vote with their 306 candidates and won twelve seats. Both Beveridge and the Liberal leader Sinclair lost their seats.

> Colonel Blimp explains: 'Gad sir, I ascribe my defeat to apathy and to the fact that 90 per cent of the electorate voted for my opponent.'

4

Politically Incorrect

If the middle ground of politics had all but disappeared by 1945, some extremes of political opinion continued to be expressed throughout the war years. In this chapter, we look at the activities of fascists, communists and others during the war, and start with those who opposed the war entirely – the conscientious objectors.

Never in the Field of Human Conflict . . .

In the First World War conscientious objectors had been the victims of considerable persecution, from both official sources and the general public. Of those who sought to register, some six thousand ended up in prison at least once and over seventy died of their treatment there.

Herbert Morrison, who for much of the Second World War was Home Secretary, had been a conscientious objector in the First World War. During that war, conscription applied only to men of military age. Now it was to be extended to everyone, including women up to the age of 55. At the same time, the criteria for conscientious objection were widened for this war, to cover not just religious beliefs but also philosophical or even political principles.

The conduct of the tribunals also changed. Gone were the questions about what the appellant would do if he saw a Hun raping his sister. Instead, the proceedings were presided over by a judge, accompanied by other worthies. Their questions were supposed to relate to the individual's role in a democracy in time of war. Do they eat foods brought in by convoy? Would they help a child injured in an air raid? Did they obey the blackout (which could be regarded as a form of passive resistance)? Did they grow food (thus freeing up space in convoys for armaments)? Thus, it was possible to demonstrate that virtually everyone was contributing something to the war effort, and the tribunal could go on from there to test the boundaries of the contribution that each individual was willing to make.

About fifteen thousand claimed exemption in the First World War. The wider criteria in the second increased the numbers of applicants to around sixty thousand. Of these, about ten thousand were refused outright, of which half were later prosecuted and, in many cases, were sent to prison for refusing to serve. A small number – about 2,900 – were able to demonstrate such a complete and principled objection that they were given total exemption. The vast majority were given conditional exemption, provided they agreed to take up agriculture, forestry or some similar activity for the duration.

Conscientious objectors were thus able to plead all sorts of cases in aid of their cause. While many did so on the basis of sincerely held religious convictions, the case put by others raised rather more questions. Lesley Stevens of Birmingham sought exemption on the grounds that he was a vegetarian. In case anyone is under the mistaken impression that Mr Stevens thought that, having killed the Germans, he would then have to eat them, his problem was rather that he thought he would find it difficult to maintain his dietary principles in service life.

Others were prompted by a higher source than vegetables. Lesley Blacknell, a clerk from Shrewsbury Park, London, decided not to take part in the war after 'a visitation from the Holy Spirit. Two days after war was declared, my mind was set at rest by a particularly vivid spiritual experience. The visitation directed me to feed my fellow men by agricultural work.' In similar vein, one man based his objection on a series of mystical experiences he had undergone on different occasions, while listening to Beethoven's Ninth Symphony, reading *King Lear* or sitting on top of a mountain. Another confused political and religious convictions:

> I felt sort of queer when I registered at the labour exchange. People seemed to think I was a coward. I am only going on one thing, and that is the Bible, although I have only read one or two pages. This war is the fault of the government and not of the working class. What is a government for, anyway?

One's calling could be a powerful influence upon one's inclination to fight. One case coming before the tribunal, told them loftily: 'I cannot permit any responsibility to my country to take precedence over my loyalty to God. My loyalty will not allow me to be transferred from the career which I have accepted.' This all sounded very grand, until it transpired that his vocation was as a clerk to the London County Council! Artistic sensibilities were also advanced as a case for exemption. Harold Matthews presented himself to the tribunal as an artist. He considered that the prosecution of war did make use of vice and immorality. He thought nudity on the stage had some connection with the war. The tribunal decided to make use of his artistic abilities and offered him the opportunity to work painting vehicles in camouflage. He refused, whereupon they agreed to register him as a conscientious objector, provided he worked in agriculture or forestry. Mr Matthews announced his intention to appeal.

Some offered in their defence membership of the Boy Scout movement, socialist principles or the fact that they were orphans. Others based their religious affiliations upon the most tenuous links; one pig dealer, who claimed to be a Seventh Day Adventist, was asked when he had last attended church. 'When I was fourteen,' he replied. 'Since then I have been too busy.' Another said his religious beliefs were a mixture of Christianity and Buddhism, though he could not say that he was exactly a Christian or a Buddhist. Others were very clear about their religious affiliations. Samuel Turner of Dudley entered his tribunal wearing a cloth inscribed 'Christ died for our sins' across his shoulders.

Few can have tried to argue the case against war in economic terms, in quite the way that unemployed Middlesex insurance salesman Albert F. Johnson did. He told the tribunal that, for the price of the First World War, it would have been possible to buy for the entire populations of Britain, the United States, Canada, New Zealand and the other belligerent countries a luxury house with five acres of land *each*, still leaving enough money over to purchase outright France and Belgium (the entire countries, that is). His application was dismissed, the tribunal adding insult to injury by telling him that his calculations were nonsense.

Not all those who applied for exemption were of the pacifist tendency. Henry Ballantine-Best of Manchester considered that he had been unjustly treated at his tribunal. He felt that the judge presiding over it had been antagonistic towards him from the outset. This may have been something to do with the fact that, at one point, the appellant had to be ordered out of the courtroom for causing a disturbance. Later, as Judge E.C. Burgis was boarding a train to go home, Ballantine-Best drew the judge's attention to his dissatisfaction by stabbing him six times with a sheath knife.

Scarcely more pacifist was the conscientious objector hauled before the court for refusing to work as a fire watcher. He explained his apocalyptic view of things: 'I object to fire watching as it appears to me to be an attempt to prevent the fulfilment of the scripture which says that the world will be destroyed by fire.'

There were even those who objected on the grounds that they supported the other side: 'I believe that the fascist creed is the only thing to bring peace to this country. I believe that all war is wrong because it leads to the destruction of man. I believe we are wrong in taking up arms against Germany because it was Britain's responsibility.' When the tribunal learned that this last case was a known fascist activist, his objection was refused.

There was public concern, not just about whether appellants' objections were genuine, but also about whether they would gain advancement in their civilian jobs while their colleagues were in the armed forces. Reading Town Council resolved that any conscientious objectors on their books should be given unpaid leave of absence for the duration of the war. Their superannuation was protected, but otherwise they were told to seek alternative employment within the war economy. Others, like Bermondsey Council, simply sacked any conscientious objectors in their employ, in some cases costing them their pensions.

The treatment of those conscientious objectors who went to prison was not always by the rule book. The following remarks were made by a detention centre inmate, and quoted by Grafton:

> What they did was, they used to bring them in, put them in a cell, strip them naked, throw a uniform in, and that's it. You put it on or you don't, and in the middle of winter that's no joke. To reinforce the point, like as not they'd put a hose on him, wet the whole bloody place out, including the uniform. Every pressure was used, but some of these people were incredibly hard.

But there was one fine body of men where there was no hiding place for the conscientious objector. As their national President,

Major-General Sir Frederick Maurice, told the press: 'in the British Legion there is no room for pacifists and there is no place for "stop the war" parties and their pernicious groups.'

The Far Right

> . . . was it not a supreme tragedy that one of the most brilliant men of our age, who might have talked to Hitler in a language that he would have understood, should have been shuffled off the stage as though he were a criminal?
>
> Beverley Nichols, writing of Sir Oswald Mosley in his autobiography, *The Unforgiving Minute*.

Hitler had many sympathisers, not to say admirers, in pre-war Britain, many of whom came to be regarded as security risks when war broke out. At the height of the government's concern about them, in August 1940, some 1,482 British nationals were detained under Regulation 18B. Overall, the importance attached to the far right of politics during the war years was probably out of all proportion to its real significance.

British Union of Fascists

> Mosley was in fact a highly gifted playboy. From the moment he modelled himself on Mussolini, he resembled nothing so much as an actor touring in the provinces in a play which someone else had made a success of in London.
>
> A.J.P. Taylor.

Oswald Mosley's British Union of Fascists was the largest and most active of the pre-war fascist parties. Mosley, the product of a privileged upbringing which included education at Winchester and Sandhurst, entered Parliament as its youngest Member, in 1918. He started out as the Conservative Member for Harrow but within six years had left them, spent some time as an Independent Liberal and then joined the Labour Party. He became Chancellor of the Duchy of Lancaster in Ramsay MacDonald's 1929 Labour government, and was given the job of finding solutions to the problem of mass unemployment. When the government rejected his radical and interventionist proposals, involving public works, tariff protection, the nationalisation of the banks, raising the school leaving age and promoting early retirement, he resigned from the government in 1930 and from the Labour Party in 1931. His proposals none the less attracted interest across a political spectrum which stretched from Harold Macmillan to Aneurin Bevan.

Having run out of mainstream parties to join, he founded his own New Party, with the help of £50,000 from the car manufacturer William Morris (later Lord Nuffield). After a dismal performance in the 1931 General Election, this transformed itself into the British Union of Fascists in 1932. In its first two years it attracted forty thousand members, and Lord Rothermere's *Daily Mail* wrote an article entitled 'Hurrah for the Blackshirts', praising Mosley's 'sound, commonsense Conservative doctrine'.

At this stage, Mosley's fascist policies were directed primarily at the running of the economy. It was his subordinates, notably his Director of Propaganda William Joyce, who succeeded in getting anti-Semitism adopted as official party policy in 1934. It was about this time, too, that their public meetings started to get seriously violent and Rothermere's support for them cooled. Relations between Mosley and Joyce also began to cool, among other things because of what Joyce saw as Mosley's reluctance to embrace anti-Semitism with enough enthusiasm. Joyce was eventually sacked from the BUF, ostensibly as a cost-saving measure, in 1937. By the outbreak of war, membership of the BUF had shrunk to about nine thousand. It was the only organisation proscribed under the Defence Regulations, though leading individuals from other groups were also interned.

Once war broke out, Mosley tried initially to maintain a relatively neutral stance, calling on supporters not to be dragged into 'an alien quarrel' caused by 'the dope machine of Jewish finance'. They should instead engage in Civil Defence activities and 'do nothing to injure our country, or to help any other power'. By May 1940 Mosley went further and put his supporters at the disposal of the British defences, in the event of an invasion. He even condemned members of the Nordic League as Nazi traitors. It later transpired that he was not, unlike some of his fellow extremists, on the Nazis' list of potential collaborators.

One of the reasons for the BUF's initial success was that many people simply could not believe that someone like Mosley could have moved so far beyond the political pale. They thought that his brand of fascism was simply some kind of robust conservatism. The Mosleys were well connected in the highest circles and remained so even after he embraced fascism. Mosley was related by marriage to Winston Churchill's wife, and Diana Mosley (second wife of Sir Oswald and the daughter of Lord Redesdale) had previously been married to Bryan Guinness, one of England's richest men.

The BUF was the largest of the pre-war fascist parties, but there were a number of other, much smaller ones. Like many of those on the political fringes, they dissipated much of their energy in squabbling among themselves about the minutiae of dogma. The main link between all these groups and Germany was the Nazis' 'Gauleiter for Britain', Dr R.G. Rosel, until he was expelled from Britain in June 1939.

The National Socialist League

The National Socialist League was set up by William Joyce and former Labour MP John Beckett, after they fell out with Mosley in 1937. It enabled Joyce to give vent to his more violent anti-Semitic instincts. He was the American-born son of an Irish-American, who moved the family back to Ireland when Joyce was only three. He grew up among the struggles for Irish independence during the First World War and, as a schoolboy, served briefly as an informer for a government-recruited auxiliary group opposing Republicanism. The family moved to Lancashire, and Joyce initially joined the British Fascisti, a group of right-wing conservatives, whose paranoia about a state takeover by trades unionists and socialists nicely suited Joyce's own feelings of persecution.

Joyce moved to the BUF and then helped to set up the League. He eventually fled to Berlin in August 1939, days before the introduction of the Emergency Defence Regulations that would have led to his detention. There, he began his wartime radio career as Lord Haw-Haw, in the company of other turncoat broadcasters such as Ralph Baden-Powell, nephew of the founder of the Boy Scouts, and John Amery, the son of Leo Amery, Secretary of State for India in the wartime Cabinet. Joyce was, along with Amery, one of the last Britons to be hanged for treason.

The Anglo-German Association

This group originally had quite an honourable pedigree. It was set up just after the First World War under the patronage of Lord D'Abernon, who was British Ambassador to Berlin during the Weimar Republic. One of its aims was to secure better treatment of the Germans following the Versailles peace treaty. Had they been more successful in this aim, they might have helped to prevent the rise of Hitler. As it was, the Association was dissolved when the Nazis took control in Germany.

It reappeared in a more sinister guise in October 1935 at the instigation of an extreme right-wing peer, Lord Mount Temple. Von Ribbentrop, the pre-war German Ambassador to Britain, also formed a sister organisation in 1936, Deutsche-Englische Gesellschaft, which was used to disseminate Nazi propaganda in Britain.

The Anglo-German Association was extremely well connected in high society. Before the war, some of its members moved among a group known as the 'Cliveden set' (named after the monumental stately home of the Astor family, near Maidenhead). Many of this group's members had fawned upon Von Ribbentrop, and regarded Britain and Germany as united bulwarks against Communism. Influential people attended its gala events, including Lord Halifax, the Foreign Secretary.

The Right Club

The Right Club was founded in 1939 by Captain Archibald Maule Ramsay, a far-right Conservative Member of Parliament for Peebles and Midlothian. Ramsay had served with some distinction in the First World War and became a Member of Parliament in 1931. He spent a number of uneventful years on the back benches, espousing strongly Christian and even more strongly anti-Communist views. But in 1938 he came to the view that the world was in danger of being dominated by a conspiracy of Jews, Bolsheviks and Freemasons. He became a firm believer in the *Protocol of the Elders of Zion*.

His tiny organisation of some three hundred members carried out what has been described as 'pro-German activities and secret subversive work, with the object of disorganising the home front and hindering the prosecution of the war'. The *Daily Express* claimed in June 1940 that Ramsay had been selected as the Gauleiter for Scotland, in the event of a German invasion. Ramsay denied it, sued them for libel, and was awarded the derisory sum of one farthing.

Ramsay was implicated in the Tyler Kent/Anna Wolkoff spy scandal, described earlier, and was imprisoned from May 1940 to September 1944. Wolkoff was herself a member of the Right Club and was caught by an MI5 infiltrator of the organisation, Joan Miller. Wolkoff had foolishly entrusted Miller with the delivery of a letter she had written to William Joyce in Berlin, advising him how best to direct his propaganda in Britain.

Despite calls from his constituents to resign, Ramsay did not allow imprisonment to interfere with his parliamentary duties, and submitted questions to ministers from his cell. On his release, he returned to the House. His last act as a Member of Parliament was to table a motion for the reintroduction of the Statute of Jewry of 1290, by which Edward I expelled the Jews from England. This was in June 1945, shortly after the full details of Hitler's concentration camps had been revealed to the world. He was not re-elected.

Imperial Fascists and Missing Links

Despite its grand title, the Imperial Fascist League never had more than two hundred members. It was founded in 1929 by a retired veterinary surgeon, A.S. Leese, previously a member of the British Fascisti. His virulent anti-Semitism is thought to have been brought about by his disapproval of the ritual Jewish methods of slaughtering animals. Leese denounced the BUF as mere 'Kosher Fascists'. Despite the tiny size of his organisation, Leese was one of only two openly fascist candidates ever to gain public office in Britain. He and another Fascisto were elected to Stamford Council in 1924.

The Link was a more extreme pro-fascist organisation, founded in 1937 by Admiral Sir Barrie Domville. Disturbingly, Domville was the head of British Naval Intelligence from 1927 to 1930. The Link was an apologist for every excess of fascism, spreading its views via a propaganda sheet called *News from Germany*, which may have been

THE COMMITTED AND THE CONFUSED

Over and above the organised support for Hitler, there were those individuals who, either for ideological reasons or simply because they were unhinged, would take up the Nazi cause in a public place. Their court cases would appear in the paper after they had been arrested, often for their own protection.

An example of the first category was Elsie Steele, aged 22, of Stamford Hill, who was charged in April 1940 with using insulting words likely to cause a breach of the peace. She addressed a crowd of some three hundred at Bethnal Green, which included many Jews, telling them that 'you won't see many of our rotten government leaders in khaki'. As the crowd grew restive, she warmed to her theme. Hitler, she told them, had done nothing to them; he had simply put an end to unemployment and turned out the rotten yids. Remember, it was Chamberlain, dictated by his Jewish masters, who declared war, not Hitler. So remember that when you kill a German, he is only defending himself, he is not attacking you. I hope I live to see the day when Chamberlain and his rotten warmongers are put on trial for their lives for the murder of thousands of British and German soldiers, too. As for Churchill, we will remember Gallipoli and the Dardanelles.

She was arrested at that point, and later told the court that nothing that she had said had been resented by a large proportion of the crowd. In fact, she said, she was acclaimed at frequent periods. It was in fact the police who had caused a breach of the peace by arresting her and denying her right of free speech. She was fined £15 with the option of 14 days' prison and bound over to keep the peace for six months.

Definitely more towards the bewildered end of the oratorical scale was the self-styled 'Reverend' Nelson Noakes of Didcot, a clerk and supposed faith healer, who was taken into protective custody when he was found staggering through the streets, shouting: 'You have not got much longer! England will soon fall and then you will see!'

The court was told that Noakes was in the habit of drinking cheap wine and becoming abusive. He was fined £1 and the court never learned exactly what it was they would see when England fell.

funded by the German government. Its membership at its highest was just 4,325, spread across thirty-five local branches.

Many other groups emerged and disappeared over the course of the war years. Some were – in their titles, at least – less overtly fascist, wrapping themselves in the cloak of Christianity (the British Council for Christian Settlement in Europe), pacifism or nationalism (like the Nationalist Association, run by a man called Jock Houston, who had been expelled even from the BUF for the extremity of his racist views). Some naive Christians or pacifists found themselves drawn into such groups.

At least four weekly anti-Semitic publications were freely available throughout the war years, and in 1943 an eccentric pretender to the Polish throne, Count Potocki, published what the *Jewish Chronicle* called: 'Probably the vilest anti-Semitic pamphlet yet produced in Britain.'

The Truth about the Jews blamed them, among other things, for 90 per cent of the nation's crime, for pornography and for the Second World War itself. It also claimed that there were no authenticated cases of Jewish deaths under Hitler. Several thousand copies of this tract were circulated.

Even the lunatic fringe had its own lunatic fringe. The Social Credit Secretariat (another front for extreme anti-Semitism) believed that the Nazi movement was itself a Jewish plot! Political and Economic Planning saw Jewish intrigue behind Air Raid Precautions, any form of planning, and evacuation (the latter being a devilish plot to pollute the countryside by introducing 'verminous Jews'). The National Health Service and the Beveridge report (and no doubt most of everything else that went on during the war years) were similarly condemned as instruments of Zion.

Later in the war, fascist groups attempted to come back more into the open. From covert activities like painting the slogan PJ (Perish Judah) on Karl Marx's tomb, they moved to open public meetings. These were generally poorly attended and often violently disrupted.

The Internment of Fascists

The outbreak of war led to calls for the arrest of Mosley and other leading fascists. During the First World War internment had only been applied to aliens, but the close association of Mosley's party with the Nazis prompted pressure for a harder line to be taken against them. Home Secretary Sir John Anderson initially resisted this pressure in Cabinet:

> Although the policy of the BUF is to oppose the war and to condemn the government, there is no evidence that they would be likely to assist the enemy. Their public propaganda strikes a patriotic note. . . . In my view, it would be a mistake to strike at this organisation at this stage by interning the leaders. Apart from the fact that there is no evidence on which such action would be justified, it is to be borne in mind that premature action would leave the organisation itself in being and other leaders could be appointed to take the place of those who had been apprehended. In my view, we should hold our hand. . . .

The law (in particular Regulation 18B, introduced at the start of September 1939) allowed British nationals who were acting in a manner 'prejudicial to the public safety or the defence of the realm' to be interned. By the end of November 1939 only forty-six Britons had been detained under this clause, almost half of whom were subsequently released. However, the Wolkoff spy scandal broke just in time to strengthen the hands of those who wanted more Draconian action to be taken. Revised Regulation 18B (1A) conferred the power of clairvoyance upon the Home Secretary, allowing him to detain any member of an organisation who, he felt, was 'likely to endanger the public safety or the defence of the realm'. A further fifty-nine people, including Mosley, other leading lights of the BUF and Frank Joyce, younger brother of Lord Haw-Haw, were detained within two days of this revised regulation coming into effect. Lady Mosley was arrested subsequently, on 29 June 1940.

It is said that, following her internment, her brother intervened on her behalf with Churchill at a Downing Street dinner party. Churchill's attitude to the Mosleys was certainly in marked contrast to the 'collar the lot!' mentality that he applied to the arrest of thousands of (largely innocent) foreign nationals. Churchill wrote to the Home Secretary, saying: 'Naturally I feel distressed at having to be responsible for an action so utterly at variance with the fundamental principles of British liberty.' He asked the Home

Secretary to ensure that they were given hot baths, exercise, books and the wireless, and inquired: 'What arrangements have been made for Mosley's wife to see her baby, from whom she was taken before it was weaned?'

Churchill was also instrumental in securing for her extra privileges, including the right to co-habit with her husband at what had previously been the exclusively female Holloway Prison. The allegedly luxurious conditions under which they were imprisoned were a source of public outrage throughout their internment. Bus conductors stopping outside Holloway Prison would announce the stop as 'Lady Mosley's suite'.

It was rumoured that the imprisoned Mosley led a life of bridge and champagne, with a prisoner valet to fetch him his silk underwear when it had returned from being laundered in Mayfair. While the details of their imprisonment were no doubt embellished by the press in the interests of a good story, and Mosley denied many of them during the course of his unsuccessful appeal against internment, it certainly appears that they enjoyed considerable privilege. They were allowed to cultivate fresh vegetables on a plot of land within the prison walls, were able to have their children come for extended visits and had other inmates to do many of the domestic chores for them.

While initially held in a men's prison, Mosley and his fellow internees used to conduct meetings of what they styled the Fascist Grand Council in their cells and he even set up a registered war charity – the 18B (British) Aid Fund in September 1942. Its ostensible aims were to raise funds for the dependents of internees and to campaign against the legislation that had put them there.

There was further public outrage when the couple were released on medical grounds in November 1943 (she had dysentery and Mosley a circulatory problem). They had to be smuggled out of prison amid cries for their re-arrest and for Mosley's hanging, and spent the remainder of the war under house arrest. However, as *The Times* pointed out:

> Sir Oswald Mosley's detention for three and a half years was preventative, not punitive; no court had convicted him, nor had he been charged with any crime. It was for what the Home Secretary thought he might do, and to prevent him doing it, that he was put in gaol.

The Hunt for a British Fifth Column

Overall, very little evidence of active treachery was found among the British population. However, this did not prevent both the authorities and the general public looking for it, often on the thinnest of pretexts. A correspondent to the *Spectator* gave an account of the experience of one of those arrested. He was taken direct from his home to prison, where, for ten days, he was held in almost complete solitary confinement, without even basic amenities such as a shaver or toothpaste and with no indication of the charges against him. Even after a month, no charges had been laid and there was no sign of any trial in prospect. And who was this threat to national security? He was a retired army officer, who had fought in the First World War and had volunteered to do so in the Second. His only crime was that, for just one month in 1934, he had been a member of the British Union of Fascists.

Many who were not even formally accused by the authorities were subject to trial by rumour. Lord Iliffe said there was an 'urgent need for the inauguration of an anti-chatter campaign in Berkshire'. He was one of its victims, with rumours circulating that he was in fact a German and had been imprisoned. The entire substance for these rumours was apparently the fact that he had once entertained the German Ambassador to a day's shooting.

Such rumours were not confined to the aristocracy. Allegations about one tradesman's family became so virulent that they prompted this editorial in the local newspaper:

> I am assured that there is not the slightest justification for the wild and wicked stories that have spread like wildfire and which have been designed to discredit the loyalty of a patriotic British subject, one of whose sons is serving in the forces; his second son is expected to be called up. The same rumour is said to have connected the names of other citizens with alleged 'Fifth Column' activities. Very probably efforts to trace the origins of this poisonous scaremongering will be unsuccessful; having started the snowball on its way they have disappeared into the background, there to watch the results of their villainous work.

The family concerned advertised in the paper, offering a reward for information identifying the source of the rumours. The nature of the gossip was kept tantalisingly hidden from the readers. But their curiosity was satisfied a few weeks later, when a member of the family was remanded in custody for the possession of two unlicensed revolvers. It transpired that Alfred Bird had been the local Secretary of the Imperial Fascist League before the war. The rumours were that he spent his holidays in Germany, attacking Jews, that he had a secret radio transmitter and used to promote the advantages of German citizenship to anyone who would listen to him.

Irish Republican Army

The republican movement was entering one of its bloodier phases when war broke out. Five people had been killed and nearly fifty injured by them in the month before the main event against Germany began. From January 1939 they blew up public utilities and underground stations, carried out arson attacks and a bombing outrage in Coventry which left five dead and several injured. They even destroyed the waxwork of Henry VIII at Madame Tussauds.

Because of doubts about the loyalties of some Ulstermen, there was no conscription in Northern Ireland during the war, though some 42,000 of their number volunteered to fight in the British Armed Forces. Nor did they form a Home Guard, since this would have necessitated arming the Catholics. At the same time servicemen returning home proved to be one of the IRA's most valuable sources of new weapons.

Hitler had no doubts as to whose side the northern Irish were on, and some 745 Ulster people were killed in an air raid on Belfast on 15 April 1941. The air raid shelters in Belfast were worse than in any other part of the United Kingdom and, following the bombing, around a hundred thousand people nightly fled the city to find safety elsewhere. Shortly after the Belfast raid, Hitler rather set back his prospects of *détente* with the Irish Free State, when his planes accidentally bombed Dublin on 31 May, killing twenty-nine people.

The British government never forgot the adage 'England's trouble is Ireland's opportunity', and their suspicion was certainly not allayed by Eamon de Valera's scrupulous observance of their neutral status. In 1945 he joined a very short queue outside the residence of the German Minister in Dublin to pay his condolences on the death of Hitler, and Eire was about the only country in the world to maintain diplomatic relations with Germany after VE-Day.

Nationalist extremism was not confined to the Irish, and the Germans tried to cultivate dissidents among all the Celtic fringes of the nation. Even as war broke out, one Barbara Jones was being charged in Cardiff with possessing sixty-nine sticks of gelignite, 'in such circumstances as to give rise to a reasonable suspicion that she did not have them in her possession for a lawful object'. The real challenge for the court might have been to try to think of any circumstances in which a young lady of twenty-three *might* have had sixty-nine sticks of gelignite in her handbag for a lawful object.

Communism and the Communist Party of Great Britain

The CPGB was seen by many as a major potential force in British politics, before, during and after the war. The party had some twenty thousand subscribing members (a membership list that grew with the outbreak of war) and its mouthpiece, the *Daily Worker*, a circulation of up to ninety thousand. Their initial anti-war point-of-view (which lasted as long as Russia remained neutral) was shared by some in the Labour Party, who feared it would descend into a war of rival imperialisms, and by the appeasers on the right of the Conservative Party.

The CPGB led a campaign from as early as 1937, complaining about the inadequacy of Air Raid Precautions for the working people. The blitz proved them to be not far wrong, but this did not stop the police from seizing some of their leaflets during their 1940 campaign. The party was also active in setting up informal committees to represent the interests of their shelterer supporters. They were strongly represented in the Coventry area, and had lobbied strongly for improved shelters there. The major raid on the city therefore proved to be something of a propaganda coup for them. For a time after the raid, the *Daily Worker* was the only newspaper on sale in the shattered city. It lay the blame for what it described as a 'reprisal raid' on 'the big factory owners, the big business and landowning interests' and called for a negotiated peace settlement.

A major 'People's Convention' was held on 12 January 1941 and its proceedings were reported in the national press. Over 2,200 delegates, claiming to represent 1.2 million people, assembled to hear messages of support from people as diverse as Paul Robeson and Mao Tse Tung; among those attending the convention was Indira Gandhi. Within days of the Convention, on 21 January, the *Daily Worker* was suppressed by the government for its opposition to the war. Though most of the national press applauded this action by the government, the *Daily Mirror* attacked it, as did much of the artistic establishment. The ban was introduced despite there being no evidence of the paper having had any effect upon the conduct of the war. Even Herbert Morrison had to concede that: 'Little or no evidence can be found that Communist propaganda is having any appreciable effect upon the morale of the nation as a whole.' The worst they could find to say about it was that it never contained 'a note of real encouragement'.

The Cabinet considered taking further action against the CPGB but ruled against it, despite Ernest Bevin's proposal to imprison party intellectuals as potential trouble-makers. But the government's real problems started when Russia entered the war and a wave of pro-Russian sentiment swept the nation. Stalin, a mass murderer on a scale to rival Hitler, became cosy 'Uncle Joe', and even Lavrenti Beria, the Head of their Secret Police, later executed by the Russians themselves for alleged crimes against humanity, became known as 'Russia's Mr Pickwick'.

The Ministry of Information recognised the problem facing the government after Russia's entry into the war. As they reported to the Home Policy Committee (quoted in Addison):

> The Russians are operating against the Germans beyond expectation so that we cannot call Communism itself inefficient. The control by government in this country of industry, the levies made upon earnings and upon capital are all integral parts of the Bolshevik theory, and the combination of all these factors . . . is bound to educate the public into assuming that Communism . . . is either a reasonable alternative to the pre-war system of democratic theory or is a logical sequence to the wartime system of control. . . .

The government could hardly attack the politics of its new ally openly. Instead, led by the Ministry of Information, it set out to hijack initiatives to support them, so that Communist elements in Britain could not claim credit. So, when Communists in Manchester started fund-raising for Russia, the MOI got the Lord Mayor of Manchester to take it over. A body called the Anglo-Soviet Public Relations Committee, populated with 'reliable' people, was set up to oversee a range of liaisons with the forces of the left, and in February 1943, the government was behind demonstrations around the country to salute the 25th anniversary of the founding of the Red Army. At the same time they carefully steered the Boy Scout movement away from what they saw as an unsuitable link with a Communist-backed Anglo-Soviet Youth Friendship Committee.

They were supported for once by right-wing trade unionists, who were equally fearful of Communist influence in their organisations. Walter Citrine, the General Secretary of the TUC, was hard-pressed to say whether he detested the Communists or the Fascists more.

At the same time, critical voices were silenced. Former British spy and anti-Bolshevik Sir Paul Dukes was banned from lecturing to the armed forces, and, at the Ministry of Information's urging, George Orwell's satire of Communism, *Animal Farm*, was rejected by his publisher Faber as being: 'Not the right point of view from which to criticise the political system at the present time.'

> Colonel Blimp explains: 'Gad sir, Lord Punk is right! We can't have the British Empire saved from defeat by Soviet Russia. Dash it, it would lower our prestige with the enemy.'

5
Civil Defence: Common Sense?

Air Raid Precautions

Air Raid Precautions began in earnest in 1938. Shelters began to be dug and the process of recruiting a hundred thousand ARP Wardens and sixty thousand Auxiliary fire-fighters started. There were pre-war rehearsals for the blackout, which came into force with the declaration of hostilities.

A whole book could probably be written about the blackout and its consequences. Road accidents doubled as motorists struggled to cope with the unfamiliar darkness. By January 1940 one person in five had had a blackout accident of some description. There were even cases of pedestrians being knocked down and killed by other pedestrians, and moves were made to introduce a 'keep left' policy on the pavements, as well as the roads.

One problem was knowing where 'left' was. It was not unknown for a driver to mistake the kerb for the white line in the middle of the road and mount the pavement. One motorist who did this only discovered the error of his ways after he had demolished a lamp standard and a tree.

In another case, in rather more serious vein, an army lorry filled with soldiers was driving through the blackout along what the driver thought was the main road. In fact it was one of the

---

LEAD, KINDLY LIGHT . . .

Over-vigorous enforcement of the blackout produced some of the war years' more ludicrous prosecutions. A man at Bridgend station was arrested, the day after war broke out, for breaking the blackout by striking a match on the platform. The excuse that he was looking for his dropped false teeth did not save him from a fine. A woman was fined for ironing in the dark with her curtains drawn, because the pilot light of her iron kept blinking on and off. Even daylight was no excuse for breaching the blackout – a garage proprietor was fined for switching on a neon sign at midday.

side roads running parallel to it. They suddenly confronted a brick wall where they expected the main road to be and, in the accident that followed, two soldiers were killed and thirteen injured. But few deaths can have been as bizarre as that of the motorist killed as a result of a collision with a bomber – he drove into the back of a low loader carrying a still-crated bomber to its new home on an RAF airfield.

It was suggested that a 20mph speed limit would help reduce the number of accidents. There were only two problems with this; the first was knowing how the police would enforce it in pitch blackness, and the second was how the motorist himself would know how fast he was going, since lights on his dashboard were themselves illegal in the blackout.

The effectiveness of the blackout as a means of defence may be judged from this account by a German pilot, quoted in Fitzgibbon:

> Painstaking observation of the blackout regulations was in Germany, too, based on the belief that the bomber pilots needed only to see the most minute speck of light in order to dump their bombs on to it. This was, of course, nonsense. Neither a single light, nor a group of lights, was of any help in navigating a plane if there was nothing else to be seen. In any event, London's approximate position was easily detected, even from very far away, owing to the concentration of searchlights. There were a number of recognisable searchlight positions, with groups of massed lights, which our more experienced bomber crews soon learned to use as navigational aids. If they did not expose, and we wished to establish our location more exactly, we would attract their attention and make them illuminate by briefly switching on our navigation lights, or firing tracer, or shooting off our guns at their supposed sites. This usually succeeded in drawing their light.

On the subject of retaliation, the nation's anti-aircraft defences were not in good shape at the outbreak of war. During the inter-war years they had been very much the Cinderella of the armed forces, not least on the grounds that they had very little hope of actually hitting anything. A 1926 exercise by the RAF, firing at a plane flying at a known and fixed course and speed, and at the ideal height for the gunners, scored just two hits out of 2,935 shots fired.

By 1938 the entire national stock of anti-aircraft equipment stood at just 100 guns and 800 searchlights, compared with the minimum considered necessary for London alone, of 216 guns and 1,056 lights. A good proportion of this meagre supply was subsequently lost in France. At the start of the blitz Britain had just 50 per cent of the heavy anti-aircraft guns it needed and 30 per cent of the light guns. Only ninety-two of the heaviest guns guarding London could fire high enough to trouble the German planes at their normal bombing altitude.

The AA batteries consequently got the bottom of the recruitment barrel, as Fitzgibbon relates:

> Out of twenty-five recruits to one battery, one had a withered arm, one was mentally deficient, one had no thumbs, one had a glass eye which fell out whenever he doubled to the guns and two were in the advanced and more obvious stages of venereal disease. Out of a thousand recruits sent to the 31st Anti-Aircraft Brigade, fifty had to be discharged immediately, twenty more were mentally deficient, and a further eighteen were below medical category B2.

One solution to the recruitment problem was to bring in women, and not surprisingly they proved a very satisfactory substitute for the recruits the batteries had previously received. A new problem was that, because the government was committed to a policy of women working in non-combatant roles only, they could do anything on the ack-ack battery other than actually fire the gun. However, they could shout 'Bang!', if that made them feel any better. In every other respect, they got equal status.

At first, the batteries did not bother firing at their targets, not least for fear of shooting down our own fighters by mistake. This led to bitter complaints from the public about the lack of defence. A decision was then made to fire the guns regardless of their chances of hitting anything, and it proved, if nothing else, a great boost to morale. It also scared the Germans, making them fly higher and causing some to jettison their bombs early and head for home.

Naturally, the defenders could not please everyone. One council called for their local battery to be removed, since the vibrations were cracking the lavatory bowls in neighbouring houses. It was also the case that the guns were almost as great a danger to those they

Aldwych tube station during the blitz, with Londoners reduced to trying to make a bed between the rails. *(IWM HU44272)*

A few pathetic remains, rescued from a bombed-out house in 'a south-east inland town' in February 1943. On the extreme left, a policeman stands guard over them and a notice in the window warns of life imprisonment or even the death sentence for looting. *(IWM HU36177)*

J.B. Priestley was second only to Churchill in his popularity as a radio broadcaster during the war, but he was dropped by the BBC for his views about the aims of the war and what should happen afterwards. He is seen here (left) with actor Leslie Howard. (IWM HU36268)

Women were not allowed to join the Home Guard, but some of them were good enough shots to train the Home Guards in shooting. Some of them set up their own organisation – the Amazons Defence Corps. They are seen here practising in Hillingdon. (IWM HU36270)

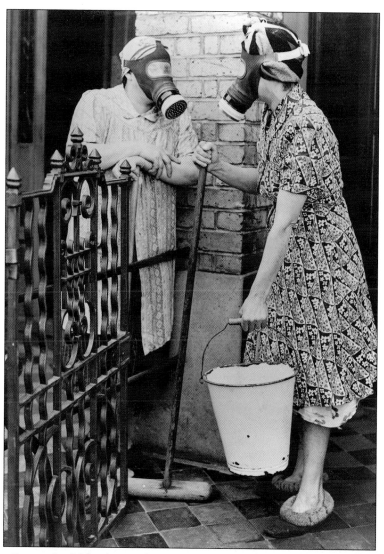

Gas-masks did for the art of conversation . . . well, they did for the art of
conversation full stop. This was a contrived photograph for propaganda
purposes, taken in Southend in 1941. As the war went on, the general
public were much less likely to carry, let alone to wear, their gas-masks.
(IWM HU36137)

May 1940, and female aliens are unceremoniously rounded up and taken under police escort to an internment camp in the Isle of Man. Their male counterparts had an armed military escort and some faced hostile crowds en route. *(IWM HU36121)*

Russian Ambassador Ivan Maisky accepts the first tank to be delivered in the 'Tanks for Russia' programme. Our alliance with the Russians was in some ways a considerable embarrassment to the wartime government. *(IWM HU57227)*

Women workers assemble a Beaufighter in 1941. Having made a huge contribution to the wartime economy, many of the advances women made in the field of employment were lost at the end of the war. *(IWM L84)*

Hitler's V-weapons brought a new reign of terror to London in the last years of the war. A V2 rocket fell on Smithfield Market on 9 March 1945 and here rescue workers pick their way through the wreckage with a badly injured woman. *(IWM HU65896)*

Many of the public ignored government advice to keep away from London and returned in droves. This is Euston Station on 12 September 1944. Railway staff were overwhelmed and Italian prisoners of war had to be brought in to help with the mountains of luggage. *(IWM AP7094)*

Many of the children evacuated overseas at the start of the war returned as young men and women at its end. These are about to disembark at Southampton in September 1945, after five years in Australia. *(IWM HU36233)*

Interned aliens, somewhere in 'the north of England' (but probably Huyton, near Liverpool), fill mattresses with straw for bedding. For some, this was the only furniture they had under the harsh conditions of their internment. *(IWM FX6641)*

For some victims of air raids, the emergency services could offer no help, and they were reduced to sleeping in a neighbour's house. *(IWM D24235)*

For those who could afford it, dining out offered a convenient solution to the problem of rationing. *(IWM D13333)*

A group of East End Jews pursue their religious studies in their bomb shelter. There was much unfounded criticism that Jews were pushing their way to the front of queues for shelter. *(IWM D1509)*

British girls dance with American GIs. Their presence in this country when so many British men were fighting overseas was a cause of considerable friction. *(IWM D14124).*

The *Ladywood* motor patrol boat, guarding the canals of Birmingham against pocket battleships in August 1940. A number of waterborne Home Guard units were founded around this time. Some may see them today as a convenient way of continuing peacetime interests, rather than as a vital arm of our home defences. *(IWM)*

The Home Guard, formerly the Mid-Devon Hunt, near Chagford on Dartmoor in July 1940. This is another example of peacetime leisure activities spilling over into war, with shotguns replacing hounds and German parachutists instead of foxes or stags. *(IWM)*

Some early Home Guard photographs were censored on the grounds that they looked too comically unmilitary. This, by contrast, would have had the Germans quaking in their jackboots – London Home Guards in August 1940 being trained as high-speed 'dispatch racers'. *(IWM)*

A small part of the devastation wrought on the town centre of Reading in the air raid of February 1943. Despite the results being rather difficult for local people to overlook, censorship did not permit the local paper for several weeks afterwards to reveal to its readers that it was their town that had been bombed. *(Reading Borough Council)*

were defending as they were to the enemy, particularly after the introduction of rocket shells, early in 1943. In the first serious raid of 1943 six Londoners were killed by shrapnel from the shells and many more by faulty shells exploding as they landed.

When the first doodlebugs came over, the anti-aircraft gunners saw how these new 'bombers' fell from the sky as they opened fire, and congratulated themselves on their improved aim. On discovering that they were crashing by design, the gunners none the less continued to fire on them, in some cases bringing them down over the crowded centre of London where they could do the maximum of damage. However, the worst of the damage to central London was subsequently avoided by British Intelligence feeding the Germans false information as to where the V1s were actually landing, leading them to make the bombs fall short of central London. While this was good news for the City, it was bad news for Croydon, which – with 142 doodlebugs and a thousand houses destroyed – became the most frequently hit target of the V1s.

> Colonel Blimp explains: 'Gad sir, Lord Flop is right! The politicians shouldn't be allowed to discuss the weakness of our defences. It saps the confidence of the War Office.'

In one of the most ill-timed political speeches of the war, Duncan Sandys announced on 7 September that the danger from the V2 rockets was remote and unlikely to amount to much. At precisely 6.40 a.m. the following day, the first of 1,054 V2 rockets to land in Britain hit Chiswick. There was no defence against these appalling weapons, and only the capture of their launching sites eventually removed the threat.

In addition to the anti-aircraft guns, great faith was also attached to the barrage balloons. This was possibly aided by the wartime propaganda film *The Lion has Wings*, which showed German pilots turning for home at the mere sight of the balloon barrage. There were various popular theories about how they worked, including one that they were magnetic and dragged the bombers in to their doom.

The balloons tended to be nicknamed after leading politicians and local dignitaries. At one point 'Archbishop Lang' broke loose from his moorings and ran amok around Lambeth Palace while another (identity unknown) tried to break into Wandsworth Prison. Another balloon fell on the Dover Castle pub in Westminster Bridge Road, where it exploded, killing two people. Ziegler records that, when they were first deployed at the time of Munich, five of the forty balloons broke loose, one of them dragging its cable across an electric railway line, shorting out services for the next half hour.

Give me Shelter

A survey carried out shortly after the start of the war showed great public dissatisfaction with the shelters being provided. After Stepney was attacked in September 1940, thousands of people went to Liverpool Street station the following evening and demanded to be allowed to shelter beneath it. At first, the authorities called in soldiers to keep them out. But the crowds would not disperse and, when it became clear that they had a near-riot on their hands, the soldiers relented and the gates were opened.

Before the war, the function of the Underground during hostilities was discussed by the Anderson Committee on civil defence. Some argued for it being closed entirely for the duration, for parts of it were extremely vulnerable to bombing. For example, the Fleet sewer passed over Farringdon Street and, if bombed, could flood the District, Metropolitan and Circle lines at the same time. Other stations, such as Embankment, were also at risk. Other people favoured closing it as a railway and using the tunnels purely as shelters. However, the decision was made to keep rail services running.

Colonel Blimp explains: 'Gad Sir John, Beaverbrook is right! We must show Hitler we have command of the air, the seas, the land and the Underground!'

None the less, the underground stations – in particular the deeper ones – became the favoured shelters for many Londoners. By the end of September 1940 an estimated 177,000 people were sheltering in eighty stations. The authorities were at first reluctant to let it happen. They feared that the public would develop a bunker mentality and refuse to come out during the day, disrupting essential war work. But it was difficult to stop people buying a 1½d platform ticket and 'waiting for a train' for the duration of the raid. However, as demand grew, people would arrive to reserve their space as early as 11 a.m., and by 5.00 p.m. travellers would have difficulty in climbing over the reclining crowds.

Conditions were at first insanitary in the extreme. Hundreds of shelterers shared a few curtained-off buckets that served as toilets and were frequently knocked over. The less fastidious among them saw nothing wrong in continuing their full range of bedroom activities there, providing some unexpected coaching in the facts of life for younger shelterers.

In order to maintain the train services, the operators painted two lines along the platform, 8 feet and 4 feet from the platform edge. People sitting or lying on the platform could not cross the 8 foot line until 7.30 p.m., when the rush hour was deemed to be over. The 4 foot line could not be crossed until 10.30 p.m., when the services stopped and the current was turned off. Thereafter, some people even slept on the tracks themselves. But not even these proved an entirely safe place to be in an air raid. Bank station suffered a direct hit and a number of the 111 victims died as a result of being blown into the path of an oncoming train. The worst disaster of its kind occurred at Balham in October, when a burst water main led to a tidal wave of sludge that suffocated many of the 680 people sheltering there.

Other subterranean communities formed at the Chislehurst Caves, where some eight thousand Londoners took refuge. Some of these even became semi-permanent homes for bomb victims, and their caves became very well appointed. One even boasted a piano. Some sixteen thousand sought shelter beneath the goods yard at Stepney, and Epping Forest also became a favoured campsite.

After the first month of bombing, there was considerable anger at the failure of the authorities to provide sufficient deep shelters, and at the shortcomings of other ARP preparations. The Communist Party in particular led the calls for deep shelters. Initially, the government resisted these, on the grounds that they would have to be widely dispersed and people would not be able to get to them in the warning time available. They also raised the fears of shelter mentality and of the spread of contagious disease in them. (Not unnaturally, the huge cost was also a consideration.)

The main target of the protesters' anger was the Home Secretary,

Sir John Anderson, and he was replaced in a Cabinet reshuffle by Herbert Morrison. Morrison was greeted in his new job by an open letter in the *Daily Herald* from journalist Ritchie Calder:

> I have seen tough London workers, of whom you and I are proud, whose homes are gone but whose courage is unflinching, goaded by neglect and seething with resentment and furious reproach. THEY LOOK TO YOU. Much of the breakdown in the last month could have been foreseen and avoided, or mastered by anyone who understood the human problem of the Londoners. GO TO IT, HERBERT.

Morrison ordered deep shelters for seventy thousand people to be constructed. Not all of these could even be completed. One had to be stopped, as it was threatening the stability of St Paul's Cathedral. Another, near the Oval, filled permanently with water. They were also completed too late to be of use for anything but the V-bomb attacks, late in the war. Even during the mini-blitz of 1944, Morrison refused to allow the public into them, since he had reserved them for vital but unspecified war services (possibly the housing of troops bound for Normandy). He said he was 'sure that these considerations will be understood by the people of London'.

Morrison also put the use of the Underground as air raid shelters on a more organised footing. Two hundred thousand bunk beds were ordered, and proper sanitation and mobile canteens provided. Shelter marshals were appointed and tickets issued to regular users. These could be withdrawn if: 'The holder or any member of his family commits any offence in the shelter or fails to do his share in keeping the shelter tidy and clean.' One unexpected effect of this was to make underground shelter places a black market commodity. Spivs sold tickets for underground sheltering places for 2/6 a time – cheaper and safer than any London hotel.

In some respects the blitz could not really be described as the communal experience of popular myth. Apart from the Underground stations and the other subterranean refuges mentioned earlier, communal sheltering was not at all popular. Only 9 per cent of the population used communal shelters of any kind. About 60 per cent of the population stayed in their beds during raids and took their chances. Around 2.25 million homes were issued with Anderson shelters (named after the Home

ANDERSON SHELTERS

The Government didn't *build* shelters for you. Council workmen just came with a lorry and dumped the bits on your front lawn and left you to get on with it. We didn't think much of the bits, lying out in the rain, gathering rainwater. Just thin bits of corrugated iron, like some old shed. People felt they'd be safer in their houses, solid bricks and mortar. They weren't going out in the middle of the night to bury themselves in a grave. Then my father saw an Anderson that had received a direct hit; he said that there was quite a lot of it left; the house it had belonged to was just a heap of bricks.

Boy aged nine, Tyneside, quoted in Westall.

We had an Anderson shelter at the bottom of the garden. The three of us shared it with Maude and Laura Rowlands (two maiden ladies who lived next door) and their fat old brown-and-white mongrel, Patch. It was very damp. My mother caught lumbago from the damp and eczema from spring-cleaning with washing soda, as there was no soap to be had. Every morning she had to drag herself backwards up the shelter steps, in time to make our breakfasts before we went to school. If you were late, and there hadn't been a raid the night before, you got caned.

Girl aged six, London, quoted in Westall.

Secretary). These shelters were semi-subterranean corrugated iron devices set into earth in the garden – and they were thought more likely to kill you by pleurisy than the Germans ever were by bombing. Around a thousand households in Fulham alone applied to have their Anderson shelters removed. Later in the war, there were also about a million Morrison shelters, which took the form of reinforced steel tables kept within the house, beneath which people could shelter during air raids.

Particularly unpopular were the brick-built communal surface shelters, found in many streets where there were no gardens to accommodate Anderson shelters. They managed to be both cold and airless, tended to double as a urinal for drunks on their way home, lacked even enough light to read by and were considered by many of the public to be death traps, since they looked like a military building and therefore were felt to invite attack. And death traps some of them were, but not for the reason people thought.

Due to an incorrect mix of cement specified for the brickwork, some of them were prone to collapse at the slightest provocation. A nearby bomb blast, for example, would cause their walls to bulge out, leaving the 9in-thick reinforced concrete roof to come crashing down on any unfortunate occupants – and earning them the grim nickname 'Morrison sandwiches'. In April 1941 the Ministry of Information was set the daunting task of trying to make these shelters popular with the public. Late in 1943 it was found that 106 of the surface shelters in Hammersmith had been built with just a 3in roof, and that they lacked many of the reinforcing bars required. The builders were charged with a £25,000 fraud.

One other item that the authorities developed for the benefit of shelterers was the siren suit. Anne Valery remembers it, not entirely fondly, as follows:

> A dark, all-in-one garment along the line of rompers, often with elasticated cuffs, and with a zip which ran from the neck to below the waist. The theory behind the design was that it could be leapt into in seconds, and the wearer kept warm while rushing to the shelter and sitting for hours in its damp depths. What the male designers had failed to take into account was that, unlike them, we could not pull out our parts, so that the contrast between its snug interior and pulling the lot down before we could pee probably gave us more colds than if it hadn't been invented.

Not everybody had to rely on siren suits or underground stations. Much of London society moved out of the capital for the duration; Mayfair and Belgravia became strangely deserted. In all, 17 out of 37 houses in Hyde Park Gardens and 13 out of 45 in Belgrave Square came on to the market as the war broke out. For those who chose to stay, the basements of luxury hotels, such as the Savoy and the Dorchester, provided a much more salubrious class of accommodation. The Savoy, sensing a good business opportunity, turned its basements into air raid shelters, a dormitory and a cabaret/restaurant. The American broadcaster Ed Murrow visited this top people's shelter in September 1940:

> We found, like everything else in this world, the kind of protection you get from bombs depends on how much money

you have. On the other hand, the most expensive dwelling places here do not necessarily provide the best shelters, but certainly they are the most comfortable. We looked in on a renowned Mayfair hotel and found many old dowagers and retired colonels settling back on the overstuffed settees in the lobby. It wasn't the sort of protection I'd seek from a half-ton bomb, but if you were a retired colonel and his lady you might feel the risk was worthwhile because at least you would be bombed with the right sort of people. . . .

Some took offence at class discrimination extending itself into air raid shelters, and on the night of 14 September 1940, a hundred or so East End residents, including some pregnant women and their local MP, presented themselves at the door of the Savoy just as the air raid alert was sounding. They announced themselves as the Stepney Tenants' Defence League and demanded use of the shelter, as they were entitled to do. This test case was of particular interest, as the hotel was packed with visiting foreign newspaper correspondents. After some confusion, it was agreed that the East Enders could go below but, before they could all take up their positions and protest, the all-clear sounded. The management promptly informed them that they could now only stay if they bought something to eat or drink, whereupon the protesters took one look at the prices and left. The British press played it down, but German papers presented it as the British working classes rising up against their oppressors in revolution. It was a short-lived revolution; no further such protests on any scale were reported.

For those seeking further escape from the blitz, pubs and cinemas provided a retreat. Some cinemas would re-run their programme if a raid were still in progress when it ended, and the Granada chain even offered a package of overnight accommodation and a mixed bag of entertainment.

Incendiary bombing increased as the winter of 1940/1 drew in. There was still no compulsory firewatching of business premises, nor a network of emergency water tanks. Both of these were ordered only after the raid on the night of 29 December, when there was a near-firestorm in the centre of London and water supplies were stretched to their very limits – and beyond.

Some of the failures of civil defence involved cock-ups of inspired proportions, such as when an air raid shelter in

Maidenhead was found to have been built right next to a reserve tank containing several thousand gallons of oil. The local paper reported their investigation with heavy irony:

> Naturally, the responsible official has had to give an explanation and to reassure the Council on the point of the safety of the shelter. He has, I believe, told them – and his statement has presently been accepted – that the oil stored in the tank is heavy oil and in the event of a hit by a bomb would not explode, but merely burn. Thus, the occupants of the shelter would not be blown to pieces; they would only be roasted alive. How comforting!

Rivalling them in incompetence, and certainly surpassing them in insensitivity, Fulham Council told some of its ARP staff that it could not afford the steel reinforcement required for their shelter, but that they would pay £7 10s towards the funeral expenses of any of their number killed on duty.

Gas Attack

Some of the most thorough preparations were made for a threat that did not materialise. After its use in the trenches of the First World War, there was a widespread terror of gas attack, and tens of thousands of its victims were still around as living warnings of the terror weapon. This fear was undoubtedly not helped by the publication of the novel *The Gas War of 1940* by 'Miles', in 1931, predicting the destruction of London from the skies.

By the beginning of 1937 civilian gas-masks were being produced at a rate of 150,000 a week, and some 38 million had been issued by the time of the Munich crisis in September 1938. They were neither easy nor comfortable to wear; beards or elaborate hairstyles both reduced the amount of protection they could provide. The Ministry of Home Security also issued the following warning to women during the first months of war: 'The attention of women is drawn to the fact that the temperature conditions inside the face-piece of the mask cause eye-black to run, leading to smarting of the eyes, profuse tears and spasms of the eyelids. This produces an urgent desire to remove the mask, with dangerous results if gas is

> ### INSIDE THE MASK
> Although I could breathe in it, I felt as if I couldn't. It didn't seem possible that enough air was coming through the filter. The covering over my face, the cloudy Perspex in front of my eyes, and the overpowering smell of rubber, made me feel slightly panicky, though I still laughed each time I breathed out, and the edges of the mask blew a gentle raspberry against my cheeks.
>
> The moment you put it on, the window misted up, blinding you. Our mums were told to rub soap on the inside of the window, to prevent this. It made it harder to see than ever, and you got soap in your eyes. There was a rubber washer under your chin, that flipped up and hit you, every time you breathed in. . . . The bottom of the mask soon filled up with spit, and your face got so hot and sweaty you could have screamed.
>
> Children, quoted in Westall.

present.' Waterproof eye make-up soon became available to overcome this problem.

It is not strictly true to say that there were no civilian casualties from gas during the war, but those that did occur were caused by our side. One ARP authority decided to test the public's readiness for gas attacks, and went to a busy street, armed with a supply of tear gas bombs and a loudspeaker van. The fact that the announcer had himself to wear a gas-mask made him totally incomprehensible to the puzzled passers-by, who found themselves rendered inexplicably tearful by the mystery cloud.

There was at first strong social pressure to carry your gas-mask with you at all times; you could be refused admission to places of entertainment or find yourself lectured by complete strangers. Two soldiers, on being sentenced to death for murder at the Old Bailey, were chastised by the police officer accompanying them for leaving their gas-masks behind as they left the dock. But as the months drew on without any sign of gas attack, the practice lapsed. Women began using their gas-mask cases as substitute handbags; small boys found them invaluable as football goalposts. Among young men, carrying a gas-mask was eventually seen as a virtual denial of one's virility.

The Local Defence Volunteers

The British government is committing the worst crime of all. Evidently it permits open preparations for the formation of murder bands. The preparations which are being made all over England to arm the civilian population for guerrilla warfare are contrary to the rules of international law. German official quarters warn the misled British public and remind them of the fate of Polish *Franc-tireurs* and gangs of murderers. Civilians who take up arms against German soldiers are, under international law, no better than murderers, whether they are priests or bank clerks.

German radio broadcast, commenting on the formation of the Home Guard.

Tuesday, 14 May 1940. Britain had a new prime minister in Winston Churchill, who had appointed Anthony Eden as his Secretary of State for War. That night, Eden made a broadcast on the Home Service that would bring millions of people on the home front into closer contact with the war:

In order to leave nothing to chance, and to supplement from sources as yet untapped the means of defence already arranged, we are going to ask you to help us in a manner which I know will be welcome to thousands of you. Since the war began, the government have received countless enquiries from all over the kingdom from men of all ages who are for one reason or another not at present engaged in military service, and who wish to do something for the defence of their country. Well, now is your opportunity.

We want large numbers of men in Great Britain, who are British subjects, between the ages of 17 and 65 . . . to come forward now and offer their services . . . the name of the new force which is now to be raised will be the Local Defence Volunteers. . . . This name describes its duties in three words. . . . This is . . . a part-time job, so there will be no need for any volunteer to abandon his present occupation. . . . When on duty, you will form part of the armed forces. . . . You will not be paid, but you will receive a uniform and will be armed . . . in order to volunteer, what you will have to do is to give your name at your local police station; and then, as and when we want you, we will let you know.

Earlier in his speech, Eden had described a new form of warfare – the dropping of troops by parachute behind the main defence lines to cause disorganisation and confusion prior to the landing of larger airborne forces. The Home Guard, as it came to be better known, was founded in large part on the misapprehension that the Germans would try to drop large numbers of parachute troops behind the defensive lines, either to act as Fifth Columnists or in support of an invasion. One of their earliest nicknames was the 'Parashots'. On 22 May, as British troops in France were making their way towards Dunkirk, the Under-Secretary of State for War explained in more detail 'the three main purposes for which the LDV were wanted':

First, observation and information. We want the earliest possible information, either from Observation Posts or from patrols, as to landings. The second purpose is to help, in the very earliest stages, in preventing movement from these enemy parties landed from the air, by blocking roads . . . so that they are hemmed in . . . from the moment they land. Their third purpose is to assist in patrolling and protecting vulnerable spots, of which there are a great number everywhere.

This mobilisation was part of a wider process to ensure that every civilian played his or her part, in the event of a German invasion. Instructions were printed in local newspapers, though the role models they prescribe for the different sexes may grate on some modern readers:

If the Enemy reaches your Village.
What can you do to help in Defence?

What will you do if the enemy comes to your village? That is a question that everyone who lives in rural England must think about now. Here is some practical advice offered to country folk by an authoritative correspondent.

Supposing the enemy motorised columns sweep across and reach your village, what are you going to do to keep him back? You have your village defenders in the LDVs and the ARP workers, and you have defences, such as barricades, which for a time will keep the enemy back. Everything possible must be done to help these men to delay the enemy, just as in every town every man, woman and child must help.

Naturally, with the enemy attacking the village with motorised forces, ordinary business must come to a standstill and young children must be moved to a safe place. But if everyone were to take cover, the enemy would soon get through, so there must not be any safety first. The enemy must be delayed. How?

The men will, of course, do the heavy work. They can rebuild damaged road blocks, hastily improvising new ones when a fresh attack is threatened. They can dig trenches, they can fill sandbags. They can destroy petrol stocks – invaluable prizes for the enemy. They can rip out vital parts from every car in the village. All this work would be done only on the orders of the officer commanding the LDVs, who takes charge of the defences of the village until the regular military forces arrive – but he will need all the help he can get when every minute is precious.

A message may have to be sent to another village. For this duty, a man with a motor cycle has a dangerous but very important job to do.

There would be important jobs for women, too – not perhaps as dangerous and spectacular jobs as those allocated to the men, but jobs which must be done. They will render first aid to any casualties. They will provide and arrange for food for the defenders. If the food in their homes is exhausted they must fetch it from the shops – take it, if necessary, for the enemy will take it without paying for it if they succeed in breaking through.

If the telephones are still working, women will be needed to send messages – and clear, cool thinking will be required of them.

The boys will have many jobs, just as the boys in the siege of Mafeking played such a big part. There must be messengers on foot or on bicycles. There are endless jobs for boys with useful hands and imagination.

The place for the girl is in the home, helping her mother with food supplies and bandages, taking care of the little ones and seeing they are kept safe and out of the way.

If your village is besieged there will be jobs for everyone but, whatever the job, there is a motto for each man, woman, boy or girl. It is this: 'Don't give in. Don't lose your head. Don't panic.' Remember that every moment gained in delaying the advance of the enemy helps your country.

Within twenty-four hours around 250,000 people had volunteered for the new force, completely overwhelming the organisers. The upper age limit was observed very much in the breach. The oldest known member was ex-Company Sergeant Major Alexander Taylor of Crieff, in Scotland, who had fought in the Sudan Campaign of 1885 and who celebrated his 80th birthday at a parade of his unit. (There was one officer who claimed to have been nursed by Florence Nightingale at Crimea, though this would have made him a minimum of 104.) Similarly, the very undemanding physical standards for entry – you had to be 'capable of free movement', whatever that meant – later had to be tightened up to weed out the obviously infirm.

The press were none the less quick to wax lyrical about the merits of the LDV, seeming quite prepared to believe that they would be able to overwhelm the invading forces with local knowledge alone (which, given the initial state of their equipment, was just as well). This example comes from the *Berkshire Chronicle* in the summer of 1940:

Berkshire's LDV Guard. Ceaseless Watch over Vital Points.
But more Volunteers are Needed.

The night watch . . . the dawn patrol . . . silent guards scanning the sunset, keen eyes piercing the morning mists, ears alert for any suspicious sound . . . the Local Defence Volunteers are at their posts.

In three weeks, the men of Berkshire have organised themselves into a miniature army to defend their homes and country from sky invaders – from parachutists and the airborne troops that the enemy might cast upon our land.

The Berkshire LDV force has sprung into being swiftly and silently and the efficiency with which its forces have been mobilised has placed it ahead of many other counties. . . .

Their strength lies not so much in their ability to fight like their brethren in the Regular Army, as in their intimate and expert knowledge of the fields, the footpaths, the lanes and the roads in and around their homes. . . . Any one of these men seeing a hostile parachutist or plane descend needs no map to tell him where the danger has come.

But how real was the threat of the parachutist, for which they had been created?

Parachute Madness:
the Myth of the German Paratroop Menace

On the first day of the invasion parachutists dropped out of the sky like a vast flock of vultures. Most of them were disguised in Allied or Dutch uniforms, others came down in the uniform of Dutch policemen and began to direct the population in the streets.

Thus the *Daily Express* of 13 May 1940 described the German invasion of Holland. Their story was without substance, but it fed the fears of those in Britain who believed the same was about to happen to them.

The fact was that there were no vast hordes of enemy paratroopers or Fifth Columnists waiting to drop on Britain. British Intelligence in Belgrade claimed to have uncovered a German invasion plan involving a massive airborne force of 5,200 planes that would, in between having neutralised the Navy and the RAF and escorted a flotilla of merchant ships across the Channel, drop a force of twelve thousand trained parachute infantry on south-east England. Churchill, a leading supporter of the airborne invasion theory since at least 1934 (when he had called for anti-invasion earthworks on British airfields), was one of the few members of the Cabinet ready to believe it. Most of the others simply thought he had a bee in his bonnet.

The German airborne forces were in fact far less numerous and less well organised than this so-called intelligence would have had us believe. Their attempts to set up such a force, following the example of the Italians and the Russians, had been delayed by inter-service wrangling (with both the Army and the Luftwaffe claiming control of them). It was only in July 1938 that the two existing battalions were united under Luftwaffe control, with the result that only five incomplete battalions existed by the outbreak of war.

These limited forces had been used with mixed success in Norway and Denmark, but enjoyed a major propaganda coup by capturing and destroying Fort Eban Emael, a supposedly impregnable fortification on the Albert Canal in Belgium. This was achieved by landing fewer than a dozen gliders, carrying eighty-five specialist troops, on its massive roof. Many of the other thirty-two gliders sent to attack it, and nearby targets, managed to get lost.

This modest force could easily have been crushed by the thousand or so defenders inside the fort, had they chosen to venture out. However, they did not, and the invaders were left with a free hand to disable the fort, destroying the ventilation shafts and immobilising the gunports. Within an hour, the pivotal point of the entire Albert defensive line had been taken out of action. The raid cost the Germans only six dead and fifteen wounded, and their propaganda made much of this success.

German airborne forces also captured three bridges over the Maas and landed paratroops on the airport at Rotterdam. By contrast, attempts to capture The Hague, the seat of the Dutch royal family, by air were almost completely disastrous. At one airfield, eleven out of thirteen transport aircraft were shot down, while at two others aircraft trying to land were wrecked by runway obstacles and the troops inside them were shot as they attempted to get out of the wreckage.

Only about four thousand paratroops were used in the invasion of Belgium and Holland. Moreover, during these campaigns, the Germans suffered the loss of a total of 184 transport planes and a substantial part of their airborne fighting force. As a further complication, parachute silk was in extremely short supply throughout Europe, and by June 1940 the Germans probably could not have mustered two thousand airborne troops. Even some of these would have had to jump without a parachute (which would no doubt have hastened their arrival in England, but would equally have reduced their usefulness once they had landed).

The Germans were, however, aided by some hysterical and extremely inaccurate reports of events which were brought to England by those fleeing the Low Countries and eagerly seized upon and elaborated by the media. They told of a parachute invasion of some twelve thousand troops, some of them dressed variously as nuns, nurses, monks and tram conductors. The press added tales of hordes of parachuting 'women' and of parachutists near Ostend using semi-transparent parachutes and sky-blue uniforms to make them less visible while descending. Clergy were particularly suspect as disguised paratroops. The Mother Superior of the Breton Convent of St Nicholas was arrested twice on suspicion. However, so far as can be ascertained, not a single nun parachuted into the Low Countries during the invasion.

Quite apart from the usual hyperbole of war, one reason for these stories may have been the keenness of the governments concerned to explain away their unpreparedness for the German invasion. Tales of devilish subterfuge and of an active Fifth Column were equally prominent and, in some cases, equally exaggerated. The traitors who massacred sentries at Gennep turned out to be Dutch-speaking members of the Abwehr. A couple of them, dressed as Dutch policemen, marched a group of German 'prisoners' across a strategically important bridge, fooling the Dutch guards just long enough for the Germans to produce concealed weapons and start firing.

This all helped to fuel a British hysteria about parachutists that even put our own airmen at risk. The only VC-winner of the Battle of Britain, Flight Lieutenant J.B. Nicholson, managed to bale out successfully from his blazing Hurricane, only to be wounded on landing by an over-zealous Home Guardsman. In order to afford some protection to our aircrew, the Air Ministry gave instructions that only groups of parachutists exceeding six in number could be safely shot (six being the largest number of crew carried by any of our bombers).

The public were also warned that the 'hands above the head' posture of parachutists (as they steered themselves towards the ground) was not in fact a sign of surrender but indicated that they were clutching a primed grenade in each hand to ward off attackers. (The dangers of making a parachute landing clutching two primed grenades did not appear to feature in the Ministry's thinking.)

The press also did its bit towards promoting parachute mania – a correspondent to the *Manchester Guardian* suggested putting anti-parachutist machine-gun nests on electricity pylons, while

> In Wapping a parachutist came down and apparently he was partially blinded. He'd obviously baled out of a plane. He jabbered away to the people that gathered around him in some foreign language. They assumed he was German and they smashed him to death. They learned later he was Polish, a Polish officer, which was tragic because he was like a British fighter pilot. This is common knowledge in Wapping. Many, many people will substantiate it, but none of course are prepared to say they took part in it, or saw it happen.
>
> London boy, quoted in Grafton.

the *Telegraph*'s letters page yielded the intelligence that German parachutists dressed as Home Guards could be expected imminently and suggested that the might of the British Legion be mobilised to round them up (offering the prospect of inter-service confusion on a grand scale). To add to the chaos, a correspondent to *The Times* suggested that the mobility and local knowledge of the AA and RAC made them ideal for rounding up parachutists, and called for them to be armed. What would have happened if the Germans had parachuted in troops dressed as AA men does not bear thinking about. There were even calls to train gun dogs as parachute spotters.

Tests were devised to establish whether descending parachutists were friend or foe. They were to be asked upon landing to say the words soothe, wrong, wretch, rats and those. If they had not already given the game away by shooting you in the meantime, their accents would apparently reveal their nationality (though how this worked for the many Polish and other foreign nationals fighting for the Royal Air Force at this time was not made clear).

Even the Germans exploited the hysteria and, in a broadcast to Britain in May 1940, claimed that they had a force of ten thousand planes ready to drop a hundred thousand airborne troops on Britain. The truth was that after the Belgian and Dutch campaigns, they had just 357 serviceable Ju52 transports, each of which could carry just 12 paratroops or 18 ground troops. Even against the depleted British forces of 1940, this did not constitute a significant part of an invasion force.

The Home Guard as a Fighting Force

Having initially established the Home Guard to protect the nation against a non-existent threat, their role changed during the course of the war. The three original functions of the LDV, outlined earlier, became translated in the popular imagination to Look, Duck and Vanish (other derisive variations on the theme included Long Dentured Veterans and Last Desperate Venture). The volunteers produced a wealth of false alarms, with everything from courting couples, swans, barrage balloons and clouds to, in one inexplicable case, a hedgehog, being mistaken for German parachutists, but precious few examples of the real thing. By 1941 the emphasis shifted to static defence, with ever-more-substantial road blocks, which were expected to be held to the last man, pending the arrival of the regular troops. By 1943 they were being trained to carry out ambushes, and 1944 saw the plot revert to chasing after parachutists, who this time were going to be dropped with a view to disrupting D-Day preparations.

> Colonel Blimp explains: 'Gad, we should continue in our present policy of victorious evacuation, luring the enemy to England and giving him influenza.'

During their more static 'roadblock' mode, they could sometimes do a good deal more harm than good. The Commander-in-Chief of British Home Forces, General Sir Alan Brooke, put it as follows:

> Another form of defence which I found throughout the country and with which I was in total disagreement consisted of massive concrete roadblocks at the entry and exit of most towns and many villages. I had suffered too much from these blocks in France not to realise their crippling effect on mobility. Our security must depend on the mobility of our reserves and we were taking the very best steps to reduce this mobility. . . . I stopped any further construction, and instructed existing ones to be removed wherever possible.

Innumerable manned road blocks, demanding to check papers, proved to be a serious obstruction to progress. Certainly, this was the case for emergency service vehicles, struggling to get to London during the height of the blitz.

The consequences of the Home Guard trying to fight real Germans on the ground, especially in the early days when the threat of invasion was greatest and their preparedness and equipment at its most rudimentary, do not bear thinking about. Many of the weapons they used, especially those they improvised, looked more likely to injure them than the Germans. They included unreliable and inaccurate Sten guns; Mills bombs, which had a lethal range rather greater than the distance most Home Guards could throw them; hedgehoppers, which were improvised anti-tank devices intended to be hurled over hedgerows (and which then had a tendency to bounce back at you); and the Northover Projector, whose glass missiles of phosphorous mixture could easily blow up in the firer's face. Catapults were also favoured by many platoons, variously hurling burning petrol cans, Molotov cocktails or anti-tank missiles consisting of a broomstick with a grenade attached. One platoon in the London Docklands improvised a new type of hand grenade, consisting of potatoes with razor blades set into them – difficult to throw, but fatal if eaten by the enemy. The 5th City of London (Press) Battalion even had an armoured car. Their Commanding Officer was press baron Lord Astor, who converted his Rolls-Royce for the purpose.

> Colonel Blimp explains: 'Even if the enemy landed here, victory could never be his. Our people would refuse to issue him ration books.'

No idea was too eccentric to merit consideration. One correspondent wrote to *Picture Post*:

> What about using the services of British and Norwegian sailors who have worked on whaling ships? A harpoon can be fired with sufficient accuracy to penetrate the vulnerable chinks in a tank's armour.

And then what? Haul it in? Another *Picture Post* reader even suggested seagoing boats, towing a lightly armoured waterskier equipped with a machine-gun, going in among the invading armada to, as they so rightly put it, 'introduce an unexpected element'. None of this stopped the press from talking up the preparedness of the Home Guard – no doubt for the benefit of civilian morale and any Fifth Columnist who might be reading. This example comes from the *Maidenhead Advertiser* in June 1941:

> . . . several new weapons have recently been perfected for the special purpose of dealing with isolated tanks. These new arms will prove an especial boon to the Home Guard in the event of invasion.
>
> Emphasis on the equipment of this new arm of our defence forces is evidence of how much the Home Guard's function has changed. It began as a unit with the job of warning regular troops of the whereabouts of the enemy in the event of invasion.
>
> Today it undertakes a bigger responsibility. It has the job of harassing and obstructing the enemy throughout its own locality. One of its great strengths is that, being a local force, it knows every nook and cranny of the land. And being an armed local force, it is capable of dealing with small bodies of the enemy on its own ground.

Tank hunting in the ill-equipped days after Dunkirk was likely to be a particularly hazardous enterprise, even for the regular army. The 6th Battalion of the Gordon Highlanders were told to form a 'tank-hunting platoon'. They were equipped for this purpose with bicycles and rifles.

Uniforms were in as short supply as weapons. In the early days, they did not even have identifying armbands (or brassards) and had to make their own with stencilling sets. Tin helmets could be substituted by items of cookware, held on by scarves. Early photographs of the LDV were banned by the censor, because they looked so comically unmilitary. Even when they finally arrived, the uniforms did nothing for the organisation's image as a fighting force, as the Commander of the 4th Buckinghamshire Battalion of the Home Guard reported:

> The issue of denim clothing forms a memorable epoch in Home Guard history. If a prize had been offered for the design of garments that would caricature the human form and present it in its sloppiest and most slovenly aspect, the artist who conceived the Home Guard denim was in a class apart.

TALLY HO! IT'S THE HUN!

Specialised troops were formed within the Home Guard, sounding today rather like a thin excuse for people to continue their pre-war hobbies. Members of local hunts formed horseback units of the force and galloped around the countryside, on the pretext that the roads might become so damaged by enemy action that their services would be indispensable.

Boating enthusiasts formed an Upper Thames River Patrol, under the command of Rear Admiral Sir Basil B. Brooke KCVO. At a time when other river users were being denied fuel and told to immobilise their craft against the threat of invasion, they attracted large numbers of volunteers for their patrols, using free government petrol. These patrols were, however, entirely successful. Not a single pocket battleship ever penetrated the upper reaches of the Thames.

In Leeds the Cobble Hall Golf Club formed its own platoon, with the object of stopping German paratroopers landing on their sacred fairways. Regular patrols were mounted round the course and, while they were there, what better than to practise repelling invaders with whatever weapons came to hand, such as golf clubs and balls. Now, just imagine that flag in the distance is a German parachutist. . . .

Though marked with different size numbers, it was always a toss-up whether a man resembled an expectant mother or an attenuated scarecrow.

On parade, NCOs avoided making their troops about turn wherever possible, since it caused their ill-fitting hats to fall off. Local tailors would be called upon to cannibalise two sets of undersized battledress into one that would fit a normal human being. Only in Harrogate did the LDV look the part. There, the locally based tailoring millionaire Sir Montague Burton had 1,500 sets of well-cut battledress run up from officer-grade barathea. Naturally, the authorities told him to stop it.

Alongside the equipping of the Home Guard, preparations were made among the civilian population to obstruct and confuse the enemy, should they land upon our shores. Unattended cars were to be immobilised, and anything which could give the enemy a hint as

THE HOME GUARD IN ACTION

My father was in the Home Guard. They guarded the main road south, at Kainies Crossing. There was a smithy with a gun-slit in the wall, under the blacksmith's furnace. They had to put the furnace out, before they put the gun in . . . someone had the bright idea of stopping the Germans by pouring petrol on the road and setting it alight. They got hold of a twenty-five gallon drum of petrol, and thought they'd try it. They poured the lot on the road and put a match to it. Unfortunately, the flaming petrol ran down the drains, and out into the Burdiehouse Burn, and down it, floating on the water, still alight. I remember the line of fire spreading, spreading as fast as the burn ran, setting fire to the fields and trees. They had to call the fire brigade out.

Quoted in Westall.

to where they were was to be removed. Milestones and direction signs were removed and station name signs were to be painted over. One inspired wartime photograph shows railway employees dutifully painting over their station nameboard, oblivious to the fact that the name was in relief lettering and thus still clearly visible!

Even private premises whose name gave a clue as to their location had to be painted out, under threat of a fine. This regulation was sometimes applied with excessive zeal. The proprietor of the Shinfield Fisheries on the Shinfield Road was fined 10s for failing to paint out the revealing name above his door. He foolishly thought that, as his premises were some miles away from the settlement of the same name, the law would not apply to him. A correspondent to *Picture Post* had an even more ingenious idea for fooling the enemy:

With a view to misleading airborne invasion, I suggest a scheme of 'adopting' the name of one town by another town in a different locality. If, for example, all the citizens in, say, Coventry, if met by a parachutist and asked the name of the town, would at once reply 'This is Bristol'. All residents in the same town would give the same reply.

The Ministry of Information had its own line on this matter, which was contained in a rhyme taught to children at the time: 'If anyone stops me to ask the way, All I must answer is "I can't say".'

The Germans ridiculed the early efforts of the Home Guard: 'Churchill has spoken about the Home Guard under arms. We ask – under what arms? Broomsticks? Or the arms of the local pub, with pots of beer and darts in their hand?'

The Home Guard's lack of weapons led *Picture Post* publisher Edward Hulton to organise training courses in guerrilla warfare for them. These were run in Osterley Park, Middlesex, and were hugely over-subscribed. Over five thousand members of the force completed this training, but Lord Haw-Haw was again predictably unimpressed by it:

Suicide Academies have apparently been set up all over Britain. The headmasters are cunning blackguards who teach their inmates to make bombs at the modest cost of 2s each, how to poison water supplies by throwing dead dogs into streams and how to kill sentries noiselessly from behind. . . . Truly the Lord has afflicted these people with blindness! So bombs at 2s a time are to be used against the German Stukas! The people of England will curse themselves for having preferred ruin from Churchill to peace from Hitler.

Descriptions of the guerrilla warfare training illustrate the improvised nature of the event. The painter Roland Penrose taught camouflage; a senior member of the Boy Scout movement taught stalking, and one participant recalls being taught unarmed combat by 'a cripple who stood about 4 feet 9 inches'. Whatever the latter lacked in stature, he made up for in blood-curdling intent. He advised his pupils: 'Forget the playing fields of Eton and the Marquess of Queensberry and remember that no way is too dirty to kill a German . . . they don't scream if you stab them from behind.'

Thus equipped, the Home Guard organised exercises, sometimes with units of the regular army, to test their mettle. The following is a contemporary press account of one such:

Elsewhere, exercises such as these attracted considerable crowds of spectators, to the extent that the combatants would sometimes find themselves tripping over the abandoned bicycles and prams of the onlookers, and the judges had difficulty in seeing enough of the

THE BATTLE OF TILEHURST. PUBLIC SHOW LITTLE
INTEREST. DISAPPOINTING LACK OF COOPERATION.

The most outstanding feature of the combined Army and Home
Guard exercise was the disappointing lack of cooperation and
interest which the civilian population took in the 'invasion of
Tilehurst'. . . . During the mimic warfare little information of the
enemy positions was received and defenders were hindered by small
groups of spectators at vital points. It must be emphasised that these
people were a danger to themselves as well as impeding the troops.

The civilian point of view was put to our representative by Mr
Arthur Fenton of City Road, Tilehurst, who complained of 'brutal
treatment' meted out by some of the soldiers to certain civilians. He
stated: 'During the exercise the invading force had broken through
and were sweeping up the road. Quite naturally, many of us were in
our front gardens watching the exercise. Suddenly and without
warning the soldiers turned into the gardens and commenced to
round up the civilian lookers-on. The garden gate of at least one of
my neighbours was damaged. Many people were forced to leave their
homes, the soldiers urging them on at the point of the bayonet.

A forces neighbour of mine, was on leave and was in civilian
garb, when two or three soldiers in civilian garb turned on him and
hustled him into the road. As they passed me, I heard one of the
soldiers tell him to "Put a ******* jerk into it". I myself escaped
being rounded up, as I had recently suffered a fractured rib and I told
them that I would stand no tomfoolery. My wife, however, was
standing by the front door and she was pushed into the road and had
her frock torn by a bayonet.

One of my neighbours was so taken aback by the sudden assault
that he instinctively grabbed the rifle of one of the attackers. There
was a bit of a struggle and an officer, on seeing this, stood in the
road, yelling like an idiot and shouting "Shoot! Shoot! Shoot!" One
soldier did actually fire a blank cartridge and injured his thumb in
doing so. I got my car out and took him to hospital in it. Another of
my neighbours, Mrs Lightfoot, had a disagreeable experience. Troops
here dashed into the house and rushed upstairs without so much as a
"by-your-leave". They forced Mrs Lightfoot downstairs and into the
road in her dressing gown.'

Mr Fenton added: 'The whole thing was just like a lot of mass
hysteria. At first, some of us thought it was something of a joke, but
these soldiers were so much in earnest that they were actually
brutal in handling civilians. The whole affair was to my mind
ridiculous.'

action to decide who had won. These judges were also given godlike powers to restore to life any participant in the exercise deemed to have been 'killed', in order that they could get more practice in before having to apply their skills for real. Some of the exercises descended into farce. Broadcasting House was infiltrated by two of the 'enemy', who gained access by showing passes in the names of Adolf Hitler and Stanley Baldwin and captured the Head of the BBC Home Guard.

How effective might the Home Guard have been, if called upon to resist real invaders? Leaving aside the inequalities of equipment, fitness and training, there was the fact that the Germans took the view, quoted earlier, that 'civilians who take up arms against German soldiers are . . . no better than murderers, whether they are priests or bank clerks'. There was the very real possibility that Home Guard attacks against German invaders would also have provoked disproportionate reprisals against the rest of the civilian population, as did the Resistance in France or the work of the Special Operations Executive elsewhere in occupied Europe.

Perhaps mercifully, their skills were never put to the ultimate test. Even so, 1,206 Home Guards were killed and 557 wounded during the life of the force – a casualty rate of something under one in a thousand. Most were killed as a result of enemy action, but a significant proportion died as a result of their own efforts. The worst single event was a training session demonstrating the workings of a No. 68 grenade in rather more detail than the men required, which cost them six dead and fourteen wounded. Members of the Home Guard also won thirteen George Medals and two posthumous George Crosses.

Morale under Attack

The whole story of the last weekend has been one of unplanned hysteria. . . . Of course the press version of life going on normally in the East End on Monday are grotesque. There was no bread, no electricity, no milk, no gas, no telephones. . . . The press versions of people's smiling jollity and fun are gross exaggerations. On no previous investigation has so little humour, laughter or whistling been recorded.

Mass Observation, 10 September 1940, following bombing raids on the East End.

Public morale was expected to collapse under the onslaught of bombing. When it did not, it helped to foster the myth that everyone in the areas being bombed acted heroically. Apart from its supposed positive effect upon morale, this myth was useful in helping the government to persuade its supporters in America and elsewhere that Britain was not being defeated. In truth, there was considerable variation in the reaction of communities to bombing, which seemed to depend to a significant degree upon the competence of the local authorities in dealing with the aftermath.

When Goering switched his attention away from London, Coventry was one of the first cities to suffer. On the night of 14 November 1940, a hundred acres of the city centre were destroyed; 2,294 buildings were lost and a further 50,000 damaged. Out of a population of 250,000, 554 were killed and a further 850 seriously hurt. The city was devastated – no shops, water supplies, telephones, pubs or communications were functioning. The rest centres, themselves often bomb damaged, were overwhelmed by the demands upon them. The roads were said to be impassable for a mile from the city centre. Coventry police estimated that in the following weeks nearly a hundred thousand people – almost half the city's population – left the city each night, returning next morning.

> Colonel Blimp explains: 'The Government are going over the edge of an abyss and the nation must march solidly behind them.'

The Home Secretary visited the scene the following day. He had been attending a champagne reception with Lord Dudley, the Regional Commissioner, at nearby Himley Hall, and had watched the glow in the sky over the city. He ordered in a thousand troops and twelve hundred building workers to help with the clearing up. Attempts were made to gauge the morale of the population. Home Intelligence reported within a few days of the raid:

The shock effect was greater in Coventry than in the East End or any other bombed area previously studied. This was partly due to the concentrated nature of the damage and to extreme dislocation of services, partly to the small size of the town which meant that many people were directly or indirectly involved. The considerable proportion of imported labour and the fact that Coventry was economically flourishing contributed to this effect.

During Friday there was a great depression, a widespread feeling of impotence and many signs of hysteria. 'This is the end of Coventry' expressed the general feeling. Many people tried to leave the city before darkness fell. A quiet night followed by a fine morning changed the atmosphere for the better.

There was very little grumbling even about the inadequacies of the shelters and in the town itself observers found no anti-war feeling. There was little recrimination or blame.

Mass Observation picked up similar views, but also made the important link between the state of morale and the priorities of the authorities:

People feel the town itself is dead, finished, and the only thing to do is to get out altogether . . . the whole tempo [of the operation to restore normality] could have been altered if the authorities had spent 5 per cent of their effort on the survivors, e.g. on mobile canteens, loudspeaker vans to give information, newspapers delivered to the streets, social workers.

The lessons from Coventry were learned too slowly by some of the other towns and cities which were to suffer after them. But after the initial shock, Coventry recovered with remarkable speed. While German propaganda was still warning of other cities about to be 'Coventrated', business resumed, often under the most extreme difficulty. The Morris engine works had lost its roof in the raid, but the workers went back to their machines and, braving the November weather, continued in the open air. Within six weeks, production was back to normal.

The south coast took its share of the attacks. Portsmouth was hit in 1941. Ironically, for a town surrounded by the sea, water shortages were a major problem for the fire-fighters. One raid coincided with an abnormally low spring tide, and the fire-fighters were not helped by the fact that incoming fire brigades' hoses would not fit on to the fire hydrants in Portsmouth (a problem encountered in many areas). Another factor that made the blazes worse than they might otherwise have been was the number of property owners who fled the city at night time, leaving their property unsupervised. Without any fire watchers, small, easily controllable fires soon grew into major blazes. Again, Home Intelligence reported on the state of morale:

> On all sides we heard that looting and wanton destruction had reached alarming proportions. The police seem unable to exercise control and we heard many tales of the wreckage of shelters and of stealing from damaged houses, and were told that some people were afraid to take shelter in an attack for fear of being robbed of their remaining possessions. This seems another illustration of the lack of community spirit. The effect on morale is bad and there is a general feeling of desperation as there seems to be no solution. Some of the trouble is caused by children, many of whom do not go to school, though attendance for half a day is again compulsory, but the worst offenders appear to be youths of 18 or 19, though it is difficult to judge as few are caught.
>
> The morale of the city may be summed up in a sentence often repeated: 'The spirit of the people is unbroken but their nerve is gone.' That is to say, though they have been badly shaken by their experiences and are afraid, they do not want to give in. The ability to return to normal may be seen in the way cinemas begin to fill and shelters empty as soon as there is a lull. . . .
>
> The following are danger points: . . .
>
> (5) Lack of home or school discipline for children.
>
> (6) Widespread looting.
>
> (7) The lack of community spirit, shown in this looting of bombed persons and also in the fact that no attempt is made by the people to organise shelters or appoint marshals, and in the reluctance to take fire-watching duty. The paternalism of the authorities may foster this and it may be, in part, temperamental. The danger should be recognised as, in a crisis, panic may spread amongst a collection of people where there is no group feeling and everyone acts for himself.

Southampton was attacked and, after a second raid, the Bishop of Winchester reported: 'the people broken in spirit after the sleepless and awful nights. Everyone who can do so is leaving the town . . .

struggling to get anywhere out of Southampton. For the time, morale has collapsed.'

Part of the problem in Portsmouth was the attitude of some of those in charge of caring for the homeless. A government report into the atrocious facilities concluded: 'The attitude of the official in charge appears to be largely responsible. . . . Apart from a personal horror of communal feeding, he expressed the opinion that it encouraged parasitism and laziness and he did not see why "workers probably earning more than I do should be encouraged by the Government".'

There was also much criticism of the lack of leadership demonstrated by the Southampton authorities, and an ARP inspector, sent there by the Home Office, described their arrangements as 'incompetent'. But, if they could do nothing else, the Southampton authorities at least knew how to prepare for a royal visit. One resident who was bombed out of her home recalls being taken to a rest centre, where she and her children were left to fend for themselves in the clothes they stood up in. Then, one day, they were unexpectedly issued with carpets, bedspreads and toys for the children. That day the rest centre received a visit from the king, who asked the woman if she was comfortable in her new accommodation. On being told that she was, the king duly left. The authorities immediately took back all her newly acquired comforts!

In Swansea the myth of British resilience in the face of bombing rebounded on the authorities, after a local newspaperman went on the radio and led the listeners to believe that the bombed residents were walking around with broad smiles on their faces, having scarcely noticed that anything had happened to disrupt their daily round. This caused great resentment among the local population, as Mass Observation reported: 'They could not possibly have behaved in that way and resented being made to feel they had fallen short of some ideal standard. Such talks do not benefit morale – people lose confidence because they do not reach this impossible ideal.' But it was on Merseyside that the authorities came under the strongest attack for their handling of the aftermath of air raids. Mass Observation talked of almost universal dissatisfaction with their efforts. On this occasion, the Home Intelligence report only hints at some of the problems:

The people seem fatalistic and there is unusual family solidarity, encouraged by the Catholic element. Though they are dour by temperament and have not the cockney resilience, they stood their eight-day ordeal with fortitude and seemed able to readjust to normal conditions. As in Portsmouth, it was remarked that the morale of the 'near bombed' suffered more than that of the bombed. It was also said that people were ready to help themselves until they realised there was official help available. They then expected everything done for them.

There seems to be some resentment against the authorities who are accused of trying to force people to stay in the city during bombing, by making it difficult for them to get out. Unless they can sleep where they feel safe, there is some fear that they may get out of our control in a new crisis. . . .

A symptom which may indicate fear is the distrust of foreign elements. Anti-Jewish feeling is said to be growing. Jews are said to be cowards who have fled to the best billets in safe areas and who avoid fire-watching duties. One restaurant recently refused to serve Jewish customers. Greeks are also disliked and there are occasional outbursts against the Chinese in shelters, though they give no trouble and are cleaner than the general shelter population. . . . In brief there seems to be a need to have someone to blame, and someone to act as a scapegoat to work off the people's own fears. The prevalence of rumours, such as the story that 30,000 were killed in the blitz, and that incendiary envelopes were to be dropped, is another sign of weakness.

Mass Observation stated the full extent of the problem much more forcefully:

There has been dissatisfaction in other towns but never with such vehemence from so many sources – from working men and businessmen, Conservatives and Labour, officials, parsons, servicemen, firewatchers, wardens. An atmosphere of ineptitude seems to oppress the town, a general feeling that there was no power and drive left to counter-attack the Luftwaffe. It was being left to the citizens of Liverpool to pick themselves up. . . .

. . . Never before has the absence of information and explanation been so apparent. Not a single poster or meeting, loudspeaker vans only giving information on transport arrangements . . . unprintably violent comments on local leadership.

There were many more rumours circulating in Liverpool than the earlier Home Intelligence report recorded. According to these, martial law had been declared; trainloads of corpses were having to be shipped out of the city; there were food riots and peace demonstrations. Despite it all, morale was said to be high, though the level of anger was higher.

By contrast, some authorities dealt with a similar situation with notable efficiency. In Hull forty thousand homeless people were billeted within two days of their last raid, and 110,000 first-aid repairs to houses were rapidly undertaken. A special information centre was set up and, where rest centres had been bombed, new ones were set up to take their place. In Sheffield sixty thousand emergency meals were served in the first twenty-four hours after their raid; a hundred schools were turned into rest centres and the school attendance officers were turned into billeting officers. Their success is shown by the fact that the raid made large numbers homeless on a Sunday, but they were all rehoused by the following Thursday.

The xenophobia reported in Liverpool also manifested itself in Manchester, where the Spanish-born widow of an Englishman found herself before the court for the rather imprecisely defined offence of 'visiting air raid shelters where her foreign accent

---

I met one poor bugger I knew at the time, who'd been blitzed. He'd been bombed out and I met him three months later. He'd been living amongst the rubble, never going to work. I've never seen a man look in such a state. His face looked like a rat. He was really a nervous animal and his eyes appeared to be trying to look behind him all the time. The bomb had smashed his house and he'd lost his wife and kids – he'd just gone beyond, with the shock of such a bashing.

London electrician, staying in Liverpool, quoted by Grafton.

alarmed people'. The court advised her: 'If you have to go into a shelter, remember not to make people afraid. You have rather a foreign accent and people are nervous.'

Rest Centres

It may be argued that the government made too much preparation for burying the dead victims of bombing and not enough for rehousing the survivors. They had expected the numbers of homeless survivors to balance out in some miraculous way with the empty accommodation remaining. But they had not allowed, among other things, for the relative failure of evacuation. Rest centres, which had been designed to accommodate homeless families for just a few hours while they were rehoused, were often asked to cope with large numbers of people on a long-term basis. At the height of the crisis, in late September 1940, some 25,000 people were living in London's rest centres, which were run under the Victorian Poor Law system for the destitute and were avoided by all who could possibly do so.

Many centres had virtually no facilities for feeding the people staying there – one was issued with cans of soup, but no can opener – or for caring for them in any other way. They were deliberately not provided with blankets, for fear that those using them would get too comfortable and would not move on as planned (there were only 25,000 blankets to serve an estimated need for 2,500,000 among displaced Londoners). One elementary school at Stepney which was used as a rest centre found itself with three hundred unexpected guests for a ten-day period. They slept on the floor with their remaining possessions and shared just ten buckets for toilets, which were often kicked over and the sewage trodden all over the building. Local government in Stepney was so incompetent that the Home Secretary finally took away their powers and appointed commissioners to run services.

Another rest centre, in West Ham, was itself bombed and 450 homeless people killed. This was another area paralysed by moribund local government. They had made little or no effective shelter arrangements before the war and their response to the suffering of the bombed-out was equally minimal. As one commentator put it: 'It was more than bricks and mortar that collapsed in West Ham . . . it was a local ordering of society which was found hopelessly wanting, as weak and badly constructed as the single brick walls which fell down at the blast.'

Bureaucratic rules also served to minimise the effectiveness of many rest centres, until the volunteer workers decided to ignore them and went out begging, borrowing or stealing whatever they needed to function. One rural rest centre greeted its bombed-out guests with a large sign containing the following uplifting information: 'Behind every social problem is revealed the hidden hand of alcohol.'

Added to these problems was the multiplicity of relief agencies which existed to helped the bombed-out to pick up the pieces of their lives. Tom Harrisson published the hypothetical but factually correct case of a Plymouth service wife with children, who would have to visit sixteen different agencies in different parts of the city after being bombed. In London, it was worse – bomb victims had to cope with six government departments, the London County Council, the Regional Commissioner, twenty-eight London boroughs and seventy other agencies, all jealously guarding their budgets, powers and lines of demarcation. Last but by no means least was the fact that many rest centres kept no records of where the people passing through them were going, thus ensuring administrative chaos in the longer term.

Londoners, at least, faced a further onslaught in 1944, with the arrival of the V1s and V2s. In some ways, these affected Londoners' morale more than the blitz had done. The V1s were random in their effects and gave no respite, coming across in a more or less continuous stream. They also provided a heart-stopping interlude after their engines cut out. The V2s, by contrast, arrived with no warning whatsoever. They led to a further hurried evacuation and other signs of panic, as Home Intelligence reported:

Evacuation has taken place on a considerable scale among those who could get away, particularly women with children, who are said to be crowding the main line stations all day. Urgent enquiries as to how to get out of London are reported from many WVS and CAB centres.

There is reported to be a growing demand for an official evacuation scheme, particularly for children. People are angry, in the belief that no plan has been put into operation, and attempts to get away are, in a few instances, said to be 'verging on panic'. . . .

Sheltering has become 'the next best thing to evacuation' for a great many Londoners. In some parts there is a general rush to the shelters when a bomb is heard, and men are said to show little signs of the 'women and children first' spirit.

Many more people are sleeping in the shelters, both public and private, than was noticed in the blitz, and some are said to refuse to leave shelters day or night.

For its part, the German propaganda machine vastly overstated the effects of the V1s:

London is in a panic. All Members of Parliament have left the capital, and a thick smokescreen hangs across south-east England.

The roads from London to the country are choked with refugees. Only a few have cars. Most take their pots and pans with them on hand-drawn carts with other improvised vehicles.

Big Ben's tower has collapsed and the Underground is severely damaged. Oil store houses at the Thames Dock have been destroyed. Never before has the world seen such a sight.

Whatever the strengths or shortcomings of the authorities in the bombed areas, and however strong the immediate trauma of bombing, the resilience of the British public in the longer term took both our government and the Germans by surprise. The numbers of mental illnesses declined, and there was no increase in insanity; suicides were reduced and drunkenness fell by 50 per cent (the limited opportunities to get to the pub and the watered-down beer may have had something to do with the latter); the only area of criminal activity to increase during the blitz was juvenile delinquency.

The German authorities, having spent a long time trying to persuade their people that the British were in a permanent state of panic and near-revolution, accounted for the failure of anarchy to break out in the following terms: 'The British masses, exploited by Jews and other monsters, have nothing to live for and meet their deaths with resignation.' They even paid the British people the 'tribute' of saying that they were a Germanic race and therefore able to withstand adversity. When British raids on Germany started in earnest in 1943, Goebbels called upon the Germans to follow the stoic example of the British civilian population.

6
Battle of the Sexes

Before the war ignorance of matters sexual was widespread throughout British society. Organisations like the Social Purity and Hygiene Movement were influential in restricting sex education in schools and encouraging controls on censorship and what was seen as obscenity in the cinemas and other media. They combined this role as self-appointed censor with some disturbing views about racial purity and the right of science to interfere with people's sexual behaviour. Contraception and other sexual aids had to be sold under pseudonyms; thus Rendel's Vaginal Cap was marketed as 'feminine hygiene' and Damaroids virility pills (the Viagra of their day) were sold as 'The Great British Rejuvenator'.

But the traditional Victorian values on these matters were showing signs of breaking down even before war broke out. Surveys of married women indicated that 39 per cent of those born in the period 1914–24 had had pre-marital sex, compared with just 19 per cent of the group born before 1904.

The relationship between warfare and heightened sexual activity had been understood long before the Second World War. In his 1917 work *Reflections on War and Death*, Sigmund Freud talked of 'war aphrodisia' – the link between violence and eroticism. Originally, it applied only to those in the armed forces, who were directly involved in conflict, but the age of total war brought soldier and civilian alike into the front line. There were periods during the Second World War when the death rate among civilians from bombing exceeded the numbers killed on active service. The sense of living for today, lest there were no tomorrow, found its way equally into the civilian population.

Women in Uniform

Those ATS girls are a disgrace. They come into this pub at night and line up against that wall. Soldiers give them drinks

> Up with the lark and to bed with a Wren.
>
> Saying of the day

and when they're blind drunk they carry them out into the street. And we're paying public money for them, too!

Quoted by Mass Observation.

Some 460,000 women served in the armed forces during the war years and a further 80,000 joined the Women's Land Army. At the same time the belief that women in uniform were 'an easy thing' gained wide currency. This is reflected in the nicknames given to the women's services: the ATS were known as 'officers' groundsheets', and WAAFs were 'pilots' cockpits'. Even the Women's Land Army had its motto 'Back to the Land' subverted into 'Backs to the land'. Military service was held to encourage a variety of behaviour in women – some of it contradictory – ranging from vampishness, through sluttishness, to lesbianism.

The Wrens tended to receive rather less of such abuse, being drawn from a much more middle-class background and therefore rather more aloof from the male other ranks, but even they were not immune:

. . . the lower deck consider they are entitled to address any Wren in uniform on the grounds that she belongs to their Service. While it is desirable to cultivate good relations between the WRNS and the Lower Deck, it must be appreciated that in a crowded port with many libertymen ashore who have not seen a white woman for some time, it becomes a matter of embarrassment to be continually addressed by sailors and, not to put it too strongly, to be pestered by requests to accompany them, or to make an appointment for some future date. I am glad to say that on this Station I have personally observed sailors and Wrens 'keeping company' to a considerable extent, but it must be admitted that a considerable percentage of Wren ratings, who are daughters of officers, or of a different social status to men of the Lower Deck, find it most embarrassing to be continually addressed by sailors and even more embarrassing to disengage themselves, without causing offence, from such well-meaning attempts to make acquaintance. On the other hand, respectable women in plain clothes are rarely addressed by sailors thanks to the natural politeness of the lower deck.

Memo, C-in-C Eastern Fleet to Admiralty, 15 August 1944.

Various possible reasons for this view of servicewomen have been advanced. One was that women in uniform were indeed more 'available' than civilians, a proposition that we will return to shortly. Another is that, because they could be drawn into barrack room badinage, it led men to believe that they were so inclined. A third possibility is that the increased emphasis on female sexual activity was used to justify the increasingly predatory behaviour of men. Some mixed army camps had cases of rape, or attempted rape, sufficiently serious to have armed guards mounted outside the female latrines with orders to shoot male intruders. Others have argued that these charges of sexual promiscuity were a respectable outlet for deep-seated male resentment of women entering traditional male preserves. The Markham Committee – discussed below – had its own variation on this last theory. This was that the British were essentially a non-militaristic race and had a deep-rooted suspicion of people – and in particular women – in uniform. Thus they became an easy target for gossip and suspicion.

The reputation for immorality became a particular problem for the ATS, which drew its numbers much more from a working-class population and whose inelegant uniforms (designed by men with few concessions to the female anatomy) did nothing for their image. Middle- and upper-class women wishing to do army-related war work opted for the more genteel and less demanding surroundings of the VAD.

The Government first tried to suppress the rising tide of concern about the matter; then, in November 1941, they set up a parliamentary committee to investigate what they coyly referred to as 'amenities and welfare conditions in the three women's services'. The Committee, under lawyer Miss Violet Markham and with a membership including the redoubtable Dr Edith Summerskill MP, looked in some detail at the conduct of the ATS:

War gives rise to many rumours. Vague and discreditable allegations about the conduct of women in the Forces have caused considerable distress and anxiety not only to friends and relations at home but to men fighting overseas. Some of these tales have suggested a high rate of illegitimate pregnancy, others that excessive drinking is a common practice. . . .

For the ATS, however, we have been supplied with detailed figures on discharges for pregnancy which prove conclusively how little truth there is in the rumour regarding illegitimate pregnancy in that service. There are in the ATS large numbers of married women and the pregnancies of these women are often, no doubt, carelessly confused with those of single women. . . .

Turning to unmarried women, the illegitimate birth rate among the age groups from which the ATS are recruited is approximately 21.8 per thousand per annum. The pregnancy rate among single ATS personnel is 15.4 per thousand per annum. It must be remembered that pregnancy and birth statistics are not identical, for a woman in the Services – or in any other occupation – discharged for pregnancy may subsequently miscarry. . . .

A number of single women come into the forces already pregnant. According to the monthly returns for the first five months of this year of single women who were discharged for pregnancy, the percentage who were pregnant before entering the ATS varied from 18 per cent to 44 per cent.

We can, therefore, with certainty, say that the illegitimate birth rate in the Services is lower than the illegitimate birth rate among the comparable civilian population. . . .

They concluded that there was: 'No justification for the vague but sweeping charges of immorality which have disturbed public opinion . . . one or two cases which, in the course of gossip, have been multiplied many times over.' In their view, the disciplines of service life were: 'A corrective, rather than an incitement, to bad conduct.'

The Committee showed that the incidence of illegitimate births and venereal disease in the women's services was less than in the comparable civilian population – in some cases half the level. The Committee also said that pregnancy figures were no guide to promiscuity, owing to the fact that condoms were (eventually) issued to servicemen (but, significantly, not to service women).

They also argued that the stigma of being PWP (Pregnant Without Permission) was a significant deterrent against promiscuity.

In fact, it sometimes worked the other way. Pregnancy was a guaranteed way of securing one's release from the female armed forces, one where the authorities could not afterwards re-enlist you. The relevant regulation was Paragraph 11 and it was not unknown for a woman seeking release from the armed forces by this means to go and stand outside the men's sleeping quarters at night and call out 'Paragraph 11!'. It rarely took long for an accommodating window – and a route out of the armed forces – to be opened to her.

The same wholesome record for propriety could not be claimed by the Women's Land Army, if this letter from one of its members to the *New Statesman* in November 1943 was to be believed:

. . . they care little about mental activities . . . and, looking for any kind of entertainment, they find their satisfaction in pub-crawling or flirting with soldiers. The girls in my hostel are mostly under twenty and know very well what they are doing, they confess that they had never been drunk before they joined up and that their parents would be very upset could they know of all this 'fun'.

Our work in the Land Army is of great importance to the nation, but sometimes I wonder whether the value of all the tons of corn and potatoes brought in by the girls does balance their really disgusting way of living. . . . The best reconstruction and security plans won't help us if those for whom they are mainly meant are left to develop into amoral and asocial beings.

Others felt that they were tarred by the brush of their less fastidious colleagues. One Land Army girl describes the reception they got in the chapel immediately opposite their camp:

We were in uniform and we sat down at the back. Suddenly the Minister, who was a real old Bible-basher, started thundering about 'heathens living across the road, who hold dances on Friday nights and spend their time fornicating with local boys'. We got up and walked out.

The Good Time had by All

'To girls brought up on the cinema who copied the dress, hairstyles and manners of the Hollywood stars, the sudden influx of Americans speaking like the films who actually lived in the magic country and had plenty of money at once went to the girls' heads'.

Home Office report 1943, quoted in Rowbotham.

Armies have attracted female camp followers from the earliest days of warfare. Popular mythology has it that the vast numbers of women who followed the Army of the Potomac in the American Civil War took their nickname from the General who led the army – Joseph Hooker – giving us the American slang term for a prostitute. During the First World War the French set up their own official military brothels, or '*maisons tolerées*' (blue lights for officers' facilities, red for other ranks), and the Germans and Italians did the same during the Second.

While the official American position on the subject (prompted by church leaders and other pressure groups) was that it would be indefensible to use women as war materiel in this way, individual commanders bowed to the inevitable and made informal arrangements for their troops. General Patton was among the more adventurous commanders in this respect, having taken the many brothels, first in Sicily and then in his part of Normandy, under *de facto* military control and subdividing them for the use of officers, white other ranks and black enlisted men. Any suggestion that the British Expeditionary Force might condone such activity had led to the government being bombarded by requests from organisations such as the Association for Moral Hygiene for: 'action to protect the men of the Home and British Empire forces by insisting that, in France and in any other country where the system of licensed brothels still exists, these houses shall immediately be declared "out of bounds".'

The War Office tried to resist such demands, partly for fear of insulting the French, and partly because the rather more regulated conditions which applied in such establishments helped to stem the spread of venereal diseases. In areas under German occupation, these places also formed an important link in the escape routes for allied airmen, since even the Germans respected the privacy of a lady and her client. Wherever the British Army went in the Second World War houses of pleasure (or ill-repute, depending upon one's perspective) grew up to service their needs. When one such in Cairo was bombed by the Germans, the British military personnel inside were officially listed as having been killed 'on active duty'.

On a darker note, many cases of rape by Allied troops against French or German women went unreported or were hushed up. The problem became sufficiently great to lead the Allies to ban all 'social intercourse' (which encompassed the other kind) with Germans, from the spring of 1945 onwards. The ban worked about as well as Prohibition, with many troops considering the $65 fine for fraternisation to be a price well worth paying.

Back at home, the arrival of large numbers of foreign troops was met by a dramatic growth in the number of British prostitutes serving their recreational needs. The most obvious sign of this was the so-called 'Piccadilly warriors', the crowds of girls who used to gather near the Rainbow Club on Shaftesbury Avenue (an establishment opened mainly for Americans in 1942). In the blackout they had no need of a room to ply their trade – the nearest shop doorway or alleyway proved perfectly adequate. This also went along with the popular misconception of the time, that a woman could not get pregnant from having intercourse standing up. More difficult was the business of attracting clients in the dark, something which many of them achieved by flashing a small torch at regular intervals. (It has been suggested that this is the origin of the term 'flashing'.) The blackout also made it considerably more difficult for the police to detect prostitution, and ladies of the night were one of the very few groups to complain about the ending of the blackout. The number of arrests for prostitution made by the Metropolitan force in 1938

MOTHER'S LITTLE HELPERS
My father was posted to India with the RAF. In early 1940, the Army took away the family's two cars. While my dad was away my mum had lots of American and Polish boyfriends. In this way we got a little more food. I used to grease my pedal car with butter.
Boy aged nine, Liverpool, quoted in Westall.

was over 3,000. By 1940, despite business apparently booming, arrests had halved, to 1,505.

A number of factors helped the trade. In addition to the extra demand occasioned by war, the exodus from central London made it easier for girls to find accommodation in some of the areas of greatest demand. They could now afford the rents, since the arrival of the American forces enabled them to charge hitherto unheard of rates, of £3–4 or, by 1945, £5. It was said that some offered preferential rates to the impoverished British militia, but hard evidence of this is understandably difficult to come by. The volume of demand also meant that they could charge these rates for very brief liaisons, and one noted courtesan – a Miss Marthe Watts – claimed in her memoirs to have obliged no fewer than forty-nine clients on VE night.

Not even a town as genteel as Leamington Spa escaped from the rise in wartime prostitution and licentiousness. Mass Observation reported that its streets were littered with condoms after an evening's partying. Much of this activity came from new entrants to the oldest profession. The town's pre-war prostitutes were forced to move out, claiming that there were 'too many gifted bloody amateurs here for a decent professional to get a living'.

This spread of the amateur was reported throughout England, a product perhaps jointly of the opportunities presented by an absent partner; the harsh economic necessities of war, especially for the wives of serving men; and the change in the moral climate, brought about by total war. It was also the case that the traditional 'management structure of the industry' tended to collapse, as many pimps were called up for military service, opening up the market to the sole practitioner. Two no-doubt-shocked members of the Public Morality Council reported being accosted by no fewer than thirty-five women in a single 120-yard stretch of Soho street. Another Canadian visitor described the areas around Hyde Park and Green Park at twilight as 'a vast battleground of sex'.

Prostitutes were able to avoid the call-up very simply. They simply wrote 'prostitute' in the box reserved for their profession on their call-up papers. The armed forces did not wish to risk the moral pollution of their girls by such a recruit, and war service (in the conventional sense) passed them by. Likewise, the taxman would not stoop to living off immoral earnings, making the occupation additionally lucrative.

Control of the problem was difficult under the existing law. It was illegal to run 'a disorderly house', as a brothel was still called, but street walkers could only be arrested if they actually accosted passers-by; and even then, all they could be charged with was obstruction. However, the market for prostitution suffered a severe decline after D-Day. The George public house near the BBC, much frequented by US Army personnel and their escorts, became colloquially known as the 'Whore's Lament'.

The abandonment of pre-war standards of morality – or, more precisely, the abandonment of the pre-war dual standards of morality for the sexes – excited a considerable amount of public concern, as Home Intelligence reported:

During the last two weeks, a good deal of comment and concern have been reported at 'the wave of moral delinquency', chiefly among young people.

Sex: particular concern is expressed about:

(a) 'Young girls who fling themselves at soldiers.' Some think that, 'with the growing number of enthusiastic amateur prostitutes', the men are not to blame, 'as the girls lie in wait for them on all sides'; but others blame 'the drunken soldiers who are always molesting women and girls'. The need for more women police is the solution most often suggested; others are – a curfew for all young women, or for U.S. troops, and a ban on the sale of alcohol to young women.

(b) The growing number of illegitimate babies, many of coloured men.

(c) The number of wives of men serving abroad who are thought to be associating with US and Dominion troops.

(d) The lack of welfare and supervision for transferred women workers. The unwelcoming attitude of some landladies, together with the small margin of money left for recreation, is blamed for some young girls' readiness to be picked up by soldiers who can show them a good time.

Home Intelligence, 28 October 1943.

Blame of the girls is more widespread, and sometimes stronger, than of the men. Their predatoriness is particularly censured; some girls are said to be dunning as many as three or four US soldiers to provide for their coming child. Some people are very concerned at what the Americans are going to say when they return home. More women police are advocated; satisfaction is expressed where their number has been increased.

Home Intelligence, 8 June 1944.

The most spectacular case of a woman playing the field in the way described above came to light in a British pub, when two American sailors produced a photograph of their wife to show each other. It turned out to be the same woman and a fight ensued. The two 'husbands' then got together to unravel the mystery and it was found that the wife, Elvira Taylor – or 'Allotment Annie' as she came to be known – was 'married' to six sailors and about to embark with a seventh when she was arrested. Bigamy also enjoyed a considerable increase in the war years, with prosecutions rising from a pre-war average of 320 a year to a peak of 649 in 1944.

But it was not just the good-time girls who were casting aside pre-war convention. Double standards, where a serviceman's extra-curricular sexual activity was condoned while his wife was expected to remain celibate, became controversial after a serviceman killed his wife upon discovering that she had become pregnant by another man. The judge released him without penalty. A letter to *Wife and Citizen* magazine in 1945 set out women's concerns at this, and a shocked nation – or at least much of the male half of it – discovered to their surprise that ordinary wives could be interested in sex!

There can be few of us who have not felt considerably irritated by the one-sided outlook portrayed by the spate of heartbreak articles which have appeared lately on the unhappy plight of Servicemen returning home to discover their wives have been sexually unfaithful. Whether mere physical satisfaction, sought while a loved partner is forced to be absent for years at a time, should be called unfaithfulness is a debatable subject. In the past it was a debatable point whether there should be licence in sexual matters.

THIS IS NO LONGER SO! The War Office, in allowing the free issue of contraceptives to men serving abroad, whether married or single, has adopted the principle that married men must be free in these matters. We civilians have acquiesced in the adoption of this principle in that we have not raised our voices against it. We have not even insisted that the issue of contraceptives should only be made to men whose wives are agreeable. There has been no suggestion of issuing contraceptives to wives, who have had to adjust themselves to living without their service husbands for four or five years or longer.

WHY THIS DIFFERENCE? The sudden cessation of their sex life has been as unendurable a privation to these women as their partners. These women, in facing the hardships of life on the Home Front, have been warriors no less courageous than their men serving abroad. Not only have men and women failed to admit and recognise that a woman's sexual needs are as urgent as a man's, but the pendulum has swung as sharply as ever in the opposite direction, giving the male partner in marriage greater freedom and at the same time attempting to tie the woman more closely. The most biting example of this was shown in the recent acquittal of a young man charged with strangling his wife in Nottingham Hospital on the grounds, claimed by the Justice, that the provocation under which the act was committed (the wife's admission that her pregnancy was due to association with another soldier and her refusal to give the man's name) was such that any man would have committed it in the circumstances.

To man has been assigned the right and protection to satisfy his sexual needs as and how he may please. To woman is denied the right and if she tries to exercise it she may be murdered, together with her unborn child and society is to be asked to wink at the slaughter.

Are we to slip back to the principles of the so-called Dark Ages or shall we go forward?

One problem that was concentrating many minds was the extreme youth of many of the girls who were getting in on the new sexual liberation. The disruption of family life by war had a profound effect upon many young people, and juvenile delinquency was a major problem for all the combatant nations by the end of hostilities. In Britain there was a 100 per cent increase in the number of teenage girls arrested in the three years after 1939 and a corresponding increase in the numbers judged to be 'in need of care and attention'. One London borough reported a six-fold increase in the numbers of teenage girls in need of care and attention in the year before D-Day. As one East End magistrate put it: 'Earlier maturity . . . (and the) jungle rhythms heard by juveniles from morning until bedtime, and slushy movies are all in part responsible for an increase in sexual delinquency among youths.'

Others complained that: 'Girls of thirteen and fourteen have attached themselves to coloured soldiers and others and been able to see films that only have the effect of arousing in them instincts that ought to be unknown to them for many years.'

GIs were held to be a major cause of sexual delinquency among young British girls. A US Army private was paid about £750 per annum, compared with £100 for their British counterpart, and many of them had nothing to spend it on but a local female population suffering from shortages of all sorts of material goods. All too often, pairs of nylons came with metaphorical strings attached – 'one before and one after' was the popular formula. The joke of the day about Utility knickers was 'One Yank and they're off'.

The BBC tried as best it could to cope with the changing moral climate. The 'radio doctor', Charles Hill, conducted a broadcast debate among young people of 16–19 under the title 'Learning about sex'. Dr Hill rapidly steered any hint of 'progressive attitudes' back to the straight and narrow of 'thou shalt not', in what was by all accounts a very stilted discussion. Even so, the suggestion by one participant that pre-marital sex

GERMAN TROOP-CARRIERS

It was not just American troops that proved popular with British women. In the Channel Islands, the only part of the British Isles to be occupied, Baron von Aufsess, the Head of Civil Affairs in the Feldkommandantur, reported: '. . . the complete amity on the beaches between the German soldiers and the local girls . . . with a few exceptions, the girl will surrender readily enough, provided this can be effected in proper privacy. The Englishwoman is astoundingly simple, effortless and swift in her lovemaking.'

There were soon quite a number of young girls expecting the babies of German soldiers. They were known to the locals as German troop carriers.

with the person you were about to marry was 'not quite right but not exactly wrong' was seized upon by some outraged listeners as the arrival of Sodom and Gomorrah in England.

At least the women's magazines could be relied upon to uphold traditional values. This is the advice on pre-marital sex dispensed respectively by *Woman* and *Woman's Own*:

> This time of all times is not one for irresponsibility. If he loves you as you say, your sweetheart will see the wisdom of patience. Remember, too, the emotions you speak of may well be the result of excitement and unnatural tension.
>
> Anyone indulging in pre-marital sex is an enemy to her country, which does not want to be faced with the further problems of unwanted children born out of wedlock.

The Disease that Dare Not Speak its Name

The British government did not have a good record in relation to the sexual behaviour of its troops overseas. In the First World War the Allies' incidence of venereal disease was seven times higher than that of the Germans and their allies, largely owing to their prudery in refusing to recognise that a problem existed. The scale of the problem was such that it could have altered the course of the war. In the first war, the Allies treated a total of 1.5 million cases of venereal disease among their troops.

The Ministry of Health anticipated the problem before the Second World War and, in 1938, put forward a proposal for a fleet of twenty mobile VD clinics to tour military bases. The Treasury refused to fund them. By 1940 they were forced to reverse that decision, partly as a result of the number of British Expeditionary Force members, evacuated via Dunkirk, who brought back their own, very personal, souvenirs of France. The problem continued into the later years of the conflict. During the Sicily campaign British medical officers there were treating forty thousand cases a month. Having no organised plan for dealing with the epidemic, the authorities spread the rumour that it was all part of an evil Axis plan to incapacitate Allied troops through the use of prostitutes.

Similar plots were alleged in relation to merchant seamen

visiting neutral ports, such as Lisbon. The increase in the incidence of syphilis was substantially greater in London and the major seaports. In Liverpool it had reached 400 per cent of its pre-war level by the middle of 1941. Merchant seamen bound for such locations were issued with special supplies of condoms, to protect their contribution to the war effort.

The epidemic in venereal diseases among British troops overseas was paralleled at home. In 1942 seventy thousand new cases of venereal disease were reported to civilian clinics alone – over and above these were cases not yet being treated, or those being treated by armed forces doctors. With a growing number of young men in the armed forces, civilian cases were increasingly an under-representation of the true scale of the problem. Even so, civilian casualties from VD in 1942 were more numerous than those from the blitz in the previous year.

A variety of factors stood in the way of the authorities tackling the epidemic. First, the 1916 Venereal Diseases Act imposed total confidentiality on cases, making it slanderous to imply that even a known prostitute was a carrier. Second, the latex for making condoms was in very short supply, following the fall of Burma, and the government gave higher priority to making teats for babies' bottles from such supplies as were available. Third, continuing prudery made the frank advertising of VD treatment centres difficult, and the green light normally used in other countries to denote the presence of such establishments was, of course, taboo in the blackout. Last but by no means least, there was consumer resistance to the use of condoms – the variety distributed to the British armed forces were said to be particularly uncomfortable to use and American GIs liked to boast that they were too small for their own lavish requirements.

It was the arrival of the GIs that produced a real explosion in sexual activity and its inevitable consequence. Cases of venereal disease among American troops rose during the first three months of 1943 from 20 per thousand troops to 60 per 1000 – three times the level among US troops in their home country and six times that of home-based British troops.

Even before the epidemic reached its height, the American and Canadian authorities were growing thoroughly alarmed at the scale of it, and put pressure on the British authorities to take action, as this Ministry of Health memorandum from October 1942 shows:

Our proposal is that compulsory powers should be conferred by Defence Regulation on Medical Officers of Health to require the examination and, if necessary, the treatment of persons who are named as the source of infection by two separate patients under treatment. . . .

. . . Canadian Military Headquarters have made representations to the War Office –

For many months the Canadian Corps Commander and this Headquarters have watched the increase in Venereal Diseases among Canadian troops with the greatest anxiety. . . . Wherever possible, we have endeavoured to identify and trace the source of the infection, and in many cases it has been determined that one woman has been the cause of a multiplicity of cases. . . .

A new control, Regulation 33B, was enacted under the 1939 Defence of the Realm Act. Its First World War predecessor had aroused much anger for pointing the finger of blame at women for spreading the disease. The Minister of Health was therefore at pains to assure potential objectors that Regulation 33B did not discriminate against women. It allowed suspected carriers of venereal disease to be investigated by the authorities if they were named by two separate people as the source of infection. In theory, it was supposed to apply equally to both sexes. In practice, it was applied almost exclusively to women. Of 417 cases investigated in 1944, 414 were women. The Minister failed to persuade Dr Edith Summerskill, for one:

What is this miserable little measure that has been introduced? Regulation 33B will provide for the treatment of individuals who have infected two others – nothing more. . . . No two men will inform on a respectable woman who has been infected innocently. This regulation will only get a few people, probably only prostitutes, and a few other unfortunate women. The vast number of victims who are infected are left – ignored. . . .

My final point concerns the women who are informed against. Probably most of them will be prostitutes. I want the House to think of the unfortunate, and probably stupid, girl who has become infected, and who is informed against by a second man, who is anxious to protect the woman who has in fact infected him. It may be that a girl will be wrongly informed against. The result will be that she is labelled as an immoral woman. . . . If this regulation is introduced, it will not only be ineffective, but it may cause hardship and injustice to some unfortunate woman.

Hansard, 15 December 1942.

Summerskill was also concerned about the risk of the disease being passed on from the husband, via the innocent wife, to their children. She wanted to see compulsory notification of the disease, and the transmission of it to be a penal offence, as it had long been in Sweden. Further opposition manifested itself in the form of a resolution at the October 1943 annual conference of the National Council of Women:

The NCW repudiates as fallacious the prevalent opinion that it is the conduct of girls and women that is mainly responsible for the present increase of Venereal Disease, and desires to emphasise the fact that in the great majority of those fleeting and irresponsible sex relationships by which the disease is spread both partners must be held responsible, and a recall to moral responsibility must necessarily be made to both sexes.

The NCW therefore calls upon the government to consider afresh its whole approach to this problem, and to initiate a bold and positive education campaign which will bring home to every citizen and every household the conviction that all who indulge in sexual promiscuity not only may be responsible for the spread of VD, but are lacking in good citizenship.

Mrs Forster (for the Association for Moral and Social Hygiene) said that the (above) resolution was concerned with the problem of irregular sex relationships. Public opinion and the press laid the blame on the woman. Giving an instance in one district where there were large concentrations of troops, one report said that forty girls under 16 were waiting to go into a Home, and it added 'little blame could be apportioned to the troops'. Girls were the menace and men the victims! . . . Yet how grossly immoral men could be towards girls, many of them young children, was abundantly proved in charges which came before the courts.

SEX AND THE STAGE

The wartime descent into permissiveness had its parallel in the theatre, but fortunately the Lord Chamberlain was on hand to save us from ourselves. For centuries, this member of the royal household had arbitrarily exercised his absolute power to prevent the staging of anything that was not to his taste. In April 1940 his attention turned to strip tease and the *Birmingham Mail*, for one, thoroughly approved:

'The wonder is that the Lord Chamberlain did not long ago find a means of banning from theatres and music halls that decadent and vulgar importation from the United States known as 'strip tease'. It is, as its name quite frankly implies, a direct appeal to prurience; and what has made it worse has been the profit motive. But nobody has yet confessed to an understanding of our stage censorship – least of all the dignitaries who have held the exalted post of Lord Chancellor!'

A conference was held in St James's Palace on 'Suggestive nudity and impropriety of gesture and speech' (a sure-fire crowd-puller of a title for an event). In the course of it:

'The point was made that indecent shows have tended to increase since the outbreak of war. This is something which must not be allowed to develop by a nation which is fighting above all things for the moral standards implicit in the Christian code; and which cannot afford to flirt with the forces of decadence. . . .

'It may also be said that the ban on suggested nudity, which is to apply to all licensed theatres and cinemas throughout England and Wales, will be welcomed as wholeheartedly by the bulk of stage artists as by the mass of people of wholesome instincts. Here and there, there are to be found "strip tease artistes", so called – mostly alien pioneers – who may be said genuinely to "glory in their shame"; just as willing patrons are not lacking, for the prurient of mind we have always with us. But many a decent chorus girl or soubrette has had to choose between losing her livelihood and accepting the indignity of following this nasty craze at the bidding of her employers. It is a choice which no girl should have to make; and though there may be occasions, even in the theatrical stage, when nudity or near-nudity is not indecent, no amount of inspired prating of "art" and "form" can excuse this species of managerial coercion.'

By October 1942 rising rates of VD forced the government into launching a publicity campaign describing the symptoms and methods of transmission of VD. This was a bold step, since public references to 'sexual intercourse' were at that time taboo and public reaction was uncertain. Immediately before the war, the national press had refused point-blank to carry such information on its pages. At the same time ignorance about the disease was rife: among the myths current then were that you could only catch VD off a professional prostitute and that sex with a virgin would cure you; that you could also rid yourself of it by 'passing it on' to another; it could be caught off toilet seats or from second-hand clothes; and one clergyman who contracted the disease swore that it was as a result of being splashed by the wheel of a passing cart!

Again, parts of the campaign gave the distinct impression that the transmission of the disease was all women's fault. One particularly striking advertisement showed a skull wearing a woman's hat, asking 'Hello boy friend, coming MY way?' and warning that 'the "easy" girlfriend spreads syphilis and gonorrhoea'. Another showed a woman leaning on a street corner with obvious intent, and the warning that 'syphilis and gonorrhoea are easy to get'.

None the less, the vast majority (92 per cent) of the public – of both sexes – agreed it was right to inform people about VD. One consequence of the campaign was that the incidence of infection fell by about two-thirds in the last years of the war (with something of a blip of gay abandon marking the introduction of the 'one-shot' cure offered by penicillin in 1944). It is estimated that the publicity campaign saved about fifteen thousand men falling prey to the disease before D-Day – the equivalent of an infantry division. It could well have had a marked impact on the outcome of the landings.

Marriage, Infidelity, Illegitimacy, Divorce

British husbands serving overseas were worried about the influx of affluent and attractive foreign servicemen while they were away, a concern which both sides in the war tried to play on with the black propaganda described elsewhere in the book. These concerns were focused by the case of Annette Pepper, a Brighton housewife whose husband was a prisoner-of-war. In his absence she had formed a relationship with a Canadian military policeman, Charles Gaultier. When she broke off the relationship to go with someone else, he machine-gunned her, a crime for which he was hanged at Wandsworth in September 1943.

Other such crimes, when committed by an American serviceman, did not find their way into the British criminal statistics. US troops were subject to American military discipline, not British law – even in the case where a GI shot an English soldier in a British pub. American public opinion apparently could not cope with the idea that the ungrateful English would thus persecute one of their boys, sent over to help them. Canadian troops were not subject to a similar dispensation, and this sometimes gives rise to the mistaken impression that they were responsible for more wartime crime than their American counterparts.

Illegitimacy saw a substantial increase during the war years, but the figures do not always tell the full story. In the First World War, for example, there was a 30 per cent increase in the proportion of births that were illegitimate, but the rapid decline in the overall birth-rate meant that the actual number of births out of wedlock did not increase. In the Second World War both the percentages and the actual numbers of illegitimate births rose, from a 1939 figure of 4.4 per 1000 to a wartime peak in 1945 of 9.1 per 1000. Based on pre-war trends, about 100,000 of these births might have been regularised by shotgun weddings had not the disruption of the war got in the way.

A wartime study in Birmingham showed that around a third of all illegitimate births recorded were to married women. Even this may have understated the case, since a child born to a married woman was deemed to be legitimate unless the mother chose to register it otherwise. A further sign of the times was a threefold rise in the numbers prosecuted for trying to procure an abortion. However, the numbers involved were relatively small, and police knowledge of these cases probably represents the very small tip of a very large iceberg.

In one unexpected way, wartime conditions militated against divorce. *Reynolds News* reported in December 1939 that: 'West End solicitors, who before the war netted five figure incomes from divorce cases, have been heavily hit by the blackout. In the winter months at any rate private enquiry agents are helpless. Adultery cannot be proved because identification is impossible in pitch darkness.'

In other respects, war conditions bought about a dramatic increase in the incidence of marital breakdown. The annual average rate of divorces over the period 1941–5 was almost twice that for 1936–40, and the high rates continued into the post-war years. However, this change had begun before the war, with new legislation in 1937 making it easier to obtain a divorce. In the final two years before the outbreak of war, the rate was 60 per cent up on the preceding two years. But not everybody found it equally easy to resolve their marital problems, as Home Intelligence reported in May 1941:

> There is a considerable increase in the number of people seeking a divorce. This is stated to be due to hasty and ill-considered marriages, thanks to the imminence of calling up, or to one of a couple, who have lived apart for many years, now wishing to marry a member of the Forces. The number of Poor Persons' Lawyers is greatly reduced, and as a result, many people are having to wait over a year before their cases can be begun. Richer people who can afford the minimal cost of £50 can have their cases heard at once, and this naturally leads to much class ill-feeling.

One change during the war years was in terms of who initiated the divorce. Before the war, it was the wife in a slight majority of cases. This shifted to a slight majority of husbands during the war as a whole, though the final year of the war saw a dramatic eightfold rise in the number of men petitioning for divorce on the grounds of their wives' adultery. Adultery petitions increased by 100 per cent each year from 1942 onwards, and in 1945 two out of three divorce petitions were filed by men. One of the reasons for this may have been the existence of an army welfare scheme, which made it easier and cheaper for the husband to initiate proceedings.

The Love that Dare Not Speak its Name

'Homosexuality had been on the increase among the upper classes for a couple of generations, though almost unknown among working people. The upper class boarding school system of keeping boy and girl away from each other was responsible. In most cases the adolescent homosexual became sexually normal on leaving school; but a large minority of the more emotional young people could not shake off the fascination of perversity. In university circles, homosexuality no longer seemed a sign of continued adolescence.'

Graves and Hodge, *A Social History of Great Britain* (1941)
quoted in Taylor.

Homosexuality presented a real dilemma for the British Army in the Second World War, just as it had in other conflicts. The official line in King's Regulations was that: 'Confirmed homosexuals, whose rehabilitation is unlikely, should be removed from the Army by the most expeditious and appropriate means.'

An Army study accused homosexuals of dominating the male groups they were in, of finding it impossible to adopt a passive position of obeying orders and of being 'a foreign body in the social microcosm'. The US Army went further, labelling them 'sexual psychopaths'. Yet, prior to the Second World War, the Americans had no procedure for vetting new recruits for their sexual inclinations and the process thereafter tended to be perfunctory in the extreme. Based upon crude stereotypes of camp effeminate behaviour, their vetting excluded only four or five thousand Americans from serving in the armed forces throughout the entire war. However, one of the few studies of gay soldiers in the US Army in the war showed their average performance to be well above the average for the service as a whole, and history is replete with cases of the valour shown by avowedly homosexual troops.

Had the armed forces made serious attempts to weed out all its homosexual members, they would have been seriously – in some cases perhaps fatally – weakened. In practice, the approach was variously to ignore or cover up cases, to offer only mild punishment, or to invalid others out, along with the offer of medical treatment or advice (which often went along the lines of 'try to find yourself a good woman and forget about it'). Only in cases of flagrant breaches of discipline (by which was meant things like relationships between officers and other ranks, thereby corrupting the line of command, or homosexual encounters with the local population) was court-martial countenanced. The Americans introduced the new category of 'undesirable discharge' – which was neither honourable nor dishonourable – for dealing with those found guilty of such offences against military discipline.

None the less the stigma of being found out was great enough to push some members of the forces over the brink. By no means unique was the British sergeant who took to leaving letters from a fake 'son' around the barracks, in an attempt to disguise his true inclinations. He ended up attempting suicide and asking, while being treated in hospital, to be castrated or imprisoned. One British Army psychiatrist estimated that 4 per cent of all military psychological cases were related to homosexuality in one form or another – some think this to be a very modest estimate.

The Germans introduced far more Draconian measures – up to and including the death sentence – for members of their armed forces found guilty of homosexuality. But even this did not prevent the number of cases prosecuted increasing by 50 per cent between 1943 and 1944. Even so, the eight thousand or so Germans court-martialled probably represented only a fraction of the true extent of the practice. It is likely that the incidence at the front line would have been higher than among the population as a whole. The enforced company of a large number of young men, without women, may result in what has been described as 'emergency' or 'deprivation' homosexuality, and the psychological pressures of war – such as prolonged bombardment – were known to lead to temporary homosexual liaisons, even if one of the parties was not normally so inclined.

Whatever their official distaste for homosexuality, most of the combatant nations were perfectly content to harness its potential for espionage. Both the Americans and the Germans maintained 'bugged' homosexual brothels in New York, at least prior to America entering the war, where visitors would be relieved of their money and any intelligence they were careless enough to pass on. Britain, meanwhile, was employing the likes of Anthony Blunt at the very centre of their Military Intelligence operations. Blunt made widespread use of homosexual blackmail to secure the participation of others in espionage. Unfortunately for Britain, the organisation he was really working for was Russian Intelligence.

By contrast, lesbianism, a disciplinary rather than a criminal offence as far as the military were concerned, was treated relatively leniently. Guidance entitled 'A special problem' was prepared but never widely distributed, apparently for fear of drawing attention to the problem. Most cases were dealt with by discreet postings, to separate the couple concerned. Only a small number of what were described as 'very promiscuous lesbians' were discharged from the service.

7
Careless Talk

It has come to my knowledge that information which might be of great value to the enemy is being discussed in hotels, bars and general meeting places. It is the duty of every citizen to refrain from discussing with their friends and acquaintances any information such as movement of troops, numbers of troops, units, stations and similar military information.

The enemy spy system is extensive and a chance remark made in complete innocence may have disastrous effects. All ranks of the forces of the Crown are forbidden to discuss in public or in private any matters concerning military or defence affairs. Failure to comply with this warning will result in severe penalties for all concerned.

Notice widely displayed in the Aldershot area.

Press Freedom

One of the freedoms the British were no doubt fighting to defend was an independent press. Britons looked with a mixture of pity and contempt at Dr Goebbels' efforts to tell the German people what to think. Had they but known it, the government of Neville Chamberlain that led Britain through appeasement into the war exercised a degree of control over the press that modern spin doctors could only dream about. After hostilities were over, a Royal Commission into the Press investigated how Chamberlain's government had gained such overwhelming support from the press for the policy of appeasement. The story was one of a complex web of informal links between government and press that reduced the media barons to the status of politicians' mouthpieces.

Even as Chancellor of the Exchequer, Neville Chamberlain proved to be an adept user of the lobby system. Yet his treatment of the press was arrogant, bordering on the contemptuous. He would refuse to accept questions with less than four hours' notice and, if cornered by a hostile question, would turn upon the questioner for being 'susceptible to Jewish-Communist propaganda'.

One of his main assistants for briefing the lobby was Sir Joseph Ball, a shadowy figure recruited from MI5 to run the Conservatives' own intelligence service. He did so using many of the techniques he had learned from his former employer. The phones of Anthony Eden and his fellow anti-appeasers were tapped and the names of other fellow Conservatives were blackened through a periodical ironically called *Truth*. This supposedly independent publication had been secretly acquired by friends of Chamberlain to act as the mouthpiece for his faction within the Conservative party. Under this ownership, it became viciously anti-Churchill, anti-Semitic, anti-American and pacifist.

Members of Chamberlain's Cabinet circle were on close personal terms with most of the big newspaper proprietors and editors of the day. In the case of the relationship between Chamberlain and Geoffrey Dawson, the editor of *The Times*, the links were so close that *The Times* became regarded as the unofficial voice of the British government, and was closely studied for that reason in government offices throughout the world.

But none of the relationships was on quite the same basis as that between Lord Beaverbrook and Sir Samuel Hoare (Lord Privy Seal in the Chamberlain War Cabinet). From 1938 Hoare was receiving secret payments of £2,000 per year from Beaverbrook, and in return lobbied for Beaverbrook to be given a Cabinet position, as Minister of Agriculture.

Another close and improper relationship was that between George Steward, Chamberlain's Press Officer and Dr Hesse, the Press Attaché at the German Embassy. Through Steward, Hesse was able to learn the true attribution of stories reported through the lobby system, and was thus able to gauge the true tenor of British government opinion in the tense negotiations on either side of the Munich agreement. Steward's relationship with Hesse has variously been described as 'strictly against his code of conduct as a civil servant' and 'treasonable'.

The British Ambassador to Berlin was Sir Nevile Henderson. He was an extreme appeaser – when the English football team played in Berlin in May 1938 he insisted that they all gave the Nazi salute, and he told a gathering of the Anglo-German Society: 'Far too many people have an erroneous conception about what the National-Socialist regime really stands for. Otherwise they would lay much less stress on Nazi dictatorship and much more emphasis on the great social experiment being tried out in this country.' Henderson very quickly picked up upon Hitler's extreme and irrational sensitivity to criticism in the British press. This message was also drummed into Lord Halifax, by Goebbels and by Hitler himself during Halifax's visit to Germany in November 1937. It was made clear to Halifax that progress on a peace settlement was dependent upon suppression of the criticism of Hitler in the British press.

Chamberlain and his colleagues duly complied by exerting pressure on newspaper owners and editors alike. Some journalists bitterly resented this regime. As J.L. Garvin, the editor of the *Observer*, put it in August 1938: 'The daily press no longer gives any true idea of the feeling of this country. There is at last – wide anxiety – a slow, eating anxiety, though silent and feeling helpless. There is not one particle of sympathy any more with Germany.' His proprietor, Lord Astor, voiced similar concerns, '. . . although the newspapers might have been silenced now . . . there was widespread uneasiness and that was likely to show itself soon'.

Questions were asked in Parliament about the muzzling of the press. First Halifax equivocated, then Chamberlain openly lied to the Commons about whether government influence was being exercised over the newspapers. But Chamberlain's hand was evident in the notorious *Times* editorial of 7 September 1938, in which it openly advocated the dismemberment of Czechoslovakia. Both Jan Masaryk, the Czech Minister to London, and his Russian counterpart, protested to the Foreign Office. As Masaryk put it, the Foreign Office's belief in the independence of *The Times* 'is not shared by a very large section of the population abroad'.

> Colonel Blimp explains: 'Gad sir, *The Times* is right! We should give Czechoslovakia a free hand in Europe.'

Beaverbrook was among the most acquiescent of the press barons. He told the government that, while the press were totally behind them, they needed a lot more guidance. A minister should be appointed to brief them directly. The minister he suggested was Sir Samuel Hoare. The proposal was accepted, and Hoare – the man on Beaverbrook's payroll – was soon dispensing daily briefings to the British press. Some journalists, frustrated by the line dictated by their employers, found an independent voice in private publications such as the *Whitehall News Letter*, which attacked Chamberlain and his entourage. By the early months of the war, these publications had a combined circulation of around 100,000.

During this period, the government sought to extend its control over public expression beyond the newspapers. The Lord Chamberlain, who at that time exercised powers to censor plays, was asked by the Foreign Office to ensure that: 'All direct references to Germany, to Herr Hitler, or to other prominent persons should be avoided . . . since they would be . . . not only dangerous, but unnecessary.' They also drew the attention of the British Board of Film Censors to a forthcoming Charlie Chaplin film, *The Great Dictator*, which they described as 'a bitter and ridiculous . . . satire which Mr Chaplin is entering into with fanatical enthusiasm', and urged the Censors 'to give the film the most careful scrutiny should it be presented to you for a licence'.

The film was only eventually released in 1940. The BBC also came under scrutiny. Its compliance had been thought for a number of years to have been guaranteed by its dependence on the government for the licence fee. However, from the mid-1930s its coverage of current affairs was watched closely by the government, resulting in what the Chief News Editor referred to as a 'conspiracy of silence'. In one example, a talk by Harold Nicolson on the Czechoslovak crisis was withdrawn at the insistence of the Foreign Secretary, and the sound engineer stood ready to fade Nicolson out, should he depart from the content of his innocuous alternative script.

Perhaps most outrageously of all, just before the invasion of Czechoslovakia, *Truth* ran a nauseating feature on 'Hitler the artist', waxing lyrical about his watercolours and the warm, human and sensitive man they portrayed. Was it, they wondered, 'possible that the real Hitler, the genuine little Adolf, is a sensitive child, intensely occupied with his own shy moods?'

Only in the very last days of peace did the press finally begin to reflect the mood of the nation. Hoare's final desperate attempts to bully the press into compliance with continued appeasement in late August fell upon deaf ears.

The press would pay a high price, in terms of public trust, for its

WAR MEANS NEVER HAVING TO SAY YOU'RE SORRY

Along with direct censorship, journalistic euphemisms for wartime reverses became commonplace. A rout became 'a retrograde movement', a 'disengagement' or simply 'straightening the line'. Insanity caused by prolonged exposure to fighting became 'battle fatigue' or 'exhaustion'. The V1 flying bombs became known as the cosy 'doodlebugs', and their successors the V2s (which arrived at such a speed that they could not even be heard coming, let alone shot down) were initially blamed on gas explosions. Cynics christened them 'flying gas mains'. The sites where they landed were 'incidents'.

Even sceptical members of the armed forces got in on the euphemism act. Bomber crews participating in a raid on a German city that spectacularly failed to find its target spoke of 'a major assault on German agriculture'. However, the prize for the finest euphemism of the war must go to Emperor Hirohito of Japan. After the two atomic bombs had fallen on Hiroshima and Nagasaki, the Emperor made a radio broadcast to the nation in which he told them that they were surrendering because: 'The war has taken a turn not necessarily to our advantage.'

spinelessness. A Mass Observation survey in March 1940 showed that the public now only ranked it third in its list of opinion-formers. Two years before, it had been first. Another survey in August 1940 found that, by a majority of more than three to one, the public now found the BBC a more reliable source of news than the press. The circulations of the main pro-Chamberlain newspapers fell sharply, while those few which had consistently opposed him – such as the *Daily Mirror* – enjoyed a correspondingly rapid rise. The newspaper industry would never fully regain the trust it had enjoyed before Chamberlain.

From the moment he was restored to government as First Lord of the Admiralty, Winston Churchill made it clear that he was also adept in manipulating the media (and not above manipulating the facts, if they stood in the way of the message he wanted to convey). The Navy already had the most effective of the forces' media organisations, and Churchill milked it shamelessly to his own ends. Good news stories were suppressed until he could announce them in his own speeches. Vice-Admiral Hallett from the Admiralty

Press Office made the unpardonable error of releasing some of these stories himself. He rapidly found himself removed from the press office and posted out to sea. Churchill said in one speech that it was 'pretty certain' that about half the U-boat fleet had been sunk. When naval intelligence told him that the true figure was no higher than 9 out of 66, Churchill simply replied that 35 was 'the lowest figure that can be accepted'.

The Mystery of Information

I may say that I have had considerable difficulty in ascertaining what are its functions.

Lord Macmillan, Minister of Information.

It was a perfectly useless body and the war would have been in no way affected if it had been dissolved and only the censorship remained.

Sir Kenneth Clark, Controller of Home Publicity in the Ministry of Information.

The Ministry of Information is a misbegotten freak bred from the unnatural union of Sir Horace Wilson and Sir Samuel Hoare (considering the progenitors, I wonder the offspring is not even more revolting).

Duff Cooper, Minister of Information.

If the Germans do not manage to bomb us to death the Ministry of Information will bore us to death.

Aneurin Bevan.

Hush, hush, chuckle who dares,
Another new Minister's fallen downstairs.

Popular rhyme at the Ministry, reflecting its rapid changes of Minister.

It takes a special talent for the organisation in charge of wartime propaganda itself to become widely unpopular and the butt of jokes, but that is what the Ministry of Information contrived to do. Frequently referred to as the Ministry for Misinformation or the Mystery of Information, when it announced that it had 999 members of staff – the same as the telephone number for the emergency services – it promptly also became known as The Disaster Department.

The Ministry of Information was planned from 1935 to 'present the national case to the public at home and abroad in time of war'. It was finally set up in 1939, and Goebbels' Ministry of Propaganda was influential in shaping its form and function. It was granted swingeing powers under the Emergency Powers (Defence) Act, to censor not just information of value to the enemy but also opinion hostile to the government and anti-war sentiment. This, and its lion's share of scarce wartime paper supplies, helped to earn it the immediate jealousy and hostility of the media.

The Ministry suffered badly from the rapid turnover of its ministers. *Time* magazine said of its first minister, the High Court Judge Lord Macmillan: 'If Lord Macmillan's first task was to undo Britain's reputation for cleverness, he could not have done it more brilliantly.' His successors, Sir John Reith and Duff Cooper, fared little better. Reith was sacked by Churchill as part of a long-running vendetta, immediately he became prime minister, and Cooper, who was described by Ponting as a 'reactionary womaniser' who was both incompetent and lazy, saw his political career ended by his failure there. It was only under Brendan Bracken that the Ministry shook off its reputation as an incompetent joke and began to perform a useful function. The recruitment of its more junior staff was no happier. It was mostly done through the old boy network, making it a hotbed of amateurism (only 43 of the 999 staff were trained journalists). The *New Statesman* referred to a 'scramble of socially favoured amateurs and privileged ignoramuses into the Ministry of Information'.

One of its leading lights, the MP Harold Nicolson, was described by a colleague as: 'a wonderful gossip but [he] seemed to know hardly anyone outside Westminster, St James and Bloomsbury. He was quite ignorant of the habits and attitudes even of the middle classes. . . . Never was there a man who represented so completely in himself the distinction between us and them.'

Originally, the Ministry was a bold idea for centralising the processing of all government information and propaganda. However, vested interests ensured that the idea got watered down in practice, and individual departmental press offices survived. The inexperience of the staff soon brought them into disrepute. Their censorship was inadequate and inconsistent and they were held responsible for the lack of news reaching the press – a charge which should more properly have been laid at the door of the press organisations of the individual government departments and armed services. The fact that only four prosecutions were carried out during the war under the censorship regulations says less about the responsible behaviour of the newspapers, and more about the difficulty the papers had tracking down any news 'hot' enough to infringe the regulations. The Ministry's accreditation of overseas war correspondents in Britain was so strict that about a hundred of them decamped for Berlin, where it was rather easier to get reliable information.

The lack of news in the early part of the war was held to be partly responsible for the proliferation of rumours (for example, that the royal family or the government were about to flee to Canada, or that the Duke of Windsor was to be appointed leader of a puppet administration). This led in turn to the establishment of the Ministry's Anti-Lies Bureau and to the doomed Silent Column campaign, referred to below.

Their coverage of the departure of the British Expeditionary Force to France illustrates their incompetence in dealing with the media. Initially, they banned the news, until they found it was being broadcast by the French. They then lifted the ban, and newspaper editors rushed it into their editions. The Ministry then decided that the media were giving too many details of the action and re-imposed the ban. The police were brought in to confiscate copies of the morning papers from newsagents and other suppliers. Finally, at 2.55 a.m., the ban was lifted for a second time, leaving newspaper editors to bite the carpet with rage.

Other aspects of the MOI's early handling of public relations were incompetent to a point that beggars belief. When war correspondent John Gunther asked for the text of some of the eighteen million leaflets that RAF bombers dropped on Germany, he was refused on the remarkable grounds that it was 'information which could be of value to the enemy'. This gave rise to a rich vein of speculation about the leaflets – that they were inaccurate, out-of-date or full of spelling mistakes. Best of all, some said that the Ministry had got the packages mixed up and had dropped a supply of our ration books on the Germans instead. In fact, a good proportion of the leaflets consisted of extracts from speeches by Neville Chamberlain and Lord Halifax. As Noel Coward, who was peripherally involved with this aspect of wartime propaganda at one time, put it: 'If it is the policy of

H.M. Government to bore the Germans to death, I do not believe we have quite enough time.'

The Ministry's first poster campaign proved disastrous in stoking up the fires of class conflict that were still smouldering from pre-war society. It said: 'Your courage, your cheerfulness, your resolution will bring us victory.'

A survey by the Daily Express showed that 33 per cent of the women questioned and 11 per cent of the men had not even noticed the posters (plastered everywhere, at the considerable cost of £44,000). A significant proportion of those who had seen them apparently did not understand them (many thought that the 'resolution' referred to was the New Year's variety). But 61 per cent of the men surveyed who had seen and understood it took exception to it. For, to those who chose to read it in such a light, the slogan meant that 'you' (the poor bloody infantry of the working classes) will make all the sacrifices that will give 'us' (the establishment) the spoils of victory. Just to complete the Ministry's success, anti-Semites began to exploit the fascist potential of the poster, and went round doctoring them to read '. . . will bring Jew victory'. It was rapidly dropped. No more successful was their 'Silent Column' campaign, launched in July 1940. The aim of this was to stop people spreading rumour and gossip, alarm and despondency. Unfortunately, it did so using characters with names like Mr Know-All, Miss Leaky Mouth and Mr Glumpot, and was written in language that was no less patronising than the names. Worst of all, it tried to turn Britain into a nation of snoopers, inviting them to inform on any transgressors.

Some did; drunks and the feeble-minded were arrested, and one soldier in a Soho pub was imprisoned for shouting 'To hell with Hitler!', when it was misheard as 'Heil Hitler!' A woman, overcome by a moment of careless rapture in a hotel bedroom, blurted out to her boyfriend: 'Who cares if Hitler does come, so long as we can have fun like this!' She was overheard by a hotel chambermaid and received a month in prison.

The newspaper advertisements lasted just three weeks, before

> Colonel Blimp explains: 'Gad sir, Mr Baldwin is right! To ensure peace, we must have plenty of aeroplanes. Otherwise how are we going to drop messages of goodwill on the enemy?'

Churchill was forced to admit in Parliament that the campaign did not look so attractive on paper as it had seemed in prospect. Dorothy L. Sayers, writing in the *Spectator*, showed how badly it had misread the mood of the nation:

> Nobody said that if Mr Churchill had put it on paper himself it would have looked very different. Mr Churchill knows how to be more insolently offensive than any man living, but he exercises his unique abilities in this direction against the enemy, not against his own people. He never suggests to us that we are a bunch of fools and cowards who need to be incessantly scolded into resolution. . . .
>   . . . We have been shown a very faint glimpse of the thing that we are fighting against, and now that we have seen it, we know for certain that we hate it beyond all imagination. To distrust our fellows, to become spies on them, to betray them to the law, to go in a continual dumb terror for fear they should spy on us – that is the thing that Nazi government means, and it is a thing we will not endure.

Home Intelligence reports also picked up the public sentiment:

> Strong resentment still felt among all classes at Silent Column campaign and at police prosecutions for spreading rumour, which are considered ridiculous. Ministry of Information becoming unpopular again; much of this feeling directed against the Minister. Indignation expressed at what people say to be 'a policy which is turning us into a nation of spies'. Labour Party candidates' meeting agreed that prosecutions for idle talking were upsetting public morale seriously. People in new positions of minor authority accused of officiousness and bullying manner, reminiscent, some say 'of the early days of the Nazis'.

The Silent Column campaign possibly marked the nadir of the Ministry's reputation, but it was by no means their last mistake. Mass Observation pilot-tested their 'Stay Put' leaflet, designed to prevent the public panicking and fleeing their homes in the event of an invasion. They found that the public were highly critical of its schoolmasterly tone and disapproved of the leaflet in a ratio of 3:1.

PROPAGANDA – CATCH THEM YOUNG

It was not just the hearts and minds of the adult population that were being won over to the war effort. The youngsters had their own diet of propaganda. As George Orwell recalled, the more traditional boys' papers, such as the *Gem* and the *Magnet*, were still stuck in an imperialistic time warp, from about 1910, in which Nazism had failed to make even an appearance by the end of September 1939. Arthur Mee's *Children's Newspaper* took a traditional patriotic line, producing a series of articles on *1940: Our Finest Hour*. However, brash newcomers like the *Beano* and the *Dandy* were most definitely at war. In them, Hitler and Goering were portrayed as Addy and Hermy, the Nasty Nazis. They would watch the British Isles through their magic telescope and reel back in horror, crying 'Himmel! Der pig-dog British are saving all their waste paper!'

Mussolini was Musso da Wop ('he's a bit of a flop') and no national stereotype was spared in the attempt to pour ridicule on him – even to the extent of his generals issuing their troops with spaghetti for bootlaces. (A contemporary riddle: 'Why does Mussolini never change his socks? Because he smells defeat'.) In its stablemate, the *Dandy Comic Annual* for 1941, Desperate Dan can be seen capturing three U-boats single-handedly, with a chain he has just knitted. 'Frizzle mein Aunt von Fanny!' cries a German submariner; 'Danny der Desperate has our goose cooked!' For the more literate consumer of comics, *Champion* had characters such as Rockfist Rogan of the RAF and The Leader of the Lost Commandos, while those of a more traditional bent could enjoy Struewwelhitler or Adolf in Blunderland, parodies of the classic children's stories.

There were children's games based on every aspect of the war – you could play Bomber Command, Air Sea Rescue, River Plate, ARP or Hang Your Washing on the Siegfried Line. Pin the Tail on the Donkey was given a new look as Decorate Goering, and darts games featuring Hitler were popular. In Plonk, you scored 100 for a dart in the Führer's mouth. (Another game (perhaps fortunately un-named) scored top marks for hitting quite the opposite end of his alimentary canal.)

Many historians would identify the entry of Russia or America into the war as turning points in the conflict, but comic readers everywhere will confirm that the Axis powers stood no chance from the moment that they took on both Desperate Dan and Lord Snooty and his Pals.

Sometimes it was the Ministry's timing that was off. In the middle of 1940 they issued a 32-page brochure, talking about there having been 'six months without any serious fighting on land'. It came out just as the British Expeditionary Force was engaging in some very serious fighting indeed, on the road back to Dunkirk. The Ministry also managed to upset the film-going public. The Ministry took over the highly regarded GPO Film Unit in April 1940 and turned it into the propaganda film-making wing of their operations. It was given the first call on scarce film stock, above the feature films the public really wanted to see, and cinemas were forced to show their propaganda short features. They were not popular with the public, who were generally cynical about them and resented having to sit through them to get to the feature they had actually paid to watch.

On one occasion the Ministry actually wanted to raise the blood pressure of the British public. There was a feeling in 1940 that the public lacked sufficient hostility to the Germans. The Ministry proposed an 'Anger Campaign', invoking the same kind of crude propaganda that had been used in the First World War (Huns bayoneting babies and Belgian nuns). This failed to recognise the cynicism which had been engendered in the public when that propaganda had subsequently been found to be untrue. This cynicism was said to be why some of the public failed at first to believe the stories of the Nazi concentration camps, when they began to emerge. The Ministry withheld some of these early stories, owing to concerns about anti-Semitism among the public at the time. The Ministry also suggested that: 'A few death sentences on traitors would have a great effect in heightening the public temper against the enemy.'

The Anger Campaign was never implemented on the scale – or with some of the wilder ideas – proposed by the Ministry.

Censorship

The possibility of introducing total press censorship was seriously considered by the wartime government, but it was felt to sit too uneasily with their self-appointed role as guardians of civil liberties in the world. Similarly, there was talk of making the BBC a department of government, but this again would have compromised its façade of independence with its world audience. Instead, they appointed civil servants as 'advisers', who in fact had powers of total direction over the Corporation's news output.

The judgement of the Ministry as to what the public should or should not be told was continually found to be faulty. After the bombing of Buckingham Palace, they busily set about suppressing all news of it. Churchill was reported to have responded as follows: 'Dolts! Idiots! Fools! Spread the news at once! Let it be broadcast everywhere. Let the people of London know that the King and Queen are sharing the perils with them.' Or, as A.J.P. Taylor put it: 'There was a difference between the King and his subjects. They had essential work to do, he could have gone through his "boxes" just as well at Windsor. He attended at Buckingham Palace solely to be bombed.'

When Noel Coward proposed making a film based on the sinking of Lord Louis Mountbatten's ship HMS *Kelly* during the battle for Crete, the Ministry initially banned it, on the grounds that a film showing a British ship sinking would be bad for morale. It was only after Mountbatten intervened through the person of King George VI himself that the ban was lifted. *In Which We Serve* went on to be probably Britain's most successful wartime film, winning Coward a special Oscar for his 'outstanding production achievement'.

Coward was once again a victim of the Ministry's censorship with his cabaret song 'Don't let's be beastly to the Germans'. The irony of the song went entirely over the heads of the civil servants, who banned it from being recorded or broadcast on the grounds that Goebbels might use some of its words for propaganda purposes. This was despite the fact that Coward had played it to Winston Churchill, to the latter's obvious amusement.

Another of the Ministry's ill-judged forays into artistic censorship was in relation to Colonel Blimp. The Colonel, created by *Evening Standard* cartoonist David Low in 1934, was a bigoted, incompetent and reactionary former military man, whose collected thoughts appear at various points in this book and whose name entered the language. George Orwell, for example, described the Home Guard as 'a people's army, officered by Blimps'. When Michael Powell announced in 1942 that he was to make a film based on the character, Churchill wrote to the Minister for Information, Brendan Bracken, in the following Blimpish terms:

Pray propose to me the measures necessary to stop this foolish production before it gets any further. I am not prepared to allow propaganda detrimental to the morale of the army and I am sure the Cabinet will take all necessary action. Who are the people behind it?

The Ministry vetted the script and eventually approved it. Quite how great their impact was is not known, but the character that emerged in *The Life and Death of Colonel Blimp* was a much more sympathetic figure, a decent and honourable man who had simply lived beyond his time – 'a lovable old walrus', as one film critic put it. The film was a huge success, helped not a little by Churchill's attempts at censorship, but Churchill none the less still tried to have its export banned. For years afterwards, the only print available of it was a heavily edited version.

Attempts by the Ministry to organise a wartime social survey earned the organisation the new nickname Cooper's Snoopers, after its then Minister, Duff Cooper. People interpreted their no-doubt well-meaning efforts to find out what was on the nation's minds as a sinister attempt to manipulate public opinion, though very few of the public declined to take part in it.

Radio broadcasts were subject to strict controls. J.B. Priestley's radio broadcasts during the early years of the war were second in popularity only to those of Churchill himself, but he made the mistake of suggesting that the war might be about something beyond just beating Hitler. His discussion of the better world that the nation might aspire to after the war earned him a number of powerful enemies. The Conservative 1922 Committee lobbied the Ministry of Information, and Churchill complained that Priestley's war aims conflicted with his own. David Margesson, the government Chief Whip, objected to the BBC about the leftward slant of Priestley's talks (which, given that Margesson was supposed to be part of a coalition government including socialists, may seem like an abuse of his position). Eventually, a terse memorandum went to a BBC Board meeting in March 1941: 'Priestley series stopping on instructions of Minister.'

The Ministry had the power to vet scripts and approve speakers. Even then, their representative sat in Broadcasting House, ready to fade out any broadcaster who might dare to depart from the approved text (an extension of the practice employed in a more limited way before the war by Chamberlain's government).

The Ministry's deference to its traditional audiences – the newspapers – also used to rebound on the BBC on occasion. They would embargo the release of important news in evening broadcasts in order to give the scoop to the morning papers. This meant, for example, that details of a Cabinet reshuffle were made public on foreign radio stations before the BBC was allowed to broadcast them.

Nothing was too innocuous to cause the authorities to take fright. Wartime radio listeners derived much innocent pleasure from listening to a radio programme called *The Brains Trust*. In this, a panel consisting of a dangerously subversive mixture of the Secretary of the London Zoological Society, a teacher of philosophy and a retired Royal Navy commander answered listeners' questions about anything under the sun. Pompous members of the Establishment began to complain about the undermining of their position as the repository of all wisdom by this programme, and the BBC duly started to vet all the questions. The absence of a member of the Established Church on the panel led them to ban questions about religion, and even to run an edition of the programme with a panel entirely composed of churchmen (not a great success). Then, any questions that might embarrass the government, such as 'should there be equal pay for men and women?' were banned. Finally, the BBC governors decided that the three individuals concerned were becoming too influential, and banned them from appearing together on the programme. Each was limited to just one appearance every three weeks.

Censorship did not even stop at words. Once Russia entered the war, Churchill was very concerned that this would promote the cause of Communism in Britain. He told the Ministry of Information to 'consider what action is required to counter the present tendency of the British public to forget the dangers of Communism in their enthusiasm over the resistance of Russia'.

One of the more ludicrous manifestations of this policy was in relation to the Russian national anthem, the 'Internationale'. Churchill issued an instruction that it was on no account to be played by the BBC. The BBC at this time had a programme on which they played the national anthems of all the Allied nations. Once Russia joined the Allied cause, they resolutely resisted all demands from the public to play the 'Internationale' on this programme, eventually scrapping the programme rather than yield

A LETTER FROM THE CENSOR

From the very start of the war, there was censorship of correspondence. A small army of over ten thousand civil servants worked in a network of offices around the country, checking letters, telegrams, books and news agency reports coming into or going out of the country. They checked not just for information that could be of value to the enemy, but also for anything defeatist, or which might bring the Allied war effort into disrepute. As the threat of invasion grew in 1940, this was extended to include internal correspondence within the British Isles. Quite how widely this latter power was used is not known, though it is thought to have been directed primarily at known or suspected dissidents. In addition, the authorities also had the power to eavesdrop on private telephone conversations.

to the pressure. Only in January 1942, and with great reluctance, was Churchill persuaded by Anthony Eden to drop his ban on the anthem, in the light of all the negative publicity it was attracting. More generally, there was a ban on playing the music of composers from Axis nations – not for any ideological reason, but for the more practical purpose of avoiding paying royalties to enemy nationals.

In another bizarre example of gratuitous censorship, the BBC cancelled a Christmas choral concert in 1940, which was due to be conducted by Sir Hugh Robertson. This was because Robertson was a pacifist who was privately critical of the government, who presumably might therefore conduct the carols in an unsuitably pacifist manner and thus promote defeatism. The Ministry of Information developed a reputation as a sanctuary for draft-dodging failed hacks and other would-be literary spirits, and was savagely lampooned in Evelyn Waugh's 1942 book *Put Out More Flags*. One other literary connection with the government's wartime propaganda efforts was the book *1984*. George Orwell's first wife was involved with the propaganda work of the Ministry of Food, and it is thought that some of the sloganising in that book (not to mention the perennial complaints about shortages) was based upon her experience.

In the interest of balance, it has to be said that some of the

Ministry's other campaigns, such as 'Careless talk costs lives' and 'Walls have ears' were so successful that they helped to fuel the paranoia about a ubiquitous Fifth Column, discussed elsewhere in this book.

Newspaper Censorship

Newspaper censorship could lead to some ludicrous anomalies. Papers could report on which German cities had been attacked by the RAF, but a raid which destroyed, for example, a substantial part of the centre of Reading could only be described for weeks afterwards in the town's newspaper as taking place in 'a home counties town' (as if the local population might not have spotted it). Even Manchester's air raids in December 1940, which left 1,000 people dead, 75,000 houses damaged and 37,000 people homeless, could not be pinpointed by the media any more specifically than 'an inland town in the north west'. The weather was also forbidden as a topic for the newspapers, on the grounds that it might aid and abet German bombers.

Any questioning of the conduct of the war soon attracted the wrath of the censors. While the Russian-German non-aggression pact lasted, the Communist *Daily Worker* was firmly anti-war, leading to its suppression by the government. Of the mainstream newspapers, the *Daily Mirror* was just about the only one seriously to question government conduct of the war. This was despite the fact that the paper had been strongly pro-Churchill during the Chamberlain administration, and had even asked Churchill to write for them.

A cartoon of a shipwrecked seaman, clinging on to some wreckage in the water, above a caption 'The price of petrol has been increased by one penny' led to threats of the paper being suppressed. The offending cartoon was supposed to illustrate the hardships endured by seamen to supply us with petrol, and the consequent need to conserve supplies, but the government misinterpreted it to be conveying some morale-sapping message about profiteering. Churchill himself was quite vituperative about the independence shown by the *Daily Mirror*. As he wrote to the proprietor, Cecil King: 'There is a spirit of hatred and malice against the government which surpasses anything I have ever seen in English journalism.

One would have thought that in these hard times some hatred might be kept for the enemy.'

Churchill's malice towards King and the *Mirror* even extended to trying to get King conscripted (he failed the medical) and having the intelligence services investigate the share ownership of the paper for evidence of subversive influences. Despite his own background as a journalist, Churchill treated the press with a similar contempt to that shown by Neville Chamberlain. He was one of the leading protagonists for tighter control over the media and even objected to factual reports of speeches by MPs critical of the government – the Ministry would censor the offending passages. Home Intelligence never uncovered any evidence that the independence of the press – such as it was – damaged morale. On the contrary, the safety valve it provided very probably had quite the opposite effect. It certainly appeared to be what the public wanted – the *Daily Mirror* enjoyed a massive rise in circulation during the war years, in contrast to some of its more compliant rivals.

With the outbreak of war, Beaverbrook's papers switched from being arch-appeasers to being arch-complainers about a war that they saw as unnecessary and avoidable. The *Express* ran campaigns against rationing, the blackout and other aspects of wartime regulation. In October 1939 the *Sunday Express* published a defeatist interview with Lloyd George, in which the former prime minister declared that Poland was not worth fighting for. But Beaverbrook's anti-war efforts, prior to his 'rehabilitation' under Winston Churchill, were not limited to editorial matters. He also attempted to get the Duke of Windsor to front a peace campaign, and sought to fund the anti-war Independent Labour Party. In fact, Beaverbrook was not at all fussy about the company he kept; he also assiduously courted the favours of Stalin, once the Russians had entered the war.

Truth magazine continued throughout the war. Sir Joseph Ball's fanatical loyalty to Chamberlain continued after the latter's death, with Ball using the magazine to attack the enemies of the Chamberlain camp, such as Eden and Churchill, even after they became members of the wartime government. He conducted a particularly unpleasant anti-Semitic campaign against Leslie Hore-Belisha, after his resignation from the Chamberlain Cabinet in January 1940. If anything, the magazine's pro-fascist tendencies grew more pronounced in wartime. At one stage, they had Major-General Fuller (Sir Oswald Mosley's one-time adviser on military affairs) writing a piece denying the existence of German concentration camps.

When British fascist sympathisers were rounded up under Regulation 18B, *Truth* championed the cause of these internees. The most disturbing aspect of this was that Ball was at the same time the Vice-Chairman of the so-called Swinton Committee, which was supposed to be responsible for rounding up the fascists. *Truth's* fascist sympathies led to calls in Parliament in 1941 for the magazine to be suppressed. Ball and fellow director Charles Crocker – also on the Swinton Committee – were forced to disentangle themselves from *Truth* rather rapidly. When Ball finally finished at the Conservative Research Department, all its records were found to have been destroyed.

Broadcasting

The lack of imagination of some of the BBC's broadcasting efforts in the early part of the war (they seemed to consist largely of Sandy Macpherson and the BBC theatre organ) made it easy for German propagandists to attract British listeners. They launched a number of stations, purporting to be dissident British broadcasters and thereby helping to foster the idea of an active Fifth Column within Britain. The first of these, the New British Broadcasting Station, went on the air on 25 February 1940, and was followed by Workers' Challenge, Caledonia and the Christian Peace Movement, appealing variously to class, nationalist and pacifist sentiments.

As long as there was little real news for the BBC to report, these stations (whose frequencies were published in the daily newspapers) attracted a good proportion of the British listening public. The Ministry of Information estimated in January 1940 that 26 per cent of the population had listened in the previous twenty-four hours to their most famous propagandist, William Joyce. Another survey suggested that no fewer than 24 million British people listened to him at least occasionally. The BBC was even forced into a ratings war, moving some of its most popular programmes around to try to win listeners back from the Germans. As one listener put it to Mass Observation: 'We nearly always turn him [Lord Haw-Haw] on at nine fifteen to try and glean some news that the Ministry of Information withholds from us.'

More worryingly, another survey showed that 17 per cent agreed with Joyce's assessment that the war was being conducted for the benefit of an international Jewish conspiracy. The *Daily Mirror* set up an 'Anti-Haw-Haw League of Loyal Britons', who vowed never to listen to, or even mention, the man. Mention of Haw-Haw could, in fact, be dangerous. A civil servant from Mansfield was prosecuted for inventing a Haw-Haw story about the schools in his area, as was a Birmingham businessman for telling his staff that Haw-Haw broadcast news of a fire before it was generally known about even in Britain.

Black Propaganda

Both sides made use of misleading or salacious propaganda, in an effort to demoralise the enemy. On the British side, efforts were co-ordinated by the Political Warfare Executive, which was established in August 1941. Like the Germans, they broadcast radio programmes purporting to be produced by dissidents within the enemy state itself. The content of the programmes was decided by Sefton Delmer, the German-born son of an Australian father and British mother, who produced a potent mixture of popular music and often-pornographic scandal about the sexual peccadilloes of the Nazi establishment. The station was called GS1 and Delmer broadcast in the character of 'Der Chef', an uncompromising, patriotic Prussian. So salacious were his reports that even the German High Command complained about his 'quite unusually wicked hate propaganda'.

Even our own side protested – one broadcast in the summer of 1942, describing an orgy involving high Nazi officials, was picked up in Moscow. It outraged the sober and humourless former British Ambassador there, Sir Stafford Cripps, who demanded that they be toned down. Delmer's chief responded robustly:

If the Secret Service were to be too squeamish, the Secret Service could not operate . . . this is a war with the gloves off, and when I was asked to deal with black propaganda I did not try to restrain my people more than M [the Head of the Secret

Service] would restrain his, because if you are told to fight you fight all out. I am not conscious that it has depraved me. I dislike the baser sides of human life as much as Sir Stafford Cripps does, but in this case moral indignation does not seem to be called for.

Delmer was none the less told to tone down the pornographic content of his scripts. In addition to GS1, there were specialised stations, such as Atlantiksender, for U-boat crews, and Soldatensenders, for German land troops in Europe. These might carry stories about Nazi officials' sex scandals with the wives of absent troops; news that much of the blood in German field hospitals was infected with syphilis; or details of married women giving birth to babies at a time when their husbands had been absent at the front for over a year.

Anything that might foster disaffection among the troops was tried: the army pay corps were stealing their pay; their parcels from home were being pilfered; the jobs they hoped to return to after the war were now being filled on a permanent basis by homosexuals and those declared unfit for military service; Gauleiters were stealing the personal effects of dead German soldiers. They mixed speculation with facts, gleaned from captured German personnel or Enigma transcripts. Not even astrological forecasts were too improbable to be pressed into service.

In retrospect, the black propaganda of both sides probably had less effect generally upon the war than on the peace which followed. The broadcasts were probably not widely believed and their entertainment content was such that they probably increased morale, rather than reducing it. The Germans took them seriously enough, however, and Goebbels felt no compunction in crying 'foul' at some of the British efforts at black propaganda: 'Whenever our High Command must keep silent about the operations on the front for military reasons, British propaganda is busy to create unrest among Germans.'

For those Germans who engaged in rumour-mongering, based on these broadcasts, he had the sternest of warnings: 'Such behaviour is not only criminal but is also utterly unfair to the soldiers who suffer such hardships on the front and to the Führer and his commanders who prepare the way to victory. Such rumour-mongers deserve death. Two have already been executed. . . .'

THE CENSOR CALLS. . . .

The zeal of mail censors could be misplaced, often along with their sense of humour. A woman in Eire sent her daughter in England some eggs. The latter sent a letter of thanks, in which she jokingly remarked 'I wish you would send me a cow!' The letter was duly returned by the censor with the following words added: 'Import of cattle into England from Eire by private individuals is not permitted. This letter, therefore, which asks for a prohibited article, is returned to sender.'

The British took an altogether more gentlemanly approach to the matter, as this Ministry of Information advertisement shows:

What do I do if I come across German or Italian broadcasts when tuning my wireless? I say to myself: 'Now this blighter wants me to listen to him. Am I going to do what he wants? I remember that German lies over the air are like parachute troops dropping on Britain – they are part of the plan to get us down – which they won't. I just remember nobody can trust a word the Haw Haws say. So, just to make them waste their time, I switch 'em off or tune 'em out.'

One, more lasting, effect of these broadcasts may have been to increase the threshold of tolerance to sexual transgressions, and thus pave the way, twenty years later, for the permissive society of the 1960s.

Careless Talk

The first days of the war led to entire British towns being destroyed by bombing, including, in some cases, attacks from Zeppelins, and the first case of a German gas attack – or at least it did according to the fertile imaginations of rumour-mongers up and down the country. The bombing raids were, of course, pure fiction, while the gas attack that somebody smelt was in fact a fire in a Southampton pickle factory.

The Ministry of Information tried, throughout the war and with varying degrees of success, to stem the flow of rumours. One explanation for their proliferation (and for the initial high audience figures for the official German rumour-monger, Lord Haw-Haw) was that the public did not believe what they were being told by the official media. Mass Observation reported that, in the early weeks of the war, people said it was useless to buy newspapers since all the front pages were identical and could not be trusted. Lack of anything happening on the war front was taken as evidence that we were not being told the truth. Another reason given for spreading rumours was that they helped to spice up the boredom that was a central part of wartime life.

Rumours in wartime take on many and varied forms – troops evacuated from Dunkirk who left their kit behind would have it docked from their pay; the London park railings, sawn down for the war effort, had been found to be useless and secretly dumped off Portsmouth; further afield, the Japanese broadcaster Tokyo Rose was in fact the missing aviator Amelia Earhart, captured in the Pacific and brainwashed; a dog was found, near Pearl Harbor after the raid, barking in morse code to an offshore submarine.

Some rumours had positive propaganda functions. The suggestion that carrots helped you see in the dark not only encouraged a healthy diet (not to mention one that was not in short supply); it was also used to account for the success of our night-fighter pilots and disguise the success of radar (or was this another rumour?) Another was that Lord Woolton's national wholemeal loaf had remarkable aphrodisiac qualities. (Ernest Bevin, for one, was not seduced by this – he claimed this unpopular bread was inedible and gave him wind.)

But there was more than mere disapproval for rumour-mongering. Douglas Sunderland of Cokington, Derbyshire, got three months in gaol for handing round a propaganda leaflet dropped by the Luftwaffe. Relaying simple information could be classed as spreading alarm and despondency and would get you into trouble. Maidenhead milkman George Kirkham was fined for telling people that there would be no newspapers that day, since London had been bombed and the presses stopped, and Charles Back of Hull got six weeks for telling people that Scarborough had been bombed. By August 1940 the Home Secretary was telling Chief Constables to deal with such cases with a caution if at all possible, unless the offence were serious or repeated. By then, he had no fewer than twenty-eight cases of such prosecutions where the case was felt to need review.

8
War Crimes

Not a week passes without the Ministry of Food prosecuting hundreds of food offenders and the Board of Trade dozens of offenders against clothes rationing and quota laws. Cheating the excess profits tax is now so universally and well tried that accountants and tax inspectors no longer trouble to cross-question. . . . When food rationing was introduced it was considered smart to circumvent the law. When clothes rationing came in June 1941 it was thought to be clever to dress round the rules, convert crepe de chine sheets into dresses or blankets into coats, buy up loose coupons from street vendors, purchase clothes without coupons at dishonest shops and in general cheat the Board of Trade.

City journalist Nicholas Davenport, from his 1942 book
Vested Interests or Common Pool.

The opening months of the war saw a marked reduction in the nation's prison population. This was not, however, the result of a patriotic outbreak of law-abiding citizenship. All prisoners with less than three months to serve were released early, to make way for the influx of aliens interned in the interests of national security. (One exception to the amnesty was IRA prisoners – they got no remission, but the government did at least pay them the backhanded compliment of allowing the operation of their Special Operations Executive to be influenced by the Republican terrorist model.) The disruption of war, not to mention the blackout, created ideal conditions for crime, and the wealth of wartime regulation added a whole new repertoire of criminal offences.

A host of different factors need to be understood to unravel the crime statistics for the war years. Reported crimes rose from their 1939 level of 303,711 (England and Wales) to 478,394 in 1945, and the number of people convicted was similarly up, by 54 per cent. There was a decline in non-serious crime, which can be explained in large part by, first, the decline in motoring offences (owing to the decline in the amount of motoring) and, second, a reduction in the recorded incidence of drunkenness. This latter was due to: (a) many of the potential drunks having been recruited into the armed forces; (b) spirits being in very short supply; and (c) beer, while unrationed, being very weak and the pubs prone to running out of it. The police also showed a markedly greater tolerance towards drunkenness in wartime, as the Police Review openly admitted.

Against this, there were new classes of offence for people to commit in a heavily regulated wartime society, and the opportunity to commit them was enhanced by the cover of the blackout and the substantial reduction in the numbers of police. (Police numbers in England and Wales, including special constables, fell from 82,232 to 59,574 over the war years.) Moreover, the average age of the force rose sharply, as younger policemen joined the armed forces, and the level of sick leave also doubled.

Looting

Looting was one crime which attracted a particularly robust response from the authorities, as this memorandum from the Home Secretary to the Prime Minister in December 1940 shows:

> There have been many cases of looting which, though not of the gravest kind, must be regarded seriously. Damage to premises, including the shattering of windows, has led to the exposure of a great deal of valuable property, and the police are finding much difficulty in providing adequate means of protection, particularly during the hours of black-out. The temptation to take exposed goods is very great and unless drastic penalties are imposed there is substantial danger that the practice may become still more widespread. Representations have been made to me from various quarters as to the need for doing everything possible to protect those who have been injured by enemy action from suffering still further injury owing to the looting of their possessions. . . . I am told that the imposition of long sentences in certain cases has already had some deterrent effect, but looting is still a serious problem.

Churchill was concerned about both the inconsistency in sentencing policy and the severity with which some cases of looting were treated, at a time when able-bodied men were in desperately short supply. When six Auxiliary Fire Service officers received five years for stealing whisky for their own immediate consumption, he wrote to the Home Secretary:

> There seems to be great disparity in these sentences. I wonder whether any attempt is being made to standardise the punishments inflicted for this very odious crime. Five years' penal servitude for stealing whisky for immediate consumption seems out of proportion when compared to sentences of three to six months for stealing valuables. Exemplary discipline is no doubt necessary, as people must be made to feel that looting is stealing. Still, I should be glad to know that such cases are being reviewed and levelled out.

Morrison resisted pressure from the Prime Minister to promote a more lenient sentencing policy for looters, not least on the grounds that sentencing policy was not part of his purview. In fact, looting had a possible maximum penalty of life imprisonment or even the death sentence, and in October 1940, the lower courts had their sentencing discretion extended from three months to a year, for those cases which came before them.

Cases of looting started to come before the courts in significant numbers more or less as soon as the bombs started to fall. September 1940 saw 539 cases come before the London courts alone, and the following month the number rose to 1,662. In February 1941 a gas company inspector reported over three thousand cases of theft from coin-operated gas meters, most of them in bombed-out houses. Intensive police efforts to combat looting in bombed areas backfired

---

A LIFETIME'S SUPPLY

Looting was widespread in the Channel Islands, as residents fled from the occupying forces. In one case, the Germans found the tiny flat of one James Rutter packed from floor to ceiling with more household goods and furnishings than he could have used in a lifetime. So bad was the case that even the Germans put him on trial.

on them when burglars turned instead to the areas that had escaped bombing, which they now found to be delightfully free of police.

Press reports gave a misleading impression of the composition of the looters – 42 per cent of the guilty parties in reported cases were people in positions of trust, such as ARP wardens or fire service officials, and about 90 per cent of the reported cases had no previous criminal record. However, a fuller analysis of the cases within the metropolitan area showed that 14 per cent of the offenders were schoolboys and a full 41 per cent were under 21. Cases involving youths tended to be reported much more rarely. Some of the looting was thought to be organised – among the most macabre examples were those who entered the bombed ruins of the Café de Paris and stripped the dead of their jewellery and wallets before even the civil defence workers got in there. But the majority was spontaneous and minor. American reporter Ed Murrow found it difficult to treat some of it as a crime:

> Most of the articles picked up from the bombed houses are of little intrinsic value: a book, or a piece of ribbon, or a bucketful of coal – that sort of thing. Many people convicted of looting are certainly not criminal types and have not taken the objects for reasons of personal gain. One has a strange feeling – or at least I have – in looking at the contents of a bombed house or shop, that the things scattered about don't belong to anyone.

At first, magistrates were quite lenient in their sentencing – albeit while making much play of the possibility of the death sentence. After receiving a good deal of criticism for such leniency, the courts became much more severe, especially to those in positions of trust, whose cases tended to be referred to the Assizes for heavier sentences.

Theft

All else being equal, one might have expected the incidence of theft to fall during the war years, since a sizeable proportion of the criminal classes would have been drafted into the armed forces. However, all that happened was that theft decreased in the inner cities and increased greatly in the areas around army camps.

The arrival of the British Expeditionary Force in France was also accompanied by a small crime wave, as a significant proportion of the Army's supplies and equipment disappeared into the arms of the French black market. Special police forces had to be sent to stamp it out.

Others of a criminal bent were able to avoid the draft by taking on essential war work, such as firewatcher, where the war offered new career opportunities, such as looting. Criminals with physical handicaps, such as weak hearts or lameness, would of course be exempted from the draft. They could thereafter supplement their criminal income to the tune of up to £150 a time by impersonating others wishing to be exempted at their medical boards.

At home, wartime shortages provided a great temptation to would-be thieves, and the war saw some substantial growth in the levels of theft. The railways lost goods carried on them to the tune of £1 million in 1941 alone. Many of the railway police had joined the armed forces, and their replacements, often called out of retirement, were not always energetic enough to cope with criminals. Similarly, on the docks, pilfering had long been seen as one of the perks of a poorly paid and insecure job, as well as part of a class war against the employers. Groups of dockers operated their own form of insurance, organising a collection for any of their number who was caught and fined.

THE POLICE ARE IN THE DARK

The blackout provided a cover for a variety of nefarious activity, as the chapter on wartime sexual activity illustrated. In the first weeks of the war, *The Times* reported an outbreak of blackout hooliganism, with assaults on police officers under the cover of darkness being a particular problem. As Detective Sergeant Hare told Mitcham Police Court: 'Gangs of roughs are taking advantage of the blackout. It is not safe for respectable people to be about.'

The courts warned of severe punishment for such behaviour and, as an example, sentenced Mary Maher (35) of Tipperary to six months' hard labour for taking on two police officers, who were trying to advise her flatmate about the blackout regulations. This case also brought to light the unexpected potential of the gas-mask as an offensive weapon.

Police action against dockyard theft was also relatively selective. Anti-theft campaigns would be discontinued when the dockers' cooperation was needed (for example, during wage negotiations) and stepped up again once a deal was struck. Even so, prosecutions for theft at Birkenhead docks, for example, increased threefold between 1939 and 1942.

Ration books were a new and lucrative item to steal, with a street value of up to £5 a book. A single raid in Romford netted ration books worth £500,000, which at today's values makes the Great Train Robbery look like petty pilfering.

Petrol became a particularly prized commodity, but not everyone was equally adept at stealing it. One group of London ambulance drivers found themselves in court, after one of their number's cars ran out of petrol. They broke into the ambulance depot at night and stole a gallon from one of the vehicles. However, while trying to steal a second gallon, one of them knocked over a hurricane lamp. The ensuing blaze destroyed the garage and fifteen ambulances.

Another man, charged with the theft of 500 gallons of petrol, offered what must have been the least plausible defence in the history of crime. He told the court that he had just switched on the tap on the tank to get a few drops of petrol for his lighter, but it had gushed out and he had been forced to direct it into a large container that had just happened to be standing next to him. The magistrates gave him twelve months' hard labour, commenting: 'This offence almost amounts to treason. In any other country, the defendant would have had his head cut off for this offence.'

However, petrol thieves did at least find a use for their redundant gas-masks. Black Market petrol, stolen from commercial or military sources, contained a tell-tale red dye. By first pouring the petrol through a gas-mask, the dye could be removed and the petrol would look just like the kind bought legitimately at the petrol station (if one had the coupons, that is).

Profiteers

Profiteers tended to be lumped together with looters in the public consciousness: 'They do not steal and they would call themselves traders or businessmen, but they are looters none the less.' There are no separate figures for profiteering – their cases form part of the 17,319 prosecutions under the Food Control Orders undertaken between September 1939 and the end of April 1941. By September 1941 over two thousand cases per month were coming before the courts.

It had become front page news in May 1941, when a strongly worded statement by the Food Price Committee, North Midland Region, claimed that 'speculation is rampant . . . people who render no service in distribution are enriching themselves at the expense of the consumer . . . prices have in consequence risen out of all reasonable proportion . . . and the trivial fines imposed by some benches are a matter of ridicule'.

However, a contrary view was that the regulations relating to price increases were a bureaucratic nightmare that made it almost impossible for even the most honest shopkeeper to stay within the law, and that some of the prosecutions showed a bureaucratic small-mindedness that bordered on the vindictive.

In January 1940 the provisions of the 1939 Prices of Goods Act came into force. This took 21 August 1939 as the base date at which, it was assumed, prices had not been inflated by the expectation of war. The Act made it a criminal offence to sell 'price regulated' goods at more than their price at that date, plus an increase representing the actual rise in costs and expenses since that time. All over the country price regulation committees were set up to investigate complaints from the public. The first prosecution was of a shopkeeper from Reading, who had an unblemished trading record going back forty-five years. In a long and complicated case, involving the services of a chartered accountant and a near-philosophical debate about the relative qualities of imported batteries and their British counterparts, it was established that the retailer had sold two torch batteries for 10½d each more than the price permitted by the Act. The case was dismissed as a first offence, on payment of £4 13s costs.

A review of the first three months' activity by the Southern Region Price Regulation Committee hardly suggested that it was single-handedly turning the tide of the war. In that time, they carried out just three prosecutions (including the one mentioned above). Even the press could not work up enough wartime patriotism to take them entirely seriously:

Not Price Regulated. Woman's Divorce Costs.
Strange Complaints to Anti-Profiteering Committee.

A woman has written to the Price Regulation Committee for the Southern Region, complaining that she is dissatisfied with the charges made by her solicitors when she divorced her husband!

A man complained that he had paid too much for his house and wanted to know if he could be assisted to get the excess money back again!

These instances were related by Mr Leo Page, the Chairman of the Committee, in a press interview this week.

The Prices of Goods Act has now been in operation for three months. During that time, the Southern Region Committee has received about a hundred complaints, and at least three-quarters of them referred to articles which are not covered by the Board of Trade order. Articles included workmen's tea cans, whisky and throat pastilles.

None the less, during the course of the war, the rules were enforced with what sometimes seemed Draconian severity. One grocer was fined 7 guineas with 7 guineas costs for making 3½d excess profit over a four-month period. In no case did an individual case of his profiteering come to more than 1s 4d. Another retailer, who sold razor blades at above the approved price, was fined the amazing sum of £376 15s (including costs). His total profit on a packet of razor blades was 1s ½d.

On occasion, even the committees rebelled at the regulations they were being asked to enforce. In Birmingham the local

---

WATCH OUT, THERE'S A SNOOPER ABOUT

Whole armies of snoopers were said to be on the prowl, ready if necessary to entrap the unwary shopkeeper into breaching the regulations. One popular story (said to be apocryphal) was that of the inspector disguised as a rain-soaked hiker, staggering off the moors into the village shop. He would then beg for dry socks without the necessary coupons, promising faithfully to mail them back to the shop.

Chairman, Mr A.L. Bill, condemned some of the cases being brought before them as 'ridiculous and trivial'. He went on: 'I hope the Committee will be more wise in future than to waste the time of the court with such trivialities.'

The cases before them on this occasion related to an overcharge of 3d on bacon and several of ¼d (i.e. a farthing) each on sugar and butter. The defendant said that the bacon overcharge was a simple oversight and that the others were simply due to a shortage of farthings. In another case a retailer confessed his ignorance of the fact that he required a licence to sell a can of peas. All but one of the cases was dismissed.

The Black Market and Hoarding

> This is not a mere matter of self-interest. It will lighten the burden on transport in the event of war.
>
> The *Evening Standard* before the war, encouraging housewives to lay in stocks of food.

Looking back in his memoirs, Lord Woolton, the Minister for Food, took a rather rosy view of the black market during the war: 'The penalties for the infringement of the food regulations were literally ruinous . . . and the consequence was that [black marketeering] became so perilous an occupation that few indeed dared embark on it. . . .' He also concluded, rather inconsistently, that: 'The fact that, in spite of all the scarcity of supplies and the rigidity of rationing, there was little or no black market in Britain was a tribute to the British people.'

His Ministry none the less managed to find enough evidence of it to occupy the time of 900 inspectors, armed with weapons like two years' imprisonment, £500 fines and forfeiture of capital up to three times the size of the offence.

The Field magazine, in March 1942, did not see it Lord Woolton's way:

> A year ago Lord Woolton, Minister of Food, made a speech in which he promised that the Black Market would be driven out of business. In the intervening period the Black Market has grown from a small individual 'racket' into an enormous, highly efficient and totally unscrupulous organisation. Now

Parliament has discussed repressive measures. So much for speeches.

Lord Woolton, one of the very few men whose Ministry has been a success, undoubtedly did his best. The Ministry of Food undertook a vast number of prosecutions, but fines mean nothing to gentry who are making enormous profits. Furthermore, these prosecutions touched only the fringe of the market. All these men with the interesting names who have been fined, and in a few cases sentenced to a month or so in prison, are the servants. The big men in business have not been touched and the big men do not object to fines at all and are not moved by prison sentences that do not touch them personally. Make no mistake about it. There are big men at the back of the Black Market; there is a big distributive organisation; there is a big warehousing organisation; there is a highly effective intelligence service. The Black Market is not made up of a large number of individuals acting independently, but a large number of individuals well organised. The thefts are on too large a scale for it to be otherwise. You cannot store 40,000 eggs nor 5 tons of meat on the kitchen shelves. And these quantities are not easy to distribute.

The Commissioner of the Metropolitan Police kept his options open in his 1944 annual report, saying that he was not able 'to substantiate by any reliable evidence the somewhat lurid descriptions published in some newspapers of super-criminals controlling a vast organisation with widespread tentacles. This may nevertheless be a true picture . . . it is significant that cases of receiving in 1944 were three and a half times as many as in 1938. . . .'

Some towns – Romford, Chelmsford, Watford and others – became particularly well known as centres of the black market. Other forms of crime – pickpocketing, gambling and illegal drinking – grew up on the back of it. Stallholders in Romford were warned by the council of instant expulsion from their pitches if they were caught in illegal dealing.

The black market grew in importance as the war went on, particularly after a military foothold was re-established in France. A popular arrangement was to take £sterling to France, where they could be sold on the black market for about 500ff each, two and a half times their official rate. This was then used to buy liqueurs, perfumes, silk stockings, cosmetics and other items unobtainable in Britain. So great was the volume of material flowing into the country (there were even reports of planes being chartered for the purpose) that black market prices were themselves depressed in a flooded market.

Another favourite trick was for a trader to buy up the short end of a lease on a shop, fill the window with a lot of flashy, cheap goods and, once potential customers were lured in, offer them all sorts of black market commodities at inflated prices. He would make his profit and be gone before the authorities caught up with him. Other traders would impose a rule that customers could not buy the item they wanted unless they also bought another, unwanted, item with it.

The officials trying to enforce trading rules were swamped with the volume of the work and boggled by the complexity of the wartime legislation. This offered a wealth of loopholes to the unscrupulous trader. Eggs sold for breeding purposes were exempted from rationing. Defective and most second-hand goods were also exempt. Health regulations were also flouted in the food shortage – horsemeat was sold as beef and diseased and otherwise unfit meat found its way on to the market.

Rationing opened up vast opportunities for fraud and theft at every stage of the process. The coupons were much easier to forge than the banknotes which had been a flourishing pre-war industry; crooked postmen would steal ration books when delivering them, in addition to the other thefts mentioned earlier. Coupons were only supposed to be removed by the shopkeeper, except when goods were being bought by mail order. This loophole opened up a massive market in the sale of coupons, especially by the poor, who did not have the cash to benefit from the ration themselves.

Various frauds were available to obtain extra coupons. In the first year of clothes rationing, around 800,000 people lost their ration books, and 27 million new coupons were issued as replacements. No doubt many of these losses were genuine, but a proportion were not. Some people adopted dual identities, and claimed the ration books to go with them. Anyone presenting themselves as being bombed out could qualify for 120 clothing coupons and £12 from the Assistance Board.

Retailers used to exchange the coupons they collected at the post office for vouchers, with which they could buy more rationed goods for sale. The GPO refused to take on the fiddly job of counting envelopes full of individual coupons, and it was left to random (and not sufficiently frequent) checks by Ministry officials. As a result, some of the envelopes handed in contained far fewer than the number of coupons claimed, or even just pieces of paper torn from the telephone directory. Finally, even used coupons, on their way to be pulped, were sometimes stolen and 'recycled'.

New classes of criminal were created by wartime rationing. Deserters from the army, of whom there were an estimated twenty thousand by the end of the war, had no ration books and no papers, and were virtually forced to turn to crime. Normally law-abiding citizens were driven to evade the ration by a scheme which, from 1942, only gave a man a new overcoat every seven years, a new pullover every five years and a new shirt every twenty months.

Hoarding

Hoarding of goods also became a serious offence during the war, though in the immediate pre-war period retailers encouraged their customers to buy in a good stock of non-perishable foods in against future shortages. The new post of Food Executive Officer was created, whose job it was to track down hoarders like this case, reported in the *Berkshire Chronicle* in 1942:

Food Hoarding Prosecution. Caversham Woman Fined.
Defence Plea that she acted Innocently.

Mrs Elsie Lilian Carter, of 10a Bridge Street, Caversham, appeared at Reading Borough Police Court on Monday on five summonses of food hoarding. It was alleged that the defendant had acquired an excessive quantity of preserves and of tinned fruit, tinned steak, fish and milk.

It was stated for the prosecution that these were the first proceedings to be taken by the Reading Borough Food Executive Officer for food hoarding. An excess quantity of food referred to anything in excess of the household's requirements for seven days. In this case, the household comprised two persons. An Inspector was sent to this address in consequence of information received. He asked Mrs Carter to show him her stores, and she opened the door of a kitchen cupboard in which there was a fairly generous supply of household commodities, such as one would expect to find in any normal household. The Inspector asked Mrs Carter if she had any other stores, to save him searching the house. She replied, 'If I have, it has slipped my memory.'

In a recess under the stairs and in an adjoining cupboard the Inspector afterwards found large quantities of food. These included 75lb of preserves, 196 tins of fish, 82 tins of milk, 81 tins of meat and 98 tins of mixed fruit. Invoices were produced in court to show that the stores were purchased wholesale from Messrs Kingham since the beginning of the war.

On behalf of his client, Mr Berry submitted that none of the goods had been purchased during a period when they had been rationed, so there could be no breach of the rationing orders. . . . Mrs Carter had acted innocently under a misapprehension that she was doing the right thing, a misapprehension due to taking notice of government pamphlets.

In announcing fines on the five summonses totalling £36 15s, the Chairman, Mr A.G. West, said that the bench considered it a bad case of hoarding. In addition to the fines, the defendant would have to pay £10 10s costs.

Mrs Carter was allowed one month to pay. Mr Edminson said that the Ministry of Food had the power, if they chose to exercise it, to requisition the food stocks upon payment of the wholesale prices. I do not know if that procedure would be followed in the case of Mrs Carter.

Officers and Gentlemen

At a time when one's rank could be the key to success, from social advancement to winning the hearts of the opposite sex, the courts saw a regular stream of cases of people impersonating officers. So it was that James Fisher, of no fixed abode, found himself up before the court for impersonating a captain in the Royal Horse Guards, complete with DSO, MC and the French Croix de Guerre (all that was missing from his set, it seems, was the Iron Cross).

He told the court that it was just vanity and over-keenness on his part. He had served in the First World War, retiring as a captain, and had applied to serve again. The result of his application was pending, but it cannot have been helped when, on learning that he had a previous conviction for a similar offence, the court put him away for three months.

In similar vein, a 27-year-old dockyard labourer from Gillingham, Alfred Hancock, got two months' hard labour for impersonating an RAF flight lieutenant. He pointed out to the court how easy it was to do. Most of the leading tailors offered a service of making officers' uniforms to measure and there appeared to be little or no control over who ordered them. The Chairman of the Magistrates observed 'it seems to us most unfortunate'.

For those who wished to take their delusion to a higher level, there was always the prospect of trying to buy yourself a proper commission. Sir Curtis George Lampson (Bart) got eighteen months for inciting a young man to offer an inducement to obtain a commission in the army. The victim was told that, for £600, a commission could be obtained within twenty-four hours. Lampson promised to see a viscount of his acquaintance, to arrange it. The viscount was, of course, non-existent. As the War Office pointed out: 'It cannot be said too strongly that there is nobody in the War Office who could be approached in this way. This sort of thing does not and cannot happen.'

Others found a far cheaper alternative than buying uniforms or commissions. Alfred Jones of Wednesfield had always fancied being a policeman, and decided, while drunk, that the time had come to get some practice in. He staggered up to a member of the public and, claiming to be a plain-clothes policeman, asked him to accompany him to the station. The person approached did not believe him, but summoned a real police officer who promptly did just what Jones had asked. He was fined £1. Another 17-year-old youth told a young lady of his acquaintance that he was a secret service agent. He gave her a 'secret' letter to take care of and later phoned her, pretending to be an air commodore. He told her that the 'secret agent' had been killed parachuting into enemy territory and asked her to bring the secret letter to a special rendezvous. The young lady sent it via a policeman and the would-be James Bond found himself in court.

Juvenile Crime and Corporal Punishment

A considerable increase in juvenile crime is causing concern in many districts; the explanation given is generally the slackening of parental control, coupled with the unsettling effect of unprecedented high wages, which are now being paid to boys who take the place of men. . . . It is thought by social workers that lack of any incentive to save, plus the fact that there are few reasonable pleasures on which to spend this 'easy money', must create serious danger for young people, at a time when violence and destruction on a vast scale are inevitably held up as an admirable human activity.

A Liverpool schoolmaster alleges that in the city there are at least 200 'cellar clubs' where boys and girls indulge in 'an orgy of gambling and drinking'.

There has been some increase in the volume of complaints . . . particularly of the immorality of young girls and the behaviour of children. There is particular concern about the damaging of property: breaking of windows, slashing of cinema seats, smashing electric light bulbs in trains, and damage to parks and gardens are alleged.

Factors blamed are:

(a) Lack of parental control, particularly where mothers are at work. Women, it is suggested, should not be able to take up full-time jobs unless they are able to satisfy the authorities that their children will be looked after in their absence.

(b) The irresponsibility of parents, particularly of working mothers 'with money to spare', who spend their time in pubs and cinemas.

These two Home Intelligence reports, from July 1941 and June 1944 respectively, highlight the growing problem of youth crime during the war years. The causes identified by the complainants are in some cases unique to the war, but in many others are common to the years of peace and prosperity that were to follow. The delinquent behaviour described in the second extract could have come just as easily from a report on 1950s teddy boys or the mods and rockers of the 1960s.

A Home Office circular published in the middle of 1941 reported

FRAUD AMONG THE DOLLY MIXTURES
We had a shop down our road; a blind lady was the proprietor. We used to put a piece of blotting paper under the sweet coupon page on the ration book, and trace round it and cut out the blotting paper in the shape of coupons. The old lady felt the texture and shape of the blotting paper and was deceived into thinking it was the coupons and we took the sweets.

Girl aged six, quoted in Westall.

that in the first year of the war there had been a 41 per cent increase in the numbers of under-14s found guilty of indictable offences. The increase in the 14–17 age group was 22 per cent. Among other causes, the government blamed unsettled wartime domestic circumstances, with many more absent fathers and mothers working, leading to increased truancy. But in some areas of major cities it was impossible at times not to be truant, since all the schools had been closed in anticipation of a total evacuation of schoolchildren. Thus eighty thousand schoolchildren were running wild in London by the end of 1940.

Amateur sociologists were not short of other explanations for the growth of juvenile crime, which had started before the war – when they had blamed unemployment and boredom. Now, for some perverse reason, it was said to be due to the high salaries payable to young people in war work. Then there was the growth of the get-rich-quick society, also marked by the import of American fashions. The Chief Constable of Nottingham, Captain Popkess, drew a comparison in his 1937 annual report between the growth in juvenile crime in Britain and its almost complete absence in Germany. This, he explained, was mainly due to the wholesome influence of the Hitler Youth movement. A more plausible explanation for a pre-war growth in recorded juvenile crime was a change in the way young people were dealt with, following the 1933 Children and Young Persons Act.

During the early years of the war, the figures cannot have been helped by the fact that all Borstal inmates who had served over six months of their sentence were freed as part of the general clearout of the prison population. Left with no support, about half of these young people had re-offended by the end of the war.

Some magistrates responded to the rising tide of crime by having a growing number of young offenders birched. But a case in Hereford drew attention to the incompatibility between birching and the right of appeal. On 12 January 1943 two boys aged 11 and 13 were found guilty of malicious damage, following break-ins at a school and a hostel. They were placed in care and sentenced to 4 strokes of the birch each. The sentence was carried out before they had a chance to have their appeal heard, making it somewhat superfluous. There was a considerable public outcry about this case, and the Home Secretary was forced to intervene, telling Parliament that corporal punishment was not considered a suitable remedy for young offenders.

Public opinion was found to be divided on the matter of birching young offenders. The majority sided with the Home Secretary, but a sizeable minority supported the Chief Constable of Renfrewshire, who said with blood-curdling relish that he would 'use a green birch and cut them with it'. A Home Office memorandum at the end of the war cast doubt on the efficacy of birching as a deterrent and showed that its use had declined steadily since 1941, well before the publicity given to the issue by the Hereford case.

9
Women at War

What changes did the war bring about in the position of women? Both wars were said to have wrought, or at least accelerated, changes, opening up new areas of career opportunity and changing their legal status. In the First World War the Representation of the People Act 1918 gave the vote to married women over 30, though it took another ten years' campaigning for women to be given the vote on an equal footing with men. There was some debate as to whether it would have happened anyway – whether the climate of opinion had been prepared for an extension of the franchise before war broke out – but it was at least presented in some government circles as a recognition of their contribution to the war effort. Was there any comparable change in the situation of women during the Second World War?

At the time the coalition government formed, in May 1940, there were only twelve women MPs in Parliament. They used to meet in a lady members' room, known as 'the boudoir', to work out common policies across party lines. Even so, there were divisions among them, between those who wanted equality and those who wanted measures to take the pressure off working-class women – what might be characterised as the 'free milk' movement. They none the less had some successes, such as promoting a cross-party Woman Power Committee.

Before the war, women in the civil service (and in some other professions) were expected to resign upon getting married. Many chose instead to live in sin, or to keep their marriage a secret, rather than lose their jobs. Some 300,000 married women were thought to be doing this at the outbreak of war. Over and above this, there were moves from among the male staff to ban all women entirely from working in the service. An anti-feminist organisation called Fairfield was set up in 1939, with this as one of its central aims. It attracted three thousand members in the first four months of its existence.

Equal Pay

Three main attempts were made to secure recognition at least of the principle of equal pay for women during the war years. In December 1941 a group of MPs attempted to block the National Service (Number Two) Act, which sought to conscript certain groups of women, unless a provision for equal pay was included. They failed in this, not least because the Act discriminated in favour of women in other ways – for example, no mother of a child aged under 14 could be conscripted, and only single women between 19 and 30 were covered by the legislation. By 1943 women up to the age of 50 could be directed into war work, but even then, a woman's duties as a housewife were sufficient to exempt her from full-time service.

The 1939 Personal Injuries Act was a long-standing target of women's interest groups. Under this, a woman suffering injuries from a bomb received 7s per week less than a man receiving comparable injuries. There was widespread public support for equality of treatment in these circumstances – Hitler's bombs, at least, did not exercise any discrimination about whom they landed on.

But even here, the case was argued (at least in part) in a way which was discriminatory towards women, treating them as chattels. One of the arguments commonly advanced against equal pay for women at the time was that they would normally be able to rely upon their husband's income, and therefore did not have the same need of independent means. However, in this case, a woman injured by a bomb was deemed to have worse prospects for marriage, and it was therefore held to be wrong in these circumstances to treat them as dependants for compensation purposes.

The government finally conceded the principle of equal compensation in this case in April 1943. One of the reasons why it was able to do so was that the circumstances related so clearly to war conditions that they offered up no precedent for the post-war world.

The third battle for equal pay came in the context of the 1944 Education Act's passage through Parliament. Here, the House narrowly voted in favour of including a provision for equal pay for teachers. The government, strongly urged by Winston Churchill, reintroduced the matter back into the House and turned it into a vote of confidence. The War Cabinet argued that: 'It would be

FAMILY ALLOWANCE – MOTHER'S BONUS

Family Allowance was one of the few parts of the Welfare State introduced during the war years. But one aspect of it which impinged upon women was the question of to whom it belonged. Eleanor Rathbone MP campaigned for twenty-five years for the payment of Family Allowance as a recognition of the value of a mother's work.

The government's Reconstruction Committee decided that either parent should be able to collect the benefit, but that it had to 'belong' to one parent or the other for legal purposes. They chose the father, as the person legally responsible for the child's maintenance, and because Family Allowance was designed to supplement family income, not to provide in full for the needs of the child. The government did not want to do anything to weaken the father's sense of responsibility for the upkeep of his children. They were heavily lobbied against this, and threatened with a coalition-breaking amendment in Parliament. It was finally decided to put the matter to a free vote, which went in favour of the mothers.

disastrous to depart from the principle of non-interference with the decisions of independent tribunals on wage questions.'

In short, they feared that the precedent would have disastrous knock-on effects throughout the economy. The proposal was defeated and the government kicked the whole business into the long grass for the duration of the war by setting up a Royal Commission on Equal Pay. This did not report until 1946, and its damp squib of a report reinforced many of the traditional prejudices against women in the workplace – that they were less efficient than men, primarily home-focused and generally not the main breadwinner.

Meanwhile, male opposition to equal pay even found its way into sabotage. Night-shift workers in a factory in Birmingham deliberately loosened the bolts on a lathe to slow down its female day-shift user, regardless of the fact that it could have caused a serious accident. One of the few recommendations the Commission did make was to introduce equal pay for equal work in the 'common classes' of the civil service, where men and women worked together, But given that the civil service operated its own version of sexual apartheid, even this modest proposal was less than met the eye. None the less the Labour government of the day rejected even that, on the grounds that the nation could not afford it.

What's Thine is Mine, Dear

Even a married woman's savings were not her own. In a controversial and widely reported case in October 1943, the Court of Appeal found against Mrs Dorothy Blackwell, ruling that her £103 10s savings were not hers, but those of her husband, from whom she had been separated since 1941. She had saved them from her housekeeping allowance and from taking in lodgers from 1936 onwards. In summing up, the judges came down strongly in favour of the wife as chattel:

> Lord Justice Goddard suggested that she might let her husband go short of food while she 'built up a bank account'. Facetiously, he pictured her giving him corned beef instead of roast beef for dinner. It would, he said, be 'a dreadful thing' to hold that her savings were her own; it would tempt husbands to stint their wives. . . . Lord Justice Goddard opined that even if a married couple agreed that the savings out of the housekeeping money should be the wife's, such agreement would not necessarily constitute a legal contract. . . .
>
> Dismissing the appeal, Lord Justice Scott said: 'There is no justification at all for the contention that where a husband hands to his wife an allowance for housekeeping purposes, the husband is not to be taken, as a matter of law, as presenting savings out of that money to the wife for her sole use.' Meanwhile, Dr (Edith) Summerskill, supported by 43 other MPs, has tabled a motion calling for the amendment of the Married Women's Property Act 1882, to secure to married women a legal right to reasonable savings from their housekeeping allowance.
>
> The Catholic Citizen, 15 November 1943.

Home Intelligence found much public criticism of what was seen to be an antiquated law, though some husbands apparently found some amusement in it. They argued that wise housewives would not support the paying of a wage by a husband, as this 'would jeopardise the comradeship of married life'. Joking aside, the idea of companionate marriage had spread into the country from America in the inter-war years, and it is sometimes argued that the rising expectations of marriage arising from this were a contributory factor to the rising divorce rate after the war, discussed elsewhere.

A Woman's Place . . . is in the Factory

Before the war there was, in many parts of society, a strong tradition that a woman's place was in the home. During the First World War there had been industrial unrest when the government had tried to introduce women into traditionally male workplaces. Safeguards, such as legislation to guarantee that everything went back to pre-war practices once hostilities finished, had to be introduced. Ernest Bevin, the wartime Minister of Labour, was the pre-war head of the Transport and General Workers' Union. He knew that if women were to replace the missing male workers, it needed to be done as far as possible with the consent of the management and unions. He therefore set up joint consultative committees to negotiate the process. By giving trades unions equal representation with management on them (a marked improvement from the trades unions' distinctly second-class status in the days of Neville Chamberlain) he eased the way for an extra 1.5 million women to move into essential industries between 1939 and 1943.

It was no easy task to achieve the shift in the workforce. Fewer than half the women made redundant from non-essential industries during the first year of Churchill's premiership found their way into war industries. This was in no small part due to the boring and unpleasant nature of much of the work. Advertising campaigns were run during 1941, including the War Work Week parades and such memorable slogans as 'Don't queue like shirkers, join the women workers'.

This slogan, portraying the hard-pressed wartime housewife as 'a shirker', occasioned some resentment from both housewives and their husbands. Women pointed out that if they went out to work, there would be war at home, and one air raid warden spoke for many husbands:

If married women are called up home life will vanish and it will be very hard to revive it after the war. . . . Men in reserved occupations will come back to cold, untidy houses with no meal ready. Friction in the home will be greatly increased and with children evacuated there will be nothing to hold it together.

Eventually, conscription became one of the main means by which Bevin expanded the workforce. He was also helped by the economic necessity forced upon many wives whose husbands had been called up.

One of the ways in which he achieved this was by 'dilution' – the automation and de-skilling of traditional craft jobs. The unions were distinctly uneasy about this, and one of the prices Bevin paid for it was the 1942 Restoration of Pre-War Practices Act, a parallel to the First World War legislation ensuring a restoration of the status quo (and a reversal of any advances women had made) at the end of hostilities.

The unions also supported equal pay for women workers doing men's work – they did not want employers to be offered any financial incentive to replace their male members on a long-term basis. This was conceded, but with a number of qualifications. First, women moved only gradually up to the full male rate for the job; secondly, they only got it if they required no additional supervision or support to do the job; thirdly, employers were able to deny women male rates for jobs commonly performed by women, even if the individual concerned actually replaced a male worker. The management spent a good deal of time trying to prove that this or that task was commonly performed by women in pre-war years, and the unions were unhappy at this 'feminisation' of their members' work.

Management generally devoted much ingenuity to getting round the demands for equal pay. Lack of skills was one of the reasons most frequently cited for women's failure to advance, yet they constituted only 5 per cent of those on Government skills training schemes (and most of these were studying typing or sewing). When male and female workers – equally untrained – were brought in to operate machines in Rolls-Royce's Hillington factory near Glasgow in 1943, the men were put on to a higher grade. This led in October to a strike by the women workers, supported by most of the men. The dispute was finally resolved by attaching a grading system to each machine. But the grading system was itself gender-related. In practice, very few of the additional women drafted in to the essential industries moved into the most skilled and highly paid grades.

The government itself had no intention of interfering with the time-honoured practice of sex discrimination in the workplace, as this Treasury evidence to a Parliamentary Committee made clear:

> The principle of sex discrimination, whether it is right or wrong, is at present a matter of government policy, and it runs right through a large part of the social structure . . . the government should provide payment and observe conditions which corresponded to the best practice in comparable outside occupations, but it was not contemplated that the Government should run ahead of outside practice, and of course, sex differentiation is deeply embedded in industrial and – though to a slightly lesser extent – in commercial practice. . . .

Home and Work

Childcare was another of the factors that gave women the ability to work, and considerable numbers of places were eventually provided at day nurseries for the children of working mothers. However, the initiative got off to a slow start: by the start of 1941 only fourteen government-sponsored nurseries had been set up. The best efforts of the Ministry of Labour were often achieved over the dead bodies of the Ministry of Health and its local representative, the Medical Officer of Health. They tended to oppose the principle of workers' nurseries, fearing epidemics and traumatised children and mothers. Mothers who wanted (or needed) to work held their own demonstrations – 'baby riots' as the tabloid press called them. They stopped the traffic with their prams and chanted 'We want war work, we want nurseries'. Even so, there were never places for more than 25 per cent of all the children of working mothers, and many of these places rapidly disappeared with the ending of hostilities, again reversing the economic progress of women in the immediate post-war years.

The government made more or less half-hearted attempts to ease the passage of women into work. Circulars were sent to factory managers, showing them how to clean up the toilets and generally make their premises more female-friendly. Women welfare officers – known as Bevin's Belles – were sent round to advise factories on improvements and to fit women to the right jobs. The advice they offered would not always pass as enlightened today. Take, for example, this, in relation to women over 35: 'A factory like ours always has a lot of more or less 'childish' jobs that would irk a lively youngster in five minutes, but which we find ideal for the grannies.'

The traditional home-centred view of women was also emphasised by the Ministry of Information. Films such as *Jane Brown Changes Her Job* and *Night Shift* introduced what must have been sickening paragons of virtue to many of the audience – women who could take on a full-time job without sacrificing any of their feminine qualities. They were expected to be a hostess in the sitting room, chef in the kitchen, lathe operator in the factory (and in the bedroom? For 1940s audiences, possibly an ARP officer, checking the blackout?). Women's magazines and newspapers also promoted the theme of 'beauty as duty'. For example:

Women can help Win the War.
Bright Clothes create Cheerful Atmosphere

That clothes make the man is not really true, because many of the best men wear the best clothes and it is no easier to judge the real quality of a man than a baked potato by its jacket.

That women's clothes make the man is, however, undoubtedly true. If they are the right kind of clothes, snappy and bright and smart, they will make him cheerful and bright, too; if they are stuffy and dowdy and uninteresting they will be as depressing as an empty tobacco pouch to an air raid warden on a cold and foggy night. This aspect of the question is surely more important at wartime than at any other.

Modern wars are fought psychologically as well as physically, and no psychological campaign will achieve a greater victory than the campaign for brightness and cheer. This is a campaign that women can fight as well as men, and it is fought not with guns and tanks and suchlike nasty rough things, but with lovely crepe, satin and lovely moiré, which can provide a variety of life and brilliance and colouring that will put miles on to the marching power of the British Army.

This rhetoric was translated into hard decisions on the munitions front. Supplies of scarce steel and rubber were set aside to safeguard the supply of ladies' corsets; a fashion couturier was brought in to design nether garments for the women's services. Supplies of high-grade cosmetics were made available to women munitions workers, whose occupation left them prone to discoloration of the skin; ladies' hairdressers were in some cases designated as key war workers.

For most women workers, the supply of corsets ranked fairly low on their scale of concerns. More immediate were the practical problems of trying to combine the interminable queues in the shops with the long hours of war work in the factories. As we saw elsewhere, this caused a good deal of ill-feeling against those middle-class women who were able to get away with 'voluntary' war work, which allowed them much more time off, when required. A Ministry of Labour study in 1942 highlighted the scale of the problems the working wife faced:

A married woman with a house, a husband and children already has a full-time job which is difficult to carry out these days. Yet thousands of them are working long hours in factories. They are trying to do two full-time jobs. If they carry on with a mere half day per week off in ordinary factory hours they are achieving something marvellous.

Mass Observation also warned against the consequences of over-stretching the female labour force:

While winning the war is the only big consideration . . . if the bonds of family and continuity are weakened beyond a certain point, the morale, unity and work effort of the country is weakened.

There are thought to be still a lot of men who are avoiding fire-watching duty; women feel that all men should be called upon first. It is suggested that the ARP Service and the Home Guard, 'who spend long hours of duty doing nothing' and older men up to 65 or 70, should be brought in to fire watch.

Fire watching is not a fit job for women; this opinion appears to be held chiefly by men, who are said to be doubtful of women's ability to tackle difficult fires, and dubious about the propriety of girls being on duty with men employees at night.

Fire watching in target areas should be left to men; women should only fire watch in residential areas.

Women's Fire Guard order, Home Intelligence report,
27 August 1942.

10

The Legacy of War

. . . the purpose of victory is to live in a better world than the old world . . . each individual is more likely to concentrate upon his war effort if he feels that his government will be ready with plans for that better world . . . if these plans are to be ready in time, they must be made now.

William Beveridge

Did the war result in dramatic changes in post-war British society? During the war years there was much talk (albeit discouraged by the Conservative part of the wartime coalition) of the better world that Britons were fighting for. *Picture Post* magazine published an influential special edition in January 1941 under the title *A plan for Britain*. In it, they discussed much of what was to be the agenda for domestic politics in the war and immediately post-war years: social security, full employment, education and health reforms, and the need for land-use planning. Their editorial forged the link between the nation's war aims and what came after:

> Our plan for a new Britain is not something outside the war, or something after the war. It is an essential part of our war aims. It is, indeed, our most positive war aim. The new Britain is the country we are fighting for. And the kind of land we want, the kind of life we think the good life, will exercise an immense attraction over the oppressed peoples of Europe and the friendly peoples of America. . . .
>
> We believe that, after this war, certain things will be common ground among all political parties. It will be common ground, for example, that every Briton – man, woman or child – shall be assured of enough food of the right kinds to maintain him in full bodily health and fitness. It will be common ground that we must reform our system of education – so that every child is assured of the fullest education he can profit by. It will be common ground that our state medical service must be reorganised and developed so as to foster health, not merely

battle with disease. It will be common ground that the agricultural land of Britain must not again be given up to thistles and bracken; and that the beauty of our country and our buildings is the nation's heritage, not to be pawned away in plots to speculative builders.

Churchill attempted to kick the whole question of post-war reconstruction into the long grass for the duration, by making some token gestures towards the reformers. He set up a toothless War Aims Committee in August 1940, and in January 1941 gave responsibility for questions of post-war reconstruction to a failing Labour politician with a drink problem, Arthur Greenwood.

One of the papers submitted to the War Aims Committee, by the historian Arnold Toynbee, effectively set out the outlines of what came to be the Welfare State. Beveridge was not working in a vacuum. Many of the ideas he and others were advancing had become accepted wisdom among progressive intellectuals before the war, and it is unlikely that something along the lines of the Welfare State would have been long delayed had the war not intervened. In some respects, what Beveridge proposed was relatively conservative: it required contributions from workers, employers and the state, had flat rates of benefit and did not even produce a bare subsistence income. Subsistence levels of payment were to be gradually phased in but, by the mid-1950s, some 27 per cent of pensioner households were still receiving means-tested National Assistance supplements to their state pensions.

The only part of the Welfare State to be implemented during the war years was the Family Allowances Act of 1945. This paid 5s weekly to the mother for each child after the first. Some liked to think that the Act was prompted by high-minded concern about child poverty, which was thrown into such sharp relief by the evacuation. In fact, Churchill and his chancellor were more concerned with stimulating the birth rate and with finding a cheaper alternative to universal wage increases for doing so.

The one other major piece of supposedly reforming legislation to surface during the war years was the 1944 Education Act – the so-called Butler Act. But this achieved neither of the goals reformers wanted – equality of opportunity and improved technical education. Local authorities were empowered, rather than required, to take action, and the lack of vision of the Act has been blamed for Britain's poor post-war economic performance. One of its provisions – the raising of the school leaving age to fifteen – had been due to happen in September 1939, had not events elsewhere intervened. This aside, the Act was to a large degree a preserver of the status quo – protecting public and direct grant schools, making religious education mandatory, but doing little

> Colonel Blimp explains: 'Education must be stopped. If people couldn't read, they wouldn't know about the depression and confidence would be restored.'

for scientific and technical education. Perhaps the greatest achievement of the Act was that it got on to the statute book at all, given Churchill's reluctance to legislate about education. It did so partly to give the Conservatives some credibility as a reforming party, at a time when they were doing their best to obstruct or water down Beveridge's welfare state proposals.

The greatest single concern for the future among the wartime public was of a return to pre-war levels of mass unemployment. The 1944 White Paper on employment was supposed to address this, but in fact papered over the gulf which divided the wartime coalition partners on the matter. It was internally inconsistent and was condemned by both Labour's Aneurin Bevan and Conservative Party Chairman Ralph Assheton as a sham.

Land-use planning was another area that bitterly divided the coalition parties. Labour wanted comprehensive planning powers to help sweep away the legacy of polluted and overcrowded Victorian slums, to prevent ribbon development and to protect areas of natural beauty. The Conservatives were instinctively opposed to the state intervention involved and again did all that they could to delay and water down the proposals, short of outright opposition to what was at the time a very popular proposal. Again, a White Paper was prepared in an effort to conceal the divisions within government. It failed to do so, and was eventually shelved. The differences were never resolved. The Labour government in 1947, freed from the constraints of coalition, introduced comprehensive land-use planning, and one of the first acts of the next Conservative government in 1951 was to repeal some of its most important provisions.

Health reform was on the Labour agenda before it entered the wartime coalition. In this case, wartime demands on medical services meant that a form of *de facto* nationalisation of the private health sector was unavoidable, and, like Social Insurance, it was an idea whose time had come, regardless of the war. Wartime surveys showed that there was a majority of the population in favour of a National Health Service in all sectors of the population. Some of the main opposition to it came from within the medical profession itself. They were supported by the caretaker 1945 Conservative government, which produced an NHS White Paper which the official history of the Service describes as 'one of capitulation (to the BMA) rather than the emergence of consensus'. This was duly scrapped by the new Labour government, whose 1946 National Health Service Act was based on its own thinking.

The war years thus did little to produce new solutions to pre-war concerns with poverty, inequality, the environment and health. Neither did they produce any advances in the role of women to rival the granting of the vote after the First World War. As the previous chapter showed, trade union pressure ensured that most of the advances women made into new areas of employment were reversed, once peace was restored. Most of the workplace nursery provision disappeared, some employers reintroduced their bans on married women employees and many more applied a very restrictive policy on working practices that made their position more difficult. The post-war baby boom (birth rates rose from their lowest ever recorded level – 13.9/1000 in 1941 – to a record high of 20.6/1000 in 1947) left an increasing proportion of women with domestic responsibilities. By 1951 the proportion of women in the workforce had fallen back to its pre-war level.

Not everyone saw the advances made by women in the wartime economy as progress. One speaker in a debate in Parliament in 1945 referred to the war years for women as 'these empty wasted years, sacrificed in war; years deprived of husband, often of home and of the children we long to have'.

The Conservatives at their 1945 Party Conference considered the following resolution:

That with the object of maintaining in the peace the partnership between men and women as full citizens that has proved so successful in war, this Conference affirms its belief that it is in the interest of the nation that opportunities and rewards shall be open equally to both sexes in order to ensure that the best mind or hand shall have the same chance to excel.

They threw it out.

But one thing had changed. If the Archbishop of Canterbury was to be believed, Britain found itself on the edge of a moral abyss. In July 1945 the Archbishop called upon his flock to reject wartime morality and return to a Christian way of life. He spoke of:

> . . . the increase in divorce, the declining birth rate, the spread of venereal disease, and the number of young couples who, as always in wartime, wed in haste without any intention of fulfilling the primary purposes of marriage. This is partly due to the influence of wartime conditions, and partly to the flaunting sale of contraceptives.

But this was one genie that would not go back into the lamp. It has been suggested that the changed moral climate that the war produced, and the increasing immunity to shock over matters sexual that came from continued exposure to black propaganda, laid the foundation for the excesses of the swinging sixties, some twenty years in the future as the first post-war generation grew to maturity.

Bibliography

Addison, Paul, *The Road to 1945* (Pimlico 1994)

Bousquet, Ben and Douglas, Colin, *West Indian Women at War* (Lawrence & Wishart 1991)

Bryant, Mark (ed), *The Complete Colonel Blimp* (Bellew 1991)

Bunting, Madeleine, *The Model Occupation* (HarperCollins 1995)

Calder, Angus, *The Myth of the Blitz* (Cape 1991)

Chamberlin, E.R., *Life in Wartime Britain* (Batsford 1972)

Cockett, Richard, *Twilight of Truth* (Weidenfeld & Nicholson 1989)

Colpi, Terry, *The Italian Factor* (Mainstream 1991)

Costello, John, *Love, Sex and War* (Collins 1985)

De Courcy, Anne, *1939: The Last Season* (Thames & Hudson 1989)

Dewey, Peter, *War and Progress: Britain 1914–45* (Longman 1997)

Donnelly, Mark, *Britain in the Second World War* (Routledge 1999)

Ferris, Paul, *Sex and the British* (Michael Joseph 1993)

Fitzgibbon, Constantine, *The Blitz* (Macdonald 1957)

Fussell, Paul, *Wartime* (Oxford University Press 1989)

Gillman, Peter and Leni, *Collar the Lot!* (Quartet 1980)

Glover, Michael, *Invasion Scare 1940* (Leo Cooper 1990)

Grafton, Pete, *You, You and You!* (Pluto Press 1981)

Haining, Peter, *The Day War Broke Out* (W.H. Allen 1989)

Hamilton, Neil, *Great Political Eccentrics* (Robson 1990)

Hinsley, F.H., *British Intelligence in the Second World War* (HMSO 1993)

Hopkins, Eric, *A Social History of the English Working Classes* (Hodder & Stoughton 1979)

Humphries, Steve, *A Secret World of Sex* (Sidgwick & Jackson 1988)

Jackson, Carlton, *Who Will Take Our Children?* (Methuen 1985)

Kushner, Tony, *The Persistence of Prejudice* (Manchester University Press 1989)

Laybourn, Keith, *Britain on the Breadline* (Sutton 1990)

Lewis, Peter, *A People's War* (Thames Methuen 1986)

Livesey, Anthony (ed), *Are We at War? Letters to the Times* (Times Books 1989)

Longmate, Norman, *The Real Dads' Army, the Story of the Home Guard* (Hutchinson 1974)

Lynton, Mark, *Accidental Journey* (Overlook 1995)

Macmillan, James, *The Way it Happened 1935–50* (William Kimber 1980)

Marwick, Arthur, *The Home Front* (Thames & Hudson 1976)

McLaine, Ian, *Ministry of Morale* (George Allen & Unwin 1979)

Miller, Neil, *Out of the Past* (Vintage 1995)

Nicholls, Beverley, *The Unforgiving Minute* (W.H. Allen 1978)

Parsons, Martin, *I'll Take That One* (Beckett Karlson 1998)

Ponting, Clive, *1940: Myth and Reality* (Hamish Hamilton 1990)

Purvis, June (ed), *Women's History: Britain 1850–1945* (UCL Press 1995)

Readers' Digest, *Life on the Home Front* (Readers' Digest 1993)

Rowbotham, Sheila, *A Century of Women* (Viking 1997)

Schactman, Tom, *The Phoney War 1939–40* (Harper & Row 1982)

Smith, Harold L (ed), *Britain in the Second World War, A Social History* (Manchester University Press 1996)

Smithies, Edward, *Crime in Wartime* (George Allen & Unwin 1982)

Spectator, *Articles of War: the Spectator Book of World War Two* (Grafton 1989)

Stent, Ronald, *A Bespattered Page? The Internment of 'HM Most Loyal Aliens'* (Deutsch 1980)

Taylor, Eric, *Women Who Went to War* (Robert Hale 1988)

Valery, Anne, *Talking About the War* (Michael Joseph 1991)

Weale, Adrian, *Renegades: Hitler's Englishmen* (Weidenfeld & Nicholson 1994)

Westall, Robert, *Children of the Blitz* (Viking 1985)

Wicks, Ben, *No Time to Say Goodbye* (Bloomsbury 1988)

Ziegler, Philip, *London at War* (Sinclair Stevenson 1995)

Index

Bogs, Baths and Basins

The Story of Domestic Sanitation

David J. Eveleigh

Toilets, baths and washbasins are taken for granted in today's privileged society, but they are some of man's most indispensable facilities. How did they come about, and how did we live without them? From Roman times right up to modern-day luxury, David J. Eveleigh leads us chronologically through the story of sanitation. With the aid of new research he briefly covers the early rather primitive sanitation devices such as cesspits and urban dung heaps, and moves on to describe the advances that came with the onslaught of developing technology from the seventeenth to the twentieth century. Victorian developments in water supply and the growth of piping and steam-powered pumps finally lead to the comparative comforts of today. The progression of baths and washbasins is also followed, with evidence of their practicality rising as they became fixed rather than moveable, eventually resulting in the arrival of the en-suite bathroom in the nineteenth century along with the introduction of decorative tiles and attachments. With first hand accounts and evidence from diaries and contemporary records, this book traces the history of inventions that have affected everyone throughout history, told with a lively combination of human interest and drama.

HBK 224PP 244 X 172
130 B/W ILLUSTRATIONS 24 COLOUR ISBN 0 7509 2793 3

SUTTON PUBLISHING

www.suttonpublishing.co.uk

ORDERS TO: HAYNES PUBLISHING, SPARKFORD, NR YEOVIL, SOMERSET, BA22 7JJ
TELEPHONE: 01963 442105 FAX: 01963 440001

Who Killed Kit Marlowe?

A Contract to Murder in Elizabethan England
M.J. & Taliesin Trow

Kit Marlowe was the bad boy of Elizabethan drama, a schemer and player who inhabited a seamy underworld in which plots, real and imagined, proliferated. When he died, apparently in a tavern brawl, in Deptford in 1593, stabbed through the eye at the age of 29, it seemed he had only met the death that had been waiting for him. But is this the whole story? Or had Marlowe become embroiled in political intrigue, touched at its edges by the dangers of alchemy, atheism and homosexual love, which made him such a threat that he had to be expunged? This new investigation of Marlowe's death – and the life which provoked it – unravels the evidence to suggest a new answer to a murder which has puzzled us for over four centuries.

ISBN 0 7509 2963 4   PBK   198 X 127   304 PP

SUTTON PUBLISHING
www.suttonpublishing.co.uk

TO ORDER PLEASE CONTACT:
HAYNES PUBLISHING, SPARKFORD, NR YEOVIL, SOMERSET, BA22 7JJ

Daggers Drawn

Real Heroes of the SAS & SBS

Mike Morgan

Twenty-five vivid stories from the soldiers of the Special Air Service about their exploits in the Second World War – an SAS Jeep patrol in France outnumbered fifty-to-one by SS troopers, who shot their way out to safety in their bullet-riddled vehicle, killing a quarter of their opposition; an SAS soldier who talked his way through enemy roadblocks in North Africa, in full British uniform, and tore a strip off the guard for neglecting to check his papers; and another, who walked the whole length of Italy to escape after his raid went wrong. Supported by a selection of rare archive and action shots, this is the first comprehensive selection of all the best stories in one book – some previously unpublished.

ISBN 0 7509 3058 6   PBK   178 X 110

SUTTON PUBLISHING

www.suttonpublishing.co.uk

TO ORDER PLEASE CONTACT:
HAYNES PUBLISHING, SPARKFORD, NR YEOVIL, SOMERSET, BA22 7JJ
TEL: 01963 442080

The Wall

Christopher Hilton

East Berlin, Sunday 13 August 1961: Reuters journalist Adam Kellett-Long sat in front of his typewriter trying to compose the day-lead. 'I suppose I was in the third sentence when the phone rang. I picked it up and a man's voice I didn't recognise said in German, "don't go to bed this night". At that moment the ADN service closed for the night as usual, End of Transmissions, but because of this extraordinary call I stayed there wondering.' At 1.11, the ADN teleprinter in Kellett-Long's office suddenly opened up again and began to run a generalised Warsaw Pact communiqué from Moscow. It read, '. . . In the face of the aggressive aspirations of the reactionary forces of West Germany and its NATO allies, the Warsaw Pact proposes reliable safeguards and effective control be established around the whole territory of West Berlin.' The unthinkable had actually happened: the border was being closed and the city permanently divided in half.

Berlin, writes Christopher Hilton, 'is positively heaving with extraordinary personal memories' like this one. Across a twelve-foot wall and the width of a white painted line at Checkpoint Charlie, East and West confronted each other for nearly thirty years, yet it is the individual stories that are perhaps most telling..

Astonishingly, these memories are largely untapped, so until now the complete story of the Berlin Wall – the people's story – has remained untold. Hilton, a journalist and writer, has been captivated by Berlin's unique past for three decades, conducting hundreds of interviews there since the Wall came down. The result is an extraordinary vivid, occasionally harrowing, sometimes touching story – the best real-life novel you'll ever read.

ISBN 0 7509 3055 1   PBK 198 X 127 464PP 16 MONO PLATES

SUTTON PUBLISHING

www.suttonpublishing.co.uk

TO ORDER PLEASE CONTACT:
HAYNES PUBLISHING, SPARKFORD, NR YEOVIL, SOMERSET, BA22 7JJ
TEL: 01963 442080

Shakespeare the Player
John Southworth

Man of the Millennium he may be but William Shakespeare is a remarkably shadowy historical figure. His writings have been analysed exhaustively but much of his life remains a mystery. This controversial biography aims to redress the balance.

A wonderfully fresh and compelling work of reinterpretation, *Shakespeare the Player* completely overturns traditional images of the Bard and his work. It retrieves the so-called 'lost years' of Shakespeare's youth and early manhood, showing that he is likely to have joined Worcester's Men, a group of travelling players, at the age of sixteen. It then follows the young William as he learns his craft and begins work on his own plays. By the time he makes his first impact on literary London he is shown to be an accomplished actor with twelve years experience, not, as generally envisaged, a great dramatist who did some acting on the side. Indeed, Southworth emphasizes that he continued to be a committed actor all his life, spending much of the year on the road right up to his death.

A work of deep scholarship and understanding, *Shakespeare the Player* presents the Bard and his plays in their proper context for the first time. Ground-breaking and contentious, it will change the way we think about the English language's greatest artist.

ISBN 0 7509 3060 8   PBK 198 X 127 336PP 8 MONO PLATES

SUTTON PUBLISHING
www.suttonpublishing.co.uk

TO ORDER PLEASE CONTACT:
HAYNES PUBLISHING, SPARKFORD, NR YEOVIL, SOMERSET, BA22 7JJ
TEL: 01963 442080

Nero

Richard Holland

Stories of Nero's tyrannical reign began before his body was cold –
the heartless tyrant who fiddled while Rome burned; the evil sadist
who murdered both his wife and his mother, and who threw
Christians to the lions – and were perpetuated in the twentieth
century by Hollywood and by historical novelists. Yet, as this new
biography and radical reassessment reveals, the man behind the
myth is a more complex, infinitely more interesting figure. This
book does not whitewash Nero, but it aims to show that he was
more of a liberator than an oppressor, that he contrived to rule in
peace rather than in the militaristic way of his predecessors, and
that he was both enlightened and civilized, a man who enjoyed
poetry, music, philosophy and the theatre, as well as erotic
delights. Cheered for his performances with the lyre by thousands
of screaming followers, his patronage of the arts also left the legacy
of the Golden Palace with its rich gold decoration and murals later
copied by Raphael and other Renaissance artists in the Vatican.
Through social, cultural, and archaeological evidence, here we
encounter Nero imaginatively as a man, not as a monster.

ISBN 0 7509 2876 X   PBK   198 X 127   320PP   8 MONO PLATES

SUTTON PUBLISHING

www.suttonpublishing.co.uk

TO ORDER PLEASE CONTACT:
HAYNES PUBLISHING, SPARKFORD, NR YEOVIL, SOMERSET, BA22 7JJ
TEL: 01963 442080

With the Jocks
Peter White

Hidden away for more than fifty years, Peter White's remarkable diary is one of the most extraordinary stories to come out of the Second World War.

In one of the most graphic and finely crafted evocations of a soldier at war, the images he records are not for the fainthearted. There are heroes aplenty within its pages, but there are also disturbing insights into the darker side of humanity, frequently brushed aside in many other war accounts – the men who broke under the strain and who ran away (sometimes with tragic results); the binge drinking that occasionally rendered the whole platoon unable to fight; the looting and the callous disregard for human life that happens when death is a daily companion.

ISBN 0 7509 3057 8 PBK 198 X 127 576PP 32 MONO PLATES

SUTTON PUBLISHING
www.suttonpublishing.co.uk

TO ORDER PLEASE CONTACT:
HAYNES PUBLISHING, SPARKFORD, NR YEOVIL, SOMERSET, BA22 7JJ
TEL: 01963 442080

Curiosities of Wine
Clinking, Drinking and the Extras that Surround the Bottles

Pamela Vandyke Price
Foreword by Oz Clarke

Who is – or was – the Bishop of Norwich? Which vineyard once belonged to a Pope? Why is one estate called 'All is Lost'? Why are sideboards unique to Britain, and what were they for? What is a Grace cup? Who invented the swizzle stick? Why do people clink glasses when they drink? Find the answers to these and many more curious questions associated with wine in this entertaining read by the doyenne of wine writers. Many books have dealt with the history of wine and spirits, but this book deals with its curiosities. From corks to corkscrews to the shape of the glasses, from loyal toasts and other drinking customs, from how to detect 'off' wine to the use of wine when launching ships to why Nelson didn't take much champagne when setting sail for Trafalgar. It also includes the politics of wine drinking, and wine and the church, the origins of Liebfraumilch and why Madeira became a patriotic drink in America. Amusing, but packed with facts, this book makes an ideal gift for all wine-drinkers, and a handy reference for the sideboard. It explains with zest and humour all those things that other books don't.

HBK 160PP 216 X 138
60 B/W ILLUSTRATIONS   ISBN 0 7509 2754 2

SUTTON
PUBLISHING
www.suttonpublishing.co.uk

ORDERS TO: HAYNES PUBLISHING, SPARKFORD, NR YEOVIL, SOMERSET, BA22 7JJ
TELEPHONE: 01963 442105   FAX: 01963 440001